THE GOLDEN AGE OF NOVELTY SONGS

THE GOLDEN AGE OF NOVELTY SONGS

BY
STEVE OTFINOSKI

BILLBOARD BOOKS
An Imprint of Watson-Guptill Publications

Senior Acquisitions Editor: Bob Nirkind
Edited by: Amy Handy
Book design: Cheryl Viker
Cover design: Howard Grossman
Production Manager: Hector Campbell

First published 1999 by Billboard Books, an imprint of Watson-Guptill Publications,
a division of BPI Communications, Inc., at 1515 Broadway, New York, NY 10036.

Library of Congress Cataloging-in-Publication Data
Otfinoski, Steven.
    The golden age of novelty songs/by Steven Otfinoski.
        p. cm.
    Includes bibliographical references (p.), discography (p.), and index.
    ISBN 0-8230-7694-6
    1. Novelty songs—History and criticism. I. Title.
ML3529.5 .O84 2000
782.42164—dc21

ISBN: 0-8230-7694-6
Manufactured in the United States of America
First printing, 2000
1 2 3 4 5 6 7 8 9 / 08 07 06 05 04 03 02 01 00

To Martha and Daniel,
who love kooky songs, clever lyrics,
and anything by Weird Al.

Acknowledgments

I would like to thank my editor at Billboard Books, Bob Nirkind, who thought a book on novelty songs was a neat idea, and Barry Hansen (aka Dr. Demento) for writing the foreword to this book and for graciously reading the manuscript and helping to make it as accurate as possible. Thanks also to Joel Whitburn at Record Research, whose scrupulous and never-ending chronicling of the Billboard charts has been an indispensable aid to writing this book and who provided me with some of the novelty songs of the golden age that I hadn't heard before. Many thanks too to Brian Korn, a dedicated collector of novelty records, who shared hours of some of the more esoteric novelties from his fabulous collection with me. Thanks as well to Stephen K. Peeples and Rhino Records, Cary Mansfield at Varese Sarabande, Heidi at Bear Family Records, Pamela Goshman at Taragon Records, Tim Livingston at Sundazed Music, and Michelle at Razor and Tie for all the wonderful CDs. Also thanks to Ron Mandelbaum at Photofest, Dave "Daddy Cool" Booth at Showtime Archives, Larry Schwartz at Archive Photos, and author Ronald L. Smith for their help in gathering the pictures for this volume. Also a warm thank you to Don McLaughlin, who has one of the world's premiere picture sleeve collections (over 9,000!), a few of which grace the pages of this book.

Special thanks to my good friend and neighbor Dewey Ewing for letting me roam freely through his vast collection of CDs and 45s. Dewey, you're the greatest.

Last, but never least, thanks to my wife, Beverly, who thinks I'm nuts but puts up with me anyway, and to my kids, who *know* I'm nuts but have developed their own twisted taste for novelty music from Spike Jones to Weird Al.

Contents

Foreword by Dr. Demento................................2

Introduction 3

Chapter 1
Flying Saucers and Singing Chipmunks................9

Chapter 2
Soul Humor..37

Chapter 3
Parody, the Sincerest Form of Flattery..............65

Chapter 4
Monsters, Madmen, and Other One-Hit Weirdos.....87

Chapter 5
Ray Stevens and Roger Miller:
Kings of Sixties Novelty...............................119

Chapter 6
Bring on the Comics!..................................134

Chapter 7
Country Corn and Funny Folk.........................152

Chapter 8
Rock Laughs at Itself.................................178

Chapter 9
A Zany Little Christmas...............................197

Chapter 10
They All Sang Novelty 212

Bibliography..232

Web Sites 238

Discography..239

Appendix: Sixty-five of the Greatest
Novelty Songs of the Rock Era 242

Index..244

Foreword

In the early years of rock 'n' roll, and for years before that in fact, funny songs (or "novelty records" if you prefer) were part of every pop music fan's experience. There was always at least one of them on the charts, it seemed. In the late sixties, though, rock music took a serious turn, and novelty songs all but disappeared from Top 40 radio.

"Good riddance," said the critics, intoxicated with the idea of rock music as a serious art form.

Oddly enough, though, people actually missed hearing songs like "The Purple People Eater," "Monster Mash," and "They're Coming to Take Me Away, Ha-haaaa!" The Dr. Demento Show began in 1970 as a more or less serious program of rare oldies, but when listeners discovered that I would play darn near anything from the Demento Archives, it was those songs that they called for, over and over again. Before long those old funny songs had taken over not only the Dr. Demento Show but my whole life as well. Soon listeners were sending in new funny songs like "Fish Heads" and "Dead Puppies (Aren't Much Fun)." When I played a homemade cassette by sixteen-year-old Alfred Yankovic one evening in 1976, a whole new saga began; Alfred would soon be known everywhere as "Weird Al."

I've been meaning to write this book for twenty-five years, but Steve Otfinoski got to it first. More power to him. If it was a funny song and a hit single, it's here. You'll win a lot of trivia contests with this book.

There's a little insanity in all of us, and what better way to let it out than by singing or enjoying a silly song. Just think—this might be your guide to lifelong mental health!

Dr. Demento

Introduction

Among the inductees at the ninth annual Rhythm and Blues Foundation Pioneer Awards ceremony in New York City in February 1998 was New Orleans singer Ernie K-Doe. K-Doe's main claim to fame was his number one novelty hit from 1961, "Mother-in-Law." After the ceremony K-Doe boasted, "I made a record that will never die till the end of the world."

Such boastfulness may seem slightly unseemly when the song in question is representative of the most ephemeral genre in pop music, one that at the dawn of the twenty-first century seems all but moribund. True, "Mother-in-Law" is one of only a handful of novelty songs that reached the top of the charts, and it was written and produced by one of the true legends of New Orleans R&B, Allen Toussaint. But immortal?

What exactly is a novelty song, anyway? Webster's defines novelty as "a new or unusual thing." Newness and novelty music seem to go hand in hand. Just as the calypso singers of the Caribbean turn to the news of the day for material for their satirical songs, so for over a century purveyors of pop music have been quick to snap up a fad, fashion, or news headline and transform it into a song.

As for "unusual," the novelty song has often shown a fondness for the wild, the strange, and the bizarre, whether it be the gimmickry of funny, high-pitched voices and ear-arresting sound effects or such taboo subject matter as sex, insanity, or death. Lighthearted or gruesome, most novelty songs have strived to be humorous and make us laugh at their silliness, wit, or weirdness. Funny, timely, and weird—seems as good a description of the novelty song as any.

It took two talented music makers in the 1940s and an intellectual upstart in the early 1950s to mix these elements anew and in the process expand the boundaries of novelty. Louis Jordan and Spike Jones were the premiere novelty artists of that time and they both had an impact on the novelty music that would follow. Jordan's influence went well beyond novelty to affect all rhythm and blues music of the '50s and '60s and even rock 'n' roll itself.

Born in Arkansas in 1908, Louis Jordan got his start in the world of entertainment in minstrel shows, eventually working in jazz bands

Louis Jordan was not only the father of black novelty songs but one of the true pioneers of rhythm and blues music of the 1950s and 1960s. (Photo courtesy of Showtime Archives, Toronto)

as an altoist and vocalist. But it was as leader of the Tympany Five (the band's size actually fluctuated from year to year) that he ruled supreme on what *Billboard* called its Harlem Hit Parade through the 1940s and into the early 1950s.

Jordan wedded urban blues to a raucous beat with such earthy songs about black life as "Beans and Cornbread," "Ain't Nobody Here But Us Chickens," and his final hit of the decade, "Saturday Night Fish Fry." This last song particularly, with its comic tone and realistic detail, would be echoed in the coming decade in the work of Jerry Leiber and Mike Stoller for the Robins and the Coasters.

There was little of reality as we know it in the music of Spike Jones and his City Slickers, who gleefully destroyed every musical sacred cow in sight. Their very first hit, "Der Fuehrer's Face" (# 3, 1942), which originally appeared in a Walt Disney cartoon, took on Hitler with a rubber razzer. The City Slickers went on to tackle insipid pop ballads ("Cocktails for Two"), fluffy instrumentals ("Holiday for Strings"), classical works ("William Tell Overture," "Dance of the Hours"), sentimental holiday songs ("All I Want for Christmas"), and even television ("The Late, Late, Late Movies"). Jones's parodies were punctuated by outlandish sound effects, weird instrumentation, and the frequently bizarre vocal talents of such regulars as Doodles Weaver, Paul Frees, and Sir Frederick Gas.

If Jordan gave novelty a beat and a heart, Jones gave it an ear and a brain. Spike's preoccupation with pop parody and musical mayhem surely influenced everyone from Stan Freberg in the '50s to "Weird Al" Yankovic in the '80s and '90s, while his quest for strange, arresting sounds led to the high-speed recording that gave birth to the Chipmunks and all their offspring.

Jones's last charting single, "I Went to Your Wedding" (# 20, 1953), with Sir Frederick sounding like a demented Frankie Laine, came out the same month as the first album of novelty songs by Harvard graduate Tom Lehrer. Lehrer's quick-witted parodies and originals were starkly set compared to Jones's three-ring circus and were sung solo by the author with only his piano for accompaniment. The tunes were beguiling, but it was the lyrics, etched in acid, that mattered most. Lehrer would produce only two more albums of original songs before retreating back into the ivy-covered towers of academia. His often controversial choice of topics ("The Old Dope Peddler," "The Masochism

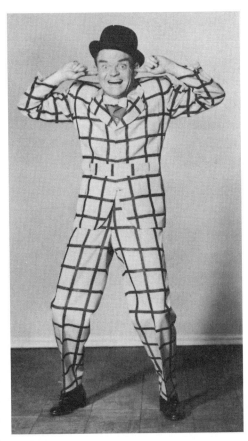

With his outrageous parodies of popular and classical music and his unceasing quest for weird and zany sounds, Spike Jones was the precursor of much of the novelty music that was to come.

Tango") would never get him much air play and a single of "Poisoning Pigeons in the Park," enhanced with strings, never came near the charts.

When rock 'n' roll burst onto the musical scene in 1955, it seemed the perfect target for a Tom Lehrer song. From the start rock 'n' roll was a novelty, just as ragtime and jazz had been in earlier decades. To adults weaned on big band music and the Hit Parade, recording artists like Elvis, Jerry Lee Lewis, Gene Vincent, and Little Richard, with their nonsense lyrics and wild and unpredictable stage performances, looked and sounded like alien creatures.

Rock musicians and songwriters, however, were in on the joke. Reading through the record reviews in *Billboard* in the '50s and '60s, as laid out by Jay Warner in his fascinating volume *Billboard's American Rock 'N' Roll in Review,* one is struck by how many times the anonymous reviewers use the word *novelty* to describe disks that normally would not be considered a part of that genre. Humor, especially self-deprecating humor about the problems of adolescence, was a mainstay of rock 'n' roll in the fifties. Rock pioneers like Chuck Berry ("School Days," "Sweet Little Sixteen"), Eddie Cochran ("Summertime Blues"), and the Everly Brothers ("Wake Up Little Susie," "Bird Dog," "Problems") all had a good measure of novelty and humor in their music. Teenagers, trapped between childhood and adulthood, learned from these songs and many more like them that they weren't alone in their misery. Better to laugh and dance than brood over your troubles.

The line between novelty and mainstream pop remains a hazy one. Novelty, like so much else, is often in the ear of the listener. To make this book as comprehensive as possible, I have given novelty a very wide definition and highlighted its many subgenres—parody, teen topical, spoken comedy, black, folk, country, Christmas, break-in, and just plain weird (remember Napoleon XIV?).

As the title indicates, the emphasis is on the golden age of novelty songs in the rock era, roughly from 1956 to 1969, when the genre peaked in popularity on the charts. But our journey will take us occasionally into the '70s and '80s (and even, briefly, the '90s) to follow the careers of artists like Ray Stevens and Dickie Goodman, who continued to work the territory beyond the '60s, and a new novelty artist like "Weird Al" Yankovic, who surfaced in the '80s. The chapters are loosely chronological, but also thematic. Thus Weird Al appears in an early chapter devoted to parody, while older artists are considered in later chapters.

The author makes no pretense of being all-inclusive. There have been literally thousands of novelty records produced since 1955 and only a small percentage of them, for space's sake, are considered in these pages. The central focus is on novelty artists and their songs that made the *Billboard* pop singles' charts and not on albums or comedy records in general, unless the comic had a hit single. I have tried to hit the high points and fashion a coherent narrative. If I've missed someone's favorite record or artist, the omission wasn't intentional.

No apologies need be made for the novelty song itself. Although not always known for its taste and sophistication, the best of novelty has been literate, challenging, and wonderfully subversive. Like all good comedy, good novelty songs puncture the balloon of pomposity, expose the darker side of ourselves, and provide some life-affirming laughter in the face of civilization's pretensions.

Granted, many novelty songs, and some of the most popular ones, have no such high aspirations. No one is about to write a doctoral dissertation on the clothing imagery in "Itsy Bitsy Teenie Weenie Yellow Polkadot Bikini" or the extra-terrestrial elements in "The Purple People Eater." (But then you never know about those academic types.) Yet both of these million-selling disks are interesting as pop artifacts of a particular time and place.

On the other hand, novelty music has attracted some of our finest talents, from Stan Freberg and Leiber and Stoller to Roger Miller and Ray Stevens. The temptation to be silly has drawn into the funny fold such "straight" artists as Johnny Cash, Bobby Bare, and Bo Diddley, and given them some of their finest, or at least most commercial, moments on vinyl. Novelty has in the past been one way for new artists to break into the business and dozens of well-known artists from Chubby Checker to Paul Simon got their start by recording novelty songs.

Good, bad, or indifferent, novelty music has for three decades held a special niche in rock music and if the last few decades have seen it largely disappear from the charts, its continuing appeal can be seen in the popularity of disk jockey Barry Hansen, better known to his fans as Dr. Demento, whose two-hour weekly radio program devoted exclusively to novelty music has been nationally syndicated since 1974 and is currently heard on a hundred radio stations coast to coast. Besides keeping classic novelty music alive, Hansen has provided a showcase for such contemporary artists as "Weird Al" Yankovic (see Chapter 3) and Barnes and Barnes.

Given its long tradition, its popularity and influence in its golden age, and the gallery of talented and colorful figures who have been a part of it, a serious study of novelty music in the rock era is long overdue.

Perhaps Ernie K-Doe was right after all. As long as there are sons-in-law and mothers-in-law, there will always be an audience for a good novelty song that makes light of our troubled existence. Times change and so do musical tastes, but human nature stubbornly stays the same—fallible, foolish, and very, very funny.

① Flying Saucers and Singing Chipmunks

"I discovered that if you double speed a song, it comes back into pitch several octaves higher."—*Sheb Wooley*

"The appearances of talking animals are a staple within novelty tune categories."—*B. Lee Cooper in* Popular Music and Society, *Fall 1988*

The year 1955 may have been the breakthrough year for rock 'n' roll, but it was not a particularly banner year for novelty songs. The year's top novelty disk was "Nuttin' for Christmas," a saccharine holiday number about a bad little kid who wasn't all that bad, sung in three versions by a trio of prepubescent boys. Among the top forty novelty runner-ups was a schmaltzy ersatz religious tune by the Cowboy Church Sunday School; a piece of rustic comedy by Andy Griffith years before he moved to Mayberry and found TV stardom; and a version of "Oh! Susanna" sung, er, barked, by the Singing Dogs.

It would take a college dropout and a young music publisher, both in their early twenties, to inject the energy and wildness of rock into novelty and breathe new life into a tired genre.

We Interrupt This Record . . .

On June 24, 1947, pilot Kenneth Arnold reported sighting a formation of strange flying objects while cruising over Washington State. He described the objects as resembling "flying saucers," thus coining a phrase that would galvanize the public's fascination with life on other planets for decades to come. By the early fifties, sightings of flying saucers were numbering in the thousands and Americans of all ages were encouraged to "look to the skies" in the closing words of one sci-fi movie.

In June 1956 Richard "Dickie" Goodman, son of an attorney with General Electric, teamed up with Bill Buchanan, a music publisher in New York City, to produce an updated recording of Orson Welles's

Bill Buchanan (left) and Dickie Goodman— sporting what look like homemade T-shirts promoting their first big hit— made their early "break-in" records on a shoestring. They initially ran their business from a pay phone in a Manhattan drugstore, which made them conveniently hard to reach when music publishers started suing them for infringement.

famous 1938 radio broadcast of H. G. Wells's *War of the Worlds.* Their version, however, would have a very contemporary slant, using snippets from current rock and pop hit records to inject some humor into the old story of a Martian invasion of earth. It was a crazy idea, but then Dickie Goodman was a crazy kind of guy. He had dropped out of New York University a short time earlier after blowing up a science lab. In four days, the two men spliced together their five-minute opus called "Back to Earth," later retitled "The Flying Saucer, Parts 1 & 2."

Buchanan and Goodman were no Orson Welles and "The Flying Saucer," with its cheap sound effects, sounds like it was produced on a shoestring, which it was. The record begins with the instrumental opening of Nappy Brown's "Open Up That Door," suddenly interrupted by announcer Buchanan intoning, "We interrupt this record to bring you this important bulletin. The reports of a flying saucer hovering over the city have been confirmed." Goodman appeared as "John

Cameron Cameron" (a parody of pioneer TV newscaster John Cameron Swayze), who from "downtown" interviews everyone from a Martian to the president. All the "answers" were quick cuts or "break-ins" from fifteen current hit records, none of which Buchanan and Goodman had bothered getting permission to use. To add insult to injury, some of the artists and records are misidentified by Buchanan in his brightest deejay voice. For example, Fats Domino becomes Skinny Dynamo and Chuck Berry, Huckle Berry. "Earth Angel" by the Penguins becomes "the Pelicans' outer space recording 'Earth . . .'" and the announcer is teasingly cut off by another interruption.

The editing of the musical snippets is razor sharp and the pace is manic, glossing over stale jokes and the shoestring production values. When the spacemen make their appearance, they speak in high-pitched voices, the result of a speeded-up tape recording of a normal voice, a process that David Seville would further refine two years later.

The zany record was turned down by numerous record companies, but tickled the funny bone of disk jockeys, including Alan Freed, who gave "The Flying Saucer" a spin on his New York radio program.★ George Goldner at Roulette Records snapped up the novelty disk and gave Buchanan and Goodman their own label, Universe. Unfortunately, there already was a Universe label, so to avoid a lawsuit, Goldner and his employees stayed up all night hand-printing "Ls" to turn "Universe" into "Luniverse," on 2,000 freshly pressed 45s and 78s.

Sales soared and "The Flying Saucer" peaked at #3 on *Billboard*'s Hot One Hundred. The record companies considered suing Buchanan and Goodman for excerpting their records without permission until they realized every record heard on the novelty was seeing a surge in sales. "Earth Angel" had even been reissued by its label, Dootone. The music publishers, however, were less compliant. They tallied nineteen separate instances of "copyright infringement and unauthorized usages." A deal was finally worked out where the publishers would receive about a penny apiece for every recording of "The Flying Saucer" sold.

Buchanan and Goodman, as impudent as ever, made their tenuous legal position the subject of their third release, "Buchanan and Goodman

★*Freed would later produce his own break-in record, "The Space Man," an almost word-for-word ripoff of "The Flying Saucer" but with the "break-in" songs recorded by anonymous artists.*

on Trial" (#80), which even topped the manic pace of "The Flying Saucer." They wisely dropped the misnaming of any of the tunes heard, but had "Skinny Dynamo" called as a witness for the prosecution. At the climax of this piece of insanity they are pronounced not guilty by a jury of Martians.

Life imitated art. Recording artists Fats Domino and Smiley Lewis ("Laughing Lewis"), along with four records labels and two publishing companies, sued the duo in New York District Court for $130,000 in compensatory and punitive damages. The judge gave the record a listen, decided it was a new work of satirical intent, and threw out the case.

Their next release, the rarely heard "The Banana Boat Story," replaced snippets of pop records with a surreal collage of radio commercials that keep interrupting Harry Belafonte's "Day-O." The disk didn't chart and the team returned to more familiar territory with "Flying Saucer the Second" in 1957, which put them back in the top twenty. In this sequel the action switches to outer space with John Cameron Cameron reporting from "downtown Mars," while his colleague John Cameron Camerovitch delivers bulletins from Moscow.

The formula was beginning to wear a little thin in "Santa and the Satellite, Parts 1 & 2" (#32). By now Buchanan and Goodman had parted ways, although Goodman continued to use the duo's name on his records until 1960. Buchanan's hip deejay was replaced by Paul Sherman, whose stolid-sounding voice undercut the manic proceedings. When he tells the listener to "turn the record over" at the end of part 1, you might think you're listening to a kiddie record.

On his own Buchanan made a few further break-in records ("The Creature," "The Invasion") with new collaborators Bob Ancell and Hal Greenfield. But Goodman was the prolific one, cranking out one break-in record after another. He had a kind of genius for seizing on the latest fad or craze in the ever-changing world of pop culture and his scenarios became increasingly more surreal. In "The Flying Saucer Goes West," Wyatt Earp is pinned down by the saucer men when General Elvis Presley (he was actually a private at the time) rides to the rescue with the army. In the '60s and '70s Goodman ransacked hit television shows ("The Touchables," "Ben Crazy," and "Batman and His Grandmother," all of which charted), the Cold War ("Berlin Top Ten," one of his wittier outings), politics ("Election Year 1964," "Watergrate"), and social issues ("Soul President Number One").

As the years went on Goodman's inspiration flagged. The records lost the manic pace that had made them so much fun; they became predictable and formulaic as Goodman the interviewer asked a series of questions of different people and the answers were snippets from contemporary hit records.

Nonetheless, his instinct for the right tie-in was still sharp and he returned to the top forty for the first time in over fifteen years with "Energy Crisis '74" and the following year splashed his way to #4 with "Mr. Jaws," which says more about the popularity of Steven Spielberg's movie than Goodman's gags. In "Election '80" he took on Reaganomics and in "Radio Russia," Communism in its waning days. His last break-in disk was "Safe Sex Report" in 1988, which skewered the topic of AIDS without ever mentioning it.

The following year, in a deep depression over the breakup of his fourth marriage and mounting gambling debts, Dickie Goodman died of a self-inflicted gunshot wound at a relative's home in Fayetteville, North Carolina. Bill Buchanan, who had retired to the Southwest years earlier, died of cancer in August 1996.

Dickie Goodman's legacy is a strange one. The argument made by Chuck Miller in a 1997 *Goldmine* profile that he and Buchanan are the grandfathers of sampling is tenuous. For all his talent, Goodman's style never evolved much beyond the format he created in 1956, and listening to more than a few of his break-in disks in one sitting can be as painful as a visit to the dentist. His occasional forays outside the break-in form are mostly negligible. His 1963 takeoff on Allan Sherman's *My Son, the Folksinger,* entitled *My Son, the Joke,* is filled with such tasteless numbers as "Balling My Zelda" ("Waltzing Matilda").

But in their heyday, Buchanan and Goodman satisfied a wide audience of listeners. Teens who loved rock could laugh along as they identified each song "break-in," while adults who loathed rock could chuckle at a space man who sounded like Little Richard or Jerry Lee Lewis. The break-in record they created has proved to have a remarkable longevity. Among the many recording artists to follow in their funny footsteps are Vik Venus ("Moonflight," #38, 1969) and the Delegates ("Convention '72," #8).

With his talent for exploiting the latest sounds and crazes and his irrepressible energy, Dickie Goodman snatched the novelty record away from singing dogs and brought it into the rock era, where it would flourish for more than a decade.

Al-vin!

If Buchanan and Goodman were the trailblazers of the modern-day novelty record, Ross Bagdasarian (aka David Seville) was its greatest popularizer. Whatever one may think of Bagdasarian's accomplishments, he showed how a little technology and a lot of savvy could sell records and just about everything else.

Ross Bagdasarian (the name is Armenian) was born in Fresno, California, a few months after the armistice of World War I was signed. His father was a grape grower, a livelihood that initially did not interest the young Bagdasarian. At the age of nineteen he headed for New York City, where he landed some acting jobs and even made it to Broadway. Young Ross was encouraged and supported by his cousin, the already famous writer William Saroyan.

During World War II Bagdasarian served four years in the Air Force in Europe. After the war he returned to Fresno, married, and started a grape farm that quickly failed. With $200 in his pocket he moved to Los Angeles, where he tried to sell a pop song he cowrote with Saroyan. Most record companies found the number "too ethnic," but Columbia's Mitch Miller took a chance on it, and "Come On-a My House" became a #1 hit in 1951 for Rosemary Clooney.

By the mid-fifties Bagdasarian was dividing his time between acting and song writing. He landed small parts in *Viva Zapata!* and *Stalag 17* and played a lonely songwriter in Alfred Hitchcock's *Rear Window.* Another Hitchcock film, *The Trouble with Harry,* inspired Bagdasarian to write a novelty song with the same title under the pseudonym Alfi and Harry. Harry was a piano player who played the same tune over and over, much to the chagrin of Alfi (Bagdasarian). Their adversarial relationship would be echoed in the Chipmunk records Bagdasarian would produce two years later. The single went to #44 in America and broke the top twenty in Great Britain. Further Alfi and Harry releases went nowhere, but an instrumental Bagdasarian dedicated to his wife, "Armen's Theme" (#42, 1956), became a hit on Liberty Records. It was released under the name David Seville, which Bagdasarian took from the Spanish city in which he had been stationed during the war.

Bagdasarian had a knack for novelty songs and in 1957 scored a modest hit with the corny "Gotta Get To Your House" (#77), about a love-struck boy prone to spoonerisms. Then in early 1958 he had an idea for a novelty song that would be considerably more novel. It was a catchy little number about another love-sick guy who went to a witch doctor for advice. There was a great nonsense chorus sung by the witch doctor that Bagdasarian decided to do in a high-pitched voice.

He was not the first recording artist to speed up the human voice for novel effect. Buchanan and Goodman had done it two years earlier in "The Flying Saucer," but it wasn't an integral part of the record. A year before that, singing cowboy Stuart Hamblen had taken a young woman's voice and accelerated it to 45 rpm so she sounded like a little girl, producing 1955's most freakish hit, "Open Up Your Heart (And Let The Sunshine In)," ostensibly by the Cowboy Church Sunday School. While corny even by 1955 standards, "Open Up Your Heart" was not meant to be a novelty. Composer Hamblen was a reformed alcoholic who had converted to Christianity at a Billy Graham prayer meeting and ran for president on the Prohibition ticket in 1952.

But Bagdasarian wanted his high-pitched voice to sound like a truly wild character. For a full two months he tinkered with his tape recorder until he came upon the formula that would make him a very rich man. He recorded his voice as the witch doctor at half speed and then played it back at normal speed. The results were truly ear-arresting. The squeaky voice gave "The Witch Doctor" just the fillip it needed and it zoomed to #1 for three weeks in April 1958. It remained in the top forty for an incredible eighteen weeks and the witch doctor's cry of "E-oo-oo-ah-ah!" became a national catch phrase.

Bagdasarian reasoned that if one funny voice was amusing, three would be even funnier. He decided to create three distinctive characters for his next record. He wanted them to be animals, but exactly what kind of animal eluded him until he took a trip through Yosemite National Park.

"He was driving along the road . . . when this chipmunk almost dared him and his huge car to drive past," said his son Ross Bagdasarian, Jr., in a 1982 *Goldmine* interview. "My dad was so impressed by this audacious behavior that he decided to make the three singing characters chipmunks."

While this story may be true, Bagdasarian might also have been influenced by the success of Walt Disney's two mischievous cartoon chipmunks, Chip 'n' Dale, whose high-pitched chatter was similar to that of his furry little friends.

© 1961 ROSS BAGDASARIAN

Ross Bagdasarian (aka David Seville) may be whispering the latest sales figures to his favorite chipmunk. By 1961, the year The Alvin Show *debuted on television, the Chipmunks were a multimillion-dollar industry, with more than a hundred licensed toys and other products. (Photofest)*

Bagdasarian named his chipmunk trio after Liberty executives Al Bennett (Alvin) and Si Waronker (Simon) and recording engineer Ted Keep (Theodore), whose skill in the sound booth would earn him and the Chipmunks a handful of Grammys.

Alvin, the leader of the group, was inspired by Bagdasarian's youngest son, Adam, who every September began asking when Christmas was coming. From this idea he wrote the song "Please Christmas Don't Be Late." Bagdasarian cleverly appeared on the record as David Seville, the adult who vainly tries to control the childlike Chipmunks' antics, only to be sabotaged by the mischievous Alvin, who wants a hula hoop for Christmas. The record fades out with Dave's now familiar cry of "Al-vin!"

Retitled "The Chipmunk Song," the record debuted on the charts on December 8, 1958, and sold three and a half million copies in just five weeks, making it the fastest-selling disk in recording history up to that time. Number one for four weeks, it won three Grammys at the first Grammy Awards, including the one for Best Comedy Performance. The record went on to chart in the top fifty during the Christmas season for the next five years, making it a perennial holiday classic alongside "White Christmas" and "Rudolph the Red-Nosed Reindeer" (which the Chipmunks recorded in 1960 and took to #21).

But Bagdasarian knew the Chipmunks were more than a seasonal act. Through April 1962 he released seven more Chipmunk singles, all but one of which charted. "Alvin's Harmonica" (#3, 1959) featured another ingratiating melody and more Alvin antics, this time with a harmonica that played a cha-cha. "Ragtime Cowboy Joe" (#16, 1959) was an evergreen from 1912, enlivened by gunshots and a closing "Hi! Ho! Alvin!"

By 1960 the trio was so pervasive that Bagdasarian released the audacious "Alvin for President." According to a *Billboard* piece, "Liberty seeks to establish its entry as the top-seller [of election disks] by unleashing a promotional push that's destined to make old ward heelers take notice." There were "Alvin for President" buttons, election sound trucks roaming the streets, and copies of the single sent to candidates Kennedy and Nixon, as well as Presidents Eisenhower and Truman. All the hoopla didn't help the record much; it only went to #95.

But by now the Chipmunks were securely entrenched in American pop culture. In October 1961 *The Alvin Show* debuted on CBS-TV, only the third animated series to run in prime time. The Chipmunks made perfect cartoon characters, with long-suffering Dave still the butt of Alvin's jokes. Baby boomers will fondly remember the supporting cast of inventor Clyde Crashcup (whose sepulchral voice was provided by Shepard Menken) and his silent assistant, Leonardo. The series lasted only one season, up against stiff competition from *Wagon Train,* but continued on Saturday mornings through 1965. The TV tie-in led to a massive merchandising campaign of more than a hundred different licensed toys and other products. In a 1963 survey Alvin was voted the number one character among kids ages four to twelve.

By the mid-sixties Bagdasarian was losing interest in his young wards. Their last new hit record, "The Alvin Twist" (#40), was three years in the past and attempts to capitalize on the British Invasion and other contemporary pop styles were less successful than earlier releases. Few adults, or even children for that matter, were anxious to hear the Chipmunks singing Beatles' songs. In 1967 Bagdasarian retired the Chipmunks and turned to more serious composing. The group made one surprise appearance the following year on a reworking of "The Chipmunk Song" with, of all people, the blues-rock band Canned Heat. This unlikely matching of '50s novelty and late '60s rock produced perhaps the Chipmunks' most delightful recording.

For all his attempts to leave the Chipmunks behind him, when Bagdasarian died of a heart attack at age fifty-two, it was the Chipmunks he was, and remains, remembered for. The furry little critters stayed dormant until his son Ross Bagdasarian, Jr., brought them back to life in 1980. With his wife providing the voice of Theodore, Bagdasarian brought the Chipmunks up to date with the album *Chipmunk Punk,* which featured the trio sporting punk haircuts and a definite attitude. The following year he released *Urban Chipmunk,* a take on the successful film *Urban Cowboy,* with covers of country hits and the Chipmunks singing along with the likes of Jerry Reed and Brenda Lee. These and subsequent albums sold well and Bagdasarian (a chip off the old chipmunk?) broadened his father's empire with a "live" touring show and a new cartoon series on NBC, even resurrecting dear old Dave as the boys' house mother.

And so after forty years as headliners, the Chipmunks have entered their fifth decade of show business with no end in sight. All of which may prompt the adults in the audience to cry out with true Sevillian anguish, "Al-vin! Enough already!"

Sons of Chipmunks

The squeaky little voices that earned a fortune for Ross Bagdasarian, along with some interesting variations, were employed successfully by a number of other novelty artists in the late '50s and early '60s.

The Nutty Squirrels, despite their name, were a more sophisticated version of the Chipmunks. It was as if Alvin, Simon, and Theodore grew up and became beatniks. Their "Uh! Oh! Parts 1 [#45] and 2 [#14]" was simply speeded-up scat-singing to a jazz combo that featured Cannonball Adderly on horn. The Squirrels were the brainchildren of jazz musician-composer Don Elliott, who led the combo, and jingle writer Alexander "Sascha" Burland, who provided the overdubbed vocals. Their double-sided hit was released in late 1959 by Hanover-Signature Records, co-owned by comic and musician Steve Allen. When the label went under a year later, Elliott and Burland continued to make Nutty Squirrel records for Columbia, MGM, and RCA. But sides like "Eager Beaver" and "Please Don't Take Our Tree for Christmas," an attempt to compete with the Chipmunks for Christmas sales, didn't squirrel away many royalties. Soon Burland returned to writing jingles and Elliott went on to score an impressive string of soundtracks for such movies as *The Pawnbroker* and *In the Heat of the Night.*

Of course, the high squeaky voice was not only the domain of small mammals. Sheb Wooley used it to good effect in "The Purple People Eater" (more on him later), which beat out both "The Witch Doctor" and "The Chipmunk Song" as the biggest novelty record of 1958.

A cuter and more cuddly alien was 1959's "The Little Space Girl," who wanted not to eat people but to marry them. The object of her desires was rockabilly singer Jesse Lee Turner, one of the more intriguing mystery figures of the novelty genre. While the squeaky voice of the four-armed Space Girl ("The better to hug you") was appealing, the most striking feature of this top twenty novelty was Jesse Lee himself, whose breathless intonations made him sound like a slightly demented Elvis. The record ends with him agreeing to this unnatural union with an enthusiastic "Why, sure!"

"Little Space Girl" was written by Floyd Robinson, whose own girlfriend song was the even stranger "My Girl," which was passed over by the record-buying public for its B-side, the more conventional

"Makin' Love" (#20, 1959). As for Jesse Lee Turner, his efforts to break out of the novelty niche proved disappointing and an attempt to regain his former momentum with "The Little Space Girl's Father"—who comes gunning for the earthling who has abandoned his daughter—fared no better. His last two singles were the novelties "The Voice Changing Song," and "The Ballad of Billy Sol Estes," about President Lyndon Johnson's larcenous crony. Wherever you are, Jesse Lee, you were an original.

Another unlikely candidate for novelty stardom was Hit Parader Betty Johnson, a graduate of radio's *Breakfast Club* and TV's *Tonight*

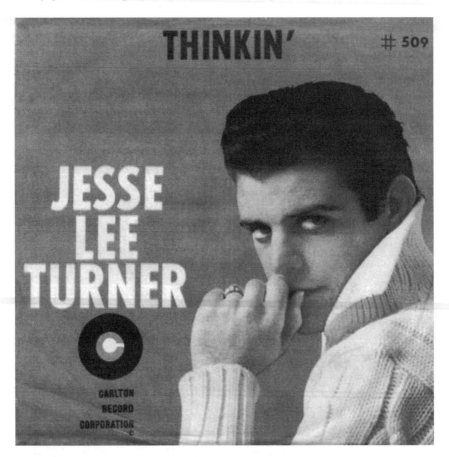

Looking every inch the cool teen idol, Jesse Lee Turner attempted to go "straight" with the follow-up to his big novelty hit "The Little Space Girl." His breathy, rockabilly vocal style, however, failed to ignite a second hit and he soon returned to the novelty form. (From the collection of Don McLaughlin)

Show with Jack Paar. Her first big hit, "I Dreamed" (#7, 1957), was a rather intriguing tale of a woman who dreams she meets up with her real-life lover in different historical scenarios. The psychological overtones were darker in "The Little Blue Man" (#17, 1958), which reversed the scenario of "The Little Space Girl." Poor Betty is pursued by the fellow of the title, who appears at the most unlikely moments pleading, "I wuv you" in an Elmer Fudd voice. The Little Blue Man is not a space alien but a figment of the woman's imagination whom she alone can see. In desperation she rushes to a rooftop and pushes her strange pursuer off. Like a Tex Avery cartoon character, he appears again unharmed to proclaim sadly, "I don't wuv you anymore." Vew-ry strange. The song's composer, Fred Ebb, would later write the lyrics for the Broadway musical *Cabaret*, a more profound study of sexual obsession. For the record, the voice of the Little Blue Man was that of ABC's retired *20-20* host Hugh Downs.

There is no squeaky voice in "Baby Sittin' Boogie," but lots of real baby gurgles and gagas provided by the two children of producer-composer John Parker. They helped this otherwise garden variety rocker by teen singer Buzz Clifford to #6 in the winter of 1961. (A German version of the song by Ralf Bendix, a director of TWA Airlines in Dusseldorf, sold a million copies in Europe.) At the end the rocking baby, who is the little brother of Buzz's girlfriend, chortles, "All-l-l-l gone." Which is what happened to Clifford's recording career after this novelty hit. He persevered, however, through a variety of musical styles and finally broke through some years later as a country artist.

A latecomer in the squeaky voice sweepstakes was veteran Italian-American singer Lou Monte. Monte was an ethnic singer who spent fifteen years in the limbo of Italian wedding dates and small New Jersey clubs before landing on the Hit Parade in 1954. That first hit was an unlikely Italian version of "At The Darktown Strutters' Ball." Monte's best '50s hit came four years later with the sly, comic "Lazy Mary," which he first sings through in Italian and then "for our American friends, the British version."

Monte had his biggest hit in 1963 with "Pepino the Italian Mouse" (#5). The relationship between Monte and his mischievous live-in mouse was similar to that of David Seville and Alvin. "You eat my food, you scare my girl, you even drink my wine," Monte lamented in the English portion of the song. Pepino's sales were undoubtedly helped by the appearance around the same time of another Italian mouse, the puppet Topo Gigo, who charmed television audiences of *The Ed Sullivan Show* with his comical tête-à-têtes with "Ed-die" himself.

Monte returned to the charts a few months later with "Pepino's Friend Pasqual (The Italian Pussy-Cat)." Pasqual's deep bass voice was an interesting counterpart to his pal's squeaky one, but the sequel was too close to the original to reach higher than #78. It was Lou Monte's

The self-styled "King of Italian-American Hit Records," Lou Monte had his biggest hit with a song about an Italian mouse with a taste for wine and cheese. Monte's career nearly ended a decade earlier when he almost died in an auto accident. (Photo courtesy of Showtime Archives, Toronto)

last appearance on the charts, although he continue to entertain audiences with his bilingual antics until his death in 1989.

Nearly all the squeaky-voiced animals and space people who rode the airwaves of novelty in its golden decade aspired to be rock 'n' roll stars. And who could blame them? Rock was the touchstone of the burgeoning youth subculture of the fifties and novelty was replete with its trappings, often as strange to many adults as the creatures who stepped out of all those flying saucers.

Teensville

By 1957 an entire teen subculture had arisen around rock music in a way that had never happened before in American society. Along with their own music, teenagers now had their own clothes, shoes, hairstyles, cars, dances, and even their own language, borrowed to a large extent from the beatniks and jazz musicians. All these accoutrements created a rich vein of material for novelty songs that record companies and songwriters were quick to capitalize on.

The iconic symbolism of clothing for rebellious youth was established, not surprisingly, by the first great songwriting team of rock 'n' roll, Jerry Leiber and Mike Stoller. In 1954 the duo, still in their teens, put together a West Coast group called the Cheers (Gil Garfield, Sue Allen, and Bert Convy) to sing demos of their songs.

"(Bazoom) I Need Your Lovin'" (#15), their first hit for the group, was a fairly conventional prerocker, but "Black Denim Trousers," released the following year, was completely original. Keen purveyors of pop culture, Leiber and Stoller got the idea for the song from the 1954 film *The Wild One,* in which Marlon Brando portrayed the tough but sensitive leader of a motorcycle gang. No film before James Dean's *Rebel Without a Cause* more convincingly portrayed the rebellious "lost" generation of the 1950s.

Unlike later musical tributes to teen rebels, such as "He's a Rebel" and "The Leader of the Pack," Leiber and Stoller did not take the figure all that seriously. Their rebel, perhaps more true to real life, was a clod with axle grease under his fingernails who treated his girlfriend badly. The comic touch to this tongue-in-cheek caricature was a shoulder tattoo that read "Mother I Love You." In the "Terror of Highway 101," the motorcyclist ends up running into an oncoming train. Prophetically, this was the same California roadway where James Dean would lose his life in a car accident only weeks after "Black Denim Trousers" became a hit.

With its insistent drum tattoo, wailing female chorus, blaring horns, and train-crossing sound effects, "Black Denim Trousers" sounded more like a Hollywood soundtrack than a pop record, and was the prototype for the brilliant playlets that the duo would shortly go on to perfect, first with the Robins and then with the Coasters (see Chapter 2).

If the Cheers were pop, Joe Bennett and the Sparkletones were pure raucous rock, at their finest in their ode "Black Slacks" (#17, 1957), which probably sold more pants than any advertising campaign, with the line "When I put 'em on, I'm a-rarin' to go."

Female fashions were not overlooked, at least not by male artists who admired the flesh they showed off. The most successful was "Short Shorts" (#3, 1958), sung and swung by the Royal Teens. As much an instrumental as a novelty song (the band started out as the instrumental group the Royal Tones), it was a teen tribal chant that had the boys asking, "Who wears Short Shorts?" and the girls responding teasingly, "We wear Short Shorts."

The Royal Teens tried to duplicate their success with "Big Name Button" which urged teens to promote their identity with a button or else "how in the heck will anyone know your name?" Name buttons might have been okay for the Mouseketeers but they didn't catch on with the teen set and the song didn't chart. The group shook off the novelty label with their last top forty hit, "Believe Me," sounding very much like Dion and the Belmonts. At least one member of the Fort Lee, New Jersey, quartet went on to bigger and better things. In 1960 Bob Gaudio joined another New Jersey vocal group that would eventually become the Four Seasons.

In "No Chemise, Please" (#23, 1958) Gerry Granahan staged a protest against changing female fashions. The novelty has a clever trick opening, starting as a slow teen ballad and suddenly breaking out into a raucous rocker as Granahan discovers that his date is wearing a sack dress instead of the usual sweater and jeans, leaving him unable to tell the "front from the back." A man of many moods, Granahan would the same year pen the classic ballad "You Were Mine" for his group the Fireflies and later lead Dicky Doo and the Don'ts, whose charters ranged from the Hit Parade corn of "Click Clack" to the bizarre novelty instrumental "Nee Nee Na Na Na Na Nu Nu." As producer of Caprice Records, Granahan went on to turn out girl group hits for Linda Scott, Patty Duke, the Angels, and the indomitable game lady of novelty, Shirley Ellis.

Footwear held a particular fascination for rock songwriters in the '50s. The classic of the form, of course, is Carl Perkins's "Blue Suede Shoes" (#2, 1956). The rockabilly artist got the inspiration for the song when he overheard a boy at a dance warn his girlfriend not to "step on my suedes." The defiant lyrics dare the listener to "do anything but don't you step on my blue suede shoes." Perkins would also wax eloquent on teen footwear on his last two charting singles, "Pink Pedal Pushers" and "Pointed Toe Shoes."

Less rebellious youth preferred Pat Boone's white bucks, immortalized by twelve-year-old Bobby Pedrick, Jr., in "White Bucks and Saddle Shoes" (#74, 1958). Fourteen years later, Pedrick would find stardom as Robert John with an updated version of the Tokens' "The Lion Sleeps Tonight." Female footwear for the teen set was the subject of Joe Bennett's follow-up hit "Penny Loafers and Bobby Socks" (#42, 1957).

The most delicious "shoe song" was "Pink Shoelaces" by another kid singer, thirteen-year-old Dodie Stevens, who had been singing professionally since age eight. "I didn't like that song one bit," Stevens confessed to Wayne Jancik in an interview. "I thought it was dumb." But it proved to be one of the biggest novelties of 1959, with a great opening choral hook and clever lyrics delivered "kooky girl" style by Stevens. "I look back on it now and it was really the first rap song," Stevens says. "I talked all the verses and only sang the chorus."

In the song Dodie's boyfriend, the eccentric and wealthy Dooley, drives her mad with his "crazy clothes"— "tan shoes and pink shoelaces and a Panama hat with a purple hat band." Like Bobby Bare's "The All American Boy," Dooley ends up in the army, that terrible destroyer of teen individuality, but writes in his will that he wants to be buried in his favorite garb.

Stevens wasn't able to repeat her initial success and landed her second-highest hit with another novelty of sorts, an answer song to Elvis's "Are You Lonely Tonight?" called "Yes, I'm Lonely Tonight" (#60, 1961). When she married at sixteen she gave up her career, only to return after a divorce five years later. She was a female singer for

Edd Byrnes is taking good care of his most valuable asset. Fame as Kookie, the parking attendant on TV's 77 Sunset Strip series, led him to a successful if brief recording career. After the series folded he found himself doing ads for a comb company. (Photofest)

Serge Medes and Brazil '77 for a while and more recently has returned to her roots with her traveling show, "Dodie Stevens and the Pink Shoelace Review." Once a novelty artist, always a novelty artist.

When it came to hair, no one paid more attention to his coiffure than Gerald Lloyd Kookson III, known familiarly as "Kookie," the parking attendant at Dino's Lodge in ABC's hit TV detective series 77 *Sunset Strip*. Efrem Zimbalist, Jr., and Roger Smith were the nominal stars, but it was cool Kookie, portrayed by Edd Byrnes, with his comb and hip talk that got all the attention. He was a fountain of hip expressions, or "Kookiesisms," such as "piling up some Zs" for sleep.

It wasn't long before such popularity landed Byrnes in a recording studio where he made the fluffy novelty hit "Kookie, Kookie (Lend Me Your Comb)" (#4, 1959). This rather lame comic skit finds Byrnes sparring with girlfriend Connie Stevens over his comb, which it turns out she only wants so he'll stop combing his hair and kiss her. Fortunately Byrnes's singing, which makes Fabian sound like Pavarotti, is kept to a minimum. But it's hard to completely hate a novelty record that ends with the line "Baby, you're the ginchiest."

Byrnes barely missed the top forty with his follow-up single, another exercise in hip talk, "Like I Love You," which paired him with another girl singer, Joannie Sommers, listed on the label as "Friend." After 77 *Sunset Strip* closed shop in 1964, Byrnes found work primarily in B movies and later in TV commercials for men's styling combs. "It's hard for some people to believe," he told England's *New Musical Express* in 1961, "but I only talk like Kookie in 77 *Sunset Strip*—never in private." Thank goodness.

Three Cool Cats

Novelty artists of the 1950s included some pretty oddball characters. The three gentlemen considered here are among the most memorable and talented of the lot. Their backgrounds could not have been more different: an old-time crooner, a singing cowboy, and a rock 'n' roll deejay. Each had a huge novelty hit, but in the range of their talents and interests they were far more than one-hit wonders.

"Transfusion" may lay claim to being one of the very first hit novelties of the rock era, hitting the charts a full two months before Buchanan and Goodman's "The Flying Saucer" in 1956. Its composer and vocalist, Jimmy Drake, was a most unlikely candidate for pop stardom. A truck driver from Oakland, California, Drake broke into show business making demos for amateur songwriters on a home tape recorder. He was a quiet crooner with a voice reminiscent of Ukelele Ike (like Ike, he also played the ukelele) and a style that was closer to the 1930s than the 1950s. His first solo record was "Gambling Fever," a country ballad, released on the Claudra label in Indiana.

He also sang backup with a pop quartet called the Four Jokers, which recorded his song "Transfusion" in early 1956 for the Diamond label. The single didn't sell and the same year Drake signed with Dot Records and made a solo version of his song, changing his nom de disque from "Singing Jimmy Drake" to the more appropriate "Nervous Norvus." This time the record took off, rising to #8 on *Billboard*'s Hot One Hundred.

Car novelty songs had been popular since "In My Merry Oldsmobile," but "Transfusion" was one of the sickest and funniest. By the mid-fifties, with the growth of the interstate highway system and the increase in the number of teen drivers, car accidents were at an all-time high and "Transfusion," with its gory humor, struck a nerve with the public. Norvus is singing from his hospital bed where he lands after all his smash-ups, each of which is punctuated by sound effects he dug out of a radio studio's library. Despite his repeated vow that he is "never, never, never gonna speed again," he continues to break every rule of the roadway from running stop signs to drinking while driving.

For all its hip talk ("I'm a twin pipe papa"), "Transfusion" betrays Drake's musical roots. He strums his ukulele and spouts rhyming tag lines after each chorus that are straight out of a 1940s jump tune ("Shoot the juice to me, Bruce," "Pour the crimson in me, Jimson"). The song concludes with a warning to "remember to slow down, today." But the rest of the record belies this tacked-on safe driving message and many radio stations banned it from the airwaves for its grisliness and humorous attitude toward bad driving. London Records, who released Dot records in the United Kingdom, refused to touch it.

"Transfusion" remains a classic novelty record—fresh, original, and, funny. Unfortunately Drake wasn't able to sustain his career as a novelty artist very long. His follow-up, "Ape Call" (#24), a comic paean to the mating rites of prehistoric man, while humorous, lacks the bite and wit of its predecessor. The most amusing part of the record is a vaudevillian

The sick humor of "Transfusion" is clearly reflected in the lettering on this sheet music cover. Nervous Norvus (aka Jimmy Drake) had fleeting fame as a novelty artist, but his classic record will live on as long as there are bad drivers. (Photo courtesy of Showtime Archives, Toronto)

vocal break in which Drake describes a pterodactyl ("Say, we haven't changed a bit, have we, cats?").

Drake released one more single for Dot and then faded from popularity, continuing to record into the late fifties on the Embee and Big Ben labels with little success. One of his last records was "Let's Worship God Each Sunday." Jimmy Drake died in 1968 at age 56; he might have been amused that year at the success of another musical throwback, Tiny Tim.

More versatile and harder to classify is the recording career of Sheb Wooley. His first ambition as a boy growing up on his dad's farm in Erick, Oklahoma, was to be a singing cowboy. Unlike many of the cowboys in Hollywood, however, Wooley was the genuine article, roping steers and riding in rodeos as a teenager. In high school he formed his own western band, the Plainview Melody Boys. He was already married and working as a welder in California when he went into the service during World War II. After the war he headed for Nashville, worked at a radio station, and began recording his own songs

The rustic air Sheb Wooley exudes in this MGM publicity still is at odds with his #1 novelty "The Purple People Eater," but Wooley was always an eclectic recording artist, equally at home with pop, country, novelty, and parody. (Photofest)

on the Bullet label. But Hollywood beckoned and Wooley headed west. He stopped off in Fort Worth, Texas, and stayed there for three years, continuing to write and record. He even had a regional hit in 1947 with "Peepin' Through the Keyhole (Watching Jole Blon)," which established a preoccupation in his music with wild country humor and shapely women. MGM Records took notice and signed him on. He would remain with the label, which offered him the greatest of freedom for his far-ranging talents, for a quarter century.

Wooley finally made it to Hollywood in 1950 and appeared in his first picture the following year, an Errol Flynn vehicle, *Rocky Mountain*. He quickly became a dependable character actor, mostly in westerns and mostly as a heavy. One of his most memorable performances was as gunslinger Ben Miller in *High Noon*. In 1961 he created the role of scout Pete Nolan on the long-running TV western series *Rawhide*.

Wooley's recording career at MGM was far more versatile than his acting career. While his early records were mostly in the hillbilly mode, by the time he recorded "Are You Satisfied?" in 1955, he was moving toward mainstream pop and this upbeat ballad crossed over from country to pop and went to #95. The next year he released "The Birth of Rock 'n' Roll," which wasn't exactly rock but showed Wooley could change with the times. He was something of a musical chameleon, sounding one minute remarkably like Dean Martin ("Recipe for Love," "Do I Remember") and the next like Don Gibson ("Running with the Night Crowd").

But it was an offbeat novelty that finally put him on the musical map in 1958. He was chatting with good friend country songwriter Don Robertson when he heard Robertson's son tell a silly joke about a creature called a "purple people eater." Wooley thought it would be a marketable novelty title in the wake of "The Flying Saucer" and more recently David Seville's "The Witch Doctor." While trying to figure out how Seville got the Witch Doctor voice, "I discovered that if you double speed a song it comes back into pitch several octaves higher," Wooley told Kevin Coffey in an interview.

Despite a spooky opening that came on like gangbusters, "The Purple People Eater" was less interested in eating earthlings than making music and yearned to "get a job in a rock 'n' roll band." The most arresting sound in the record was not the squeaky voice of the Purple People Eater, but the final double-speeded sax solo by veteran saxman Plas

Johnson which simulates the creature blowing through the horn in his head. For good measure Wooley threw in a couple of references to another current novelty hit, "Short Shorts," and the Champs' #1 instrumental "Tequila."

Never a great novelty record, "The Purple People Eater" was the perfect silly song for a silly time and zoomed to #1, where it took up residence for six weeks. It set off a national craze for Purple People Eater hats (with a horn on top), T-shirts, and even ice cream.

Wooley continued to mine the novelty field for years but never struck pay dirt again. He recycled the Purple People Eater's high-pitched voice as African natives ("Pygmy Love"), a juvenile delinquent (the Coasters-like "Luke the Spook"), and more space aliens (1963's "Who Who Wallikins" featured a trio of them, like the Chipmunks). One of his best post-People Eater novelties was the snappy hot rod item "The Chase," every bit as good as Charlie Ryan's "Hot Rod Lincoln." Nothing, however, made the pop charts except for two comic country songs, "Sweet Chile" (#70, 1959), about a bayou Baby Doll with Wooley's delicious suggestive comments delivered sotto voce, and "That's My Pa" (#51, 1962), about an irascible cuss fond of fighting and yodeling, which went to #1 on the country charts. The same year saw the birth of another unruly character who would become Wooley's alter ego, Ben Colder, who parodied pop and country songs (see Chapter 3).

Wooley's parodies far outsold his novelty numbers, but even at their most formulaic his records are often funny and always interesting. As for the "Purple People Eater," he has become a part of American pop culture. As recently as March 1998, Jesse Jackson was quoted in the *New York Times* as saying that President Bill Clinton "doesn't have one eye in his forehead, like a Purple People Eater. He can be circumspect."

Few events in the history of rock are invested with more tragic significance than the plane crash near Mason City, Iowa, on February 2, 1959, that took the lives of Buddy Holly, Ritchie Valens, and the man known as the Big Bopper, J. P. Richardson. Holly was already a legend to many at the time of his death, while Valens had just had a two-sided smash, "Donna" and "La Bamba," and seemed on the verge of becoming the first major Hispanic rock star. Of the three, Richardson seems the least likely to have left much of a legacy behind him. After all, he was only a novelty artist, a one-and-a-half-hit wonder who left behind little musical material to perpetuate his memory. But on closer examination, Richardson is revealed as an artist and songwriter of striking originality and a much wider range than he has been given credit for. His death at age twenty-nine was possibly no less a loss to the world of rock than that of his plane mates.

The persona of the Big Bopper, whom Richardson portrayed in the last few years of his life, was a boisterous character who loved good times and loose women. In real life Richardson himself wasn't so far removed from the character he played. He was born in Sabine Pass, Texas, on October 24, 1930, the eldest of three sons of an oil field worker. He hated his Christian name, Jiles Perry, and went by J. P., or Jape, which seemed to fit his brash, boisterous personality. In high school he was nicknamed Killer by his teammates on the football team, where he was a defensive linesman. But he loved music too and as a choir member won the Huntsville, Texas, Regional Meet with his rousing rendition of "Old Man River."

After high school, Richardson went to Lamar College of Technology in Beaumont, Texas, and worked as a part-time deejay on the local radio station, KTRM. After graduation he was drafted and served a two-year hitch in the army as a radar instructor. He returned to KTRM in 1955 and soon was the most popular radio personality in the region. Needing a radio name, he first chose "The Big Yazoo," after one of his local sponsors, a lawn mower company. But he soon changed it to "The Big Bopper," which better fit the black dialect he used to introduce black rhythm and blues records on the air.

Richardson's popularity with listeners moved him from the "Dishwasher's Serenade" in the late morning to the more desirable 3:00 to 6:00 afternoon slot on "The Big Bopper Show." His ebullient spirit led him to perform endless promo stunts to increase ratings. His most ambitious stunt was his "Discathon" in May 1957 in which he successfully broke the world's record for continuous broadcasting. Fueling his body with a high-sugar and -protein diet and taking cold showers to stay awake, he remained at the studio turntable for six days and nights, spinning 1,821 records. After sleeping for twenty straight hours, Richardson swore he'd never do it again.

Already he was recording demos of songs he had written. "Sippin' Cider" was his first foray into novelty, recorded for tiny Feature Records in Louisiana. A while later he signed with Mercury Records

J. P. Richardson (aka the Big Bopper) isn't liking what he hears from his girlfriend, but the sky-rocketing sales of his novelty hit "Chantilly Lace" must have eased the pain. A deejay before he became a recording artist, Richardson originally called himself "The Big Yazoo" on his radio program, in honor of a local lawn mower sponsor. (Photofest)

and recorded under the name Jape Richardson. "Beggar to a King," from an early Mercury session, is a heartfelt country ballad that revealed him to be a good "straight" vocalist within the limitations of his bass range. "Monkey Song" was a wild novelty in which he employed a convincing Buddy Holly hiccup, imitating the fellow Texan whose fate he would share a few years later.

In mid-1958 Richardson recorded another self-penned novelty that brought together the characters from the year's two biggest novelty records. "The Purple People Eater Meets the Witch Doctor" was actually a better number than the title would indicate and was a hit when covered by a very young Joe South (see Chapter 10). But much better was the flip side, a kind of vaudeville-type skit in which the Bopper conversed with his girlfriend on the telephone. Richardson titled it "That's What I Like," the Bopper's catchphrase on his radio show, but Starday Record owner Pappy Daily felt that "Chantilly Lace," which was also in the lyrics, was a more salable title and Richardson reluctantly agreed to change it.

"Chantilly Lace" struck a chord with teens everywhere and it quickly became a national hit, rising to #6. When the Bopper croons "Baby, you knooww what I like!" you know he's not talking about frilly clothes. The patter is great fun, the rocking beat is irresistible, and the famous chorus sums up the Bopper's devil-may-care character to a fare-thee-well. "Chantilly Lace" remains not only one of the great novelty records of the rock era, but one of the best rockers of the fifties.

The follow-up, "Big Bopper's Wedding" (#38), is nearly as good as its predecessor. Picking up where the first record left off, Bopper's manipulative girlfriend has somehow managed to get him to the altar, where he expresses his last-minute doubts in a freewheeling soliloquy that follows the same patter-repeating chorus of "Chantilly Lace." When the Bopper gasps, "This is it!" he speaks for every red-blooded male who has second thoughts before taking the marital plunge. The flip side, "Little Red Riding Hood," also charted and was a delicious concept, with the Big Bopper playing the Bad Big Wolf. The execution, however, is rather commonplace and disappointing after the comic inventiveness of his first two hits.

By January 1959 the Big Bopper was a qualified star and solidified his importance by signing on as a headliner with Buddy Holly's "Winter Dance Party" tour of the Midwest. Dion and the Belmonts and newcomer Ritchie Valens were also on board. The tour quickly proved a disappointment for everyone. The weather was miserable and the bus they rode in from show to show was cold and uncomfortable. To top it all, Richardson caught the flu in midtour. But it was his physical bigness that led to his untimely death. When he learned that Holly had chartered a four-seater Beechcraft Bonanza to take him to the next gig in Fargo, North Dakota, Richardson quickly talked Holly sideman Waylon Jennings out of his seat. "These bus seats bug me," he told Jennings.

Bad weather and an inexperienced pilot led to tragedy, and the plane crashed in a frozen cornfield only a few miles from their airport destination. All four passengers died on impact. Richardson's body was throw forty feet from the plane. Only a few days later he was to receive an award for "Chantilly Lace."

Richardson's death cut short a career that looked more than promising. Mercury released an album in 1959 that showed some of that promise. "White Lightning," which Richardson also wrote, was a great country novelty number that George Jones recorded that year and took to #1 on the country charts. "It's the Truth, Ruth," with its hard-hitting Bo Diddley beat and barnyard imagery, showed Richardson's instinctive feel for American folk material, both in the lyrics and his down home delivery. "Pink Petticoats" was another irresistible teen rocker cut from the same colorful cloth as "Chantilly Lace" and "Someone Watching Over You" was a heartfelt religious ballad with a fervent gospel touch that revealed Richardson to be no mere facile imitator of black Southern music.

Some months before his death, Richardson had written a song for his good friend and fellow Texan Johnny Preston, inspired by a Dove soap commercial. "Running Bear," on which Richardson can be heard whooping in the background, was a sentimental ballad of the *Hiawatha* school and a less than fitting last testament from this gifted performer. Richardson left behind him a sizable legacy of laughter and good times, rolled up in one of the most high-spirited characters in rock 'n' roll.

If the Big Bopper was a white man masquerading as a black man, there were plenty of real black artists who would bring their own unique world experience to the recording studio and in the process considerably widen the curious world of the novelty song.

② Soul Humor

"What you want for nothin'? A rubber biscuit?"—*The Chips*

In early 1957, a rather unique recording artist from New Orleans emerged on the national scene. His name was Clarence Henry and his song was a comic lament called "Ain't Got No Home," which he sang vigorously in three octaves—falsetto, tenor, and bass. This feat quickly earned him the nickname Frogman for the deep frog voice he used.★

The flip side of "Ain't Got No Home," initially intended as the A side, was a less humorous complaint entitled "Troubles, Troubles." Henry's easy Fats Domino delivery and the enticingly syncopated beat softened the despair of the lyrics, which implied that the only way out of life's troubles was suicide.

Trouble was something that black Americans were intimately familiar with, going back to their arrival in this country on the first slave ships. There were other "ways out" than suicide, however, and one of them was the ability to laugh at their troubles. Black humorists from Bert Williams to Langston Hughes to Richard Pryor have found laughter to be the best defense in a world of racism, prejudice, and economic deprivation. And so the tradition continued into the 1950s, as black rhythm and blues artists used the humor of novelty songs to deal with their "troubles" and gave this much-maligned genre some of its finest moments.

Meanwhile, Back in the Jungle . . .

The history of black entertainment in white American society until relatively recently was one of racial denigration. From the nineteenth-century minstrel shows to Broadway revues like *Blackbirds of 1928,* which made a star of William "Bojangles" Robinson, black entertainers have had to grin and bear it, singing and dancing their way into the heart of white America, but never as equals. Blacks on stage and screen

---

★*Henry disappeared from the scene after his lone hit, only to reappear on the charts four years later without the froggy voice, singing sentimental ballads like the old standard "You Only Hurt The One You Love."*

often had to play one of two stereotypical roles: dumb and gutless native "coons" or exotic savages from darkest Africa, their ancestral homeland. In both cases black performers began to twist the stereotypes to their own advantage. Josephine Baker became the toast of Paris in the 1920s by becoming the most exotic of the exotic. Part of her act was doing the shimmy wearing only a skirt of giant bananas at the Folies-Bergère. While back on Broadway, Ethel Waters played an African queen in "Hottentot Potentate," a production number from a 1933 Irving Berlin revue. At the other end of the spectrum, pioneering rhythm and blues artist Louis Jordan celebrated rural Southern black culture in such classic novelties of the 1940s as "Ain't Nobody Here But Us Chickens" and "Beans and Cornbread."

By the 1950s R&B groups were intermingling the trappings of exotica with Southern black folklore to create some of the funniest records of the decade. One of the most famous examples of this subgenre and one of the earliest of rock novelties is "Stranded in the Jungle," a song that brought fame to two black groups. Written by James Johnson, lead singer for the Jayhawks, an R&B quintet from Los Angeles, "Stranded in the Jungle" tells a tale as old as *The Odyssey*. The hero is a rich playboy whose plane crashes in Africa while he's en route to a date with his girl, who in his absence is besieged by another suitor. The song shifts back and forth from the hero's misfortunes, narrated by Johnson, to "back in the States," where the bad guy is wooing his girl to a rock beat sung by the rest of the group. The lyric unfolds like a tall tale. After the hero makes his escape from a tribe of cannibals he hitches a ride on a whale "who was heading my way,/And I reached the States in a half a day."

The Jayhawks' version was quickly covered by another L.A. group, the Cadets, who were known as "King of the Covers" for their many versions of other people's hits, even including Elvis Presley's "Heartbreak Hotel." Their "Stranded" charted in early July, and the Jayhawks' original three weeks later. The song became so popular that both versions made the top twenty. The Cadets' version is technically superior, featuring lion snarls and bird calls over the tribal drums and chanting. But Johnson's inimitable nasal tenor lead tops Cadet Aaron Collins's more typical baritone vocal for attention.

The Cadets actually led a double life, moonlighting on the Modern label as the Jacks, a doo-wop group that sang ballads, and had their only

STRANDED IN THE JUNGLE

Words and Music by
ERNESTINE SMITH, JAMES JOHNSON and AL CURRY

50c

as RECORDED BY
The JAYHAWKS
on FLASH RECORDS

SHAG MUSIC PUBLISHING CO.
Sole Selling Agent:
PEER INTERNATIONAL CORPORATION

The Jayhawks gave '50s R&B one of its earliest and best novelties. Written by baritone James Johnson, "Stranded in the Jungle" was one of the few comic songs of the period that could hold its own with the work of the Robins and the Coasters. The Jayhawks never had another hit, but returned to the charts years later as the Vibrations and the Marathons. (Photo courtesy of Showtime Archives, Toronto)

pop hit with "Why Don't You Write Me" (#88), which was also a cover. Neither the Jayhawks nor the Cadets ever had another hit under those names, but continued to rack up hits in other permutations. Collins and Cadets' second tenor Willie Davis later joined the Flares, who struck in 1961 with the infectious dance hit "Foot Stomping," while bassman Will "Dub" Jones would later join the Coasters. The Jayhawks transmuted into the Vibrations and had a hit the same year with "The Watusi," a dance named for an African tribe of giants. Three years later they had another hit with "My Gal Sloopy," which the white band the McCoys took to even greater heights as "Hang on Sloopy."

"Stranded in the Jungle" remains one of the best and most influential novelty records of the '50s. Its story-telling technique is similar to Leiber and Stoller's story songs for the Robins and the Coasters and would set a pattern for many other groups to follow.

Among the best-known black groups to "go native" were Little Anthony and the Imperials, who, according to lead Anthony Gourdine, were not eager to record "Shimmy Shimmy, Ko-Ko-Bop" (#24) in late 1959. The well-produced novelty opens with the memorable line "Sittin' in a native hut, all alone and blue," and has a wonderful tribal chanting chorus by the Imperials, accentuated by a tantalizing sigh. In its review, *Billboard* oddly claimed the song had "an attractive Latinish flavor." Four years later they would reinvent themselves with the help of producer Teddy Randazzo as one of the classiest R&B groups of the mid-sixties. From the grass hut to the supper club—some jump.

Screamin' Jay Hawkins never made it to the supper club circuit, but his outrageous act has been a staple of rock shows for forty-five years. Screamin' Jay, who got his name from an enthusiastic patron who encouraged him to "scream, Jay, scream," took exotica to its logical conclusion, creating a persona that rivaled the Wild Man of Borneo for shock value. If the Jayhawks and the Cadets were stranded in the jungle, Hawkins was right at home there, howling with the monkeys and cooking up spells with the witch doctors. The wailing chants of other jungle novelties are sweet music compared to the animal-like grunts, growls and groans he exudes. His preoccupation with demonology, voodoo, and all things grisly and gruesome makes him as much a precursor as a descendant, inspiring generations of shock rockers from Alice Cooper to Marilyn Manson.

Hawkins was born, by his own account, in a bus terminal in Cleveland, Ohio, on July 18, 1929. Although he took early to music, playing piano and sax, his first career choice was boxing and he became middleweight champion of Alaska during military service. He lost his title to Billy McCann in 1949 and gave up the ring for the stage at age twenty-three. A versatile performer, Hawkins played sax and piano and sang in Tiny Grimes's Rocking Highlanders in 1952, donning his first stage costume, a kilt. His clowning and wild behavior got him fired from some shows, most often because he was upstaging the star.

Hawkins began his solo recording career with such numbers as "Baptize Me in Wine" and "She Put the Whammy on Me." He wrote the complementary "I Put a Spell on You" as a love ballad and recorded it for the tiny Grand label to little fanfare in 1954. Two years later he signed with Okeh, a subsidiary of Columbia, where producer Arnold

Striking a characteristic pose, Screamin' Jay Hawkins fully lives up to his reputation as the wild man of rock 'n' roll. His use of such performance-enhancing props as a coffin, skulls, and smoke machines paved the way years later for such Grand Guignol acts as Alice Cooper and Kiss. (Frank Driggs/ Archive Photos)

Maxim liked the song but thought a wilder version would sell better. Determined to bring out the beast in Hawkins, Maxim sent out for a case of Italian Swiss Colony muscatel and fried chicken and got Hawkins and the band smashed. Then he set the tape rolling.

The results were truly astonishing. The clipped, tight musical tempo set by saxman Sam "The Man" Taylor and guitarist Mickey Baker was the perfect counterpoint for the ranting and ravings of Screamin' Jay. It all ended in a paroxysm of groans and screams that the shocked public found "cannibalistic" and Okeh was forced to withdraw the single. They quickly released a more sanitary version (the one heard most frequently today), but a radio ban on the song was already in effect. All the exposure helped sell more than a million copies of the record, although it never registered on the *Billboard* charts. "I Put a Spell on You" has attracted countless covers by everyone from Nina Simone to Creedence Clearwater Revival, who had a hit with it in 1968.

The original record was a breakthrough for the twenty-seven-year-old Hawkins. It made him a star of sorts, but doomed him to play a role he professes has ruined his health, largely because he had to get drunk before each live performance of his signature song. Much of the impetus for his act came from fellow Clevelandite and disc jockey Alan Freed, who encouraged Hawkins to put together a live theatrical act for Freed's Rock 'n' Roll Revues. It was Freed's idea to have Hawkins jump out of a coffin on stage for his opening number, which he offered the reluctant star $300 to perform for the first time. Dressed in a cape, surrounded by chicken bones, live snakes, and a skull named Harry, Hawkins was a decidedly more threatening male version of Josephine Baker. He quickly earned his reputation as the wild man of rock, bringing a theatricality to the music that went beyond anything dreamed of by Little Richard, Jerry Lee Lewis, or Elvis.

While teens flocked to see his act, Hawkins faced continuing criticism from adults. His scene in Freed's movie *Mister Rock and Roll* (1957) was deemed in bad taste and cut from the film before distribution. He found little comfort in the recording studio. His follow-up single, "Alligator Wine," which boasted of the properties of this homemade aphrodisiac, was written by none other than Jerry Leiber and Mike Stoller. It failed to sell and Hawkins was dropped by Okeh in 1958.

The artist took to the road. The National Casket Company banned him from renting its coffins because of what it felt was bad publicity and he was forced to buy his own coffin. Some of the other acts enjoyed poking fun at his melodramatic act. At a performance at the Apollo Theater in Harlem, the Drifters, who shared the bill and were his "pall bearers," locked him in his casket. He rocked himself off the stand and broke open the coffin, then chased the Drifters off stage, cursing them. The amused audience thought it was all part of the act!

In 1969 Hawkins released his first album in years, *What That Is,* which contained two classics, the truly unappetizing "Feast of the Mau Mau" and the hilariously scatological "Constipation Blues." ("Let it go!" screams Jay in pain, ending in orgiastic gasps of relief as he imitates a flushing toilet.)

In the eighties Screamin' Jay become a cult hero to a new generation when film maker Jim Jarmusch included "I Put a Spell on You" in the soundtrack of his first movie, *Stranger Than Paradise,* then cast the singer as the manager of a seedy hotel in his next film, *Mystery Train.* But Hawkins is not without his regrets. He insists he'd rather be known as an opera singer than a creep who jumps out of a coffin on stage. (He calls himself "Pavarotti of the Blues.") If this sounds faintly ridiculous, check out his lung power on "I Love Paris" from the 1957 album *At Home with Screamin' Jay Hawkins,* reprised on the Rhino collection *The Best of Screamin' Jay Hawkins: Voodoo Jive.*

For all his grousing about the sacrifices he has made, one wonders if Screamin' Jay would have had it any other way. When he received a Pioneer Award of the Rhythm and Blues Foundation in New York in February 1998, he appeared on stage wearing a white tie and tails along with his customary bone and skull. "My mom told me, 'Son, you know, you got a big mouth,'" he said in accepting the first award of his long career. "But for the first time I don't have any words." Maybe a scream or two would have sufficed.

Like "I Put a Spell on You," "Rubber Biscuit" by the Chips (1956) never made the *Billboard* charts, but it remains a classic novelty song. The entire record consists of one of the most outrageous of all doo-wop chants ("Chou chou homa laga duga laga") broken by the interjections of the baritone who describes such down-home culinary delights as a ricochet biscuit, a Sunday-go-to-meeting bun, and a wish sandwich ("It's the kind of a sandwich that you're supposed to take two pieces of bread and wish you had some meat.") Underneath the nonsense, the record speaks volumes about being poor and black and the saving grace of laughter. According to Jay Warner in his comprehensive *Billboard Book of American Singing Groups,* the Chips made no further recordings at that time because "presumably no one felt they could top 'Rubber Biscuit.'"

The Clown Princes

It seems oddly inadequate to refer to the Coasters as a "novelty act." A better description might be one given by songwriter Jerry Leiber, who has called them "a vaudeville comedy act." There was certainly vaudeville in the three-minute playlets that Leiber and his partner, Mike Stoller, wrote for the Coasters, but there was also satire, wit, and a generous dollop of anarchy. Perhaps the best moniker for the group is the clown princes of rock 'n' roll, for like Elvis, Chuck Berry, and Little Richard, they are definitely rock royalty, and in novelty music they're in a class by themselves.

No song the Coasters recorded is as beloved as "Charlie Brown," the definitive tribute to the class clown and their second-biggest-selling single. Each boisterous chorus ends with the threat "He's gonna get his/

The finest novelty act in rock history, the Coasters used humor to explore both the black experience and the world of teenagers through their inimitable interpretations of the songs of Jerry Leiber and Mike Stoller.

Just you wait and see," at which Charlie, portrayed by baritone Billy Guy, laments, "Why's everybody always pickin' on me?" The line succinctly sums up the Coasters' view of the world as an uncertain place where danger lurks around every corner in the form of homicidal boyfriends (and monkeys!), overbearing parents, and enticing teen beauties. The response of the Coasters is to flee for their lives, looking over their shoulders with a laugh. Their songs, all the best of which were written and produced by Leiber and Stoller, are about the misadventures of two groups that everybody always seemed to be picking on—teenagers and blacks. While their work is universal and color-blind (like the work of all great humorists), the specifics of time and place—America at the middle of the twentieth century—give it its special resonance. "Actually I think we wanted to be black," Leiber told Ted Fox in an interview. "Being black was being great. . . . As far as we were concerned the worlds that we came from were drab by comparison."

Jerry Leiber grew up in Baltimore and Mike Stoller in New York City. Both lived in borderline neighborhoods with black culture and music all around them. Their paths finally crossed in 1950 in far-off Los Angeles, where their respective families had relocated. Within a year they were writing songs together, permeated with the blues and boogie-woogie that they had fallen in love with. One song, "That's What the Good Book Says," was bought and recorded by the Robins, a veteran R&B group, on the Modern label. It was, as Leiber now admits, "a pretty bad song," but others they wrote were much better, especially "Hound Dog," a down-and-dirty blues number recorded by Big Mama Thornton, light years from Elvis's sanitized rock version, and "K.C. Loving," recorded by Little Willie Littlefield, later to become the rock classic "Kansas City" when recorded by Wilbert Harrison.

By 1953 Leiber and Stoller were confident enough to start up their own record label, Spark, with old hand Lester Sill, one of the unsung pioneer producers of rock. One of the groups they signed was the Robins and their first Spark release, written and produced by Leiber and Stoller, set the pattern for a new kind of R&B song that displayed a keen intelligence and wit under the rocking beat.

"Riot in Cell Block No. 9" literally opens like gangbusters, that is, the radio drama "Gangbusters," of which Jerry Leiber was an avid fan in his younger days. The wailing sirens and rapid machine-gun fire set the stage for the cool, offhand narrative of Richard Berry, composer of

"Louie, Louie," who was brought in because Leiber and Stoller felt that none of the Robins could give the song the right delivery.

In seriocomic tones, punctuated by sharp rhythm breaks and the Robins' wailing chorus of "There's a riot goin' on," the narrative tells of an aborted jail break at a penitentiary. Although order is restored at the end, Berry intones ominously, "It's quiet now but every now and then, there's a riot goin' on. . . ."

"Riot" was fresh and funny, and dealt with a raw side of life rarely glimpsed in conventional pop music of the day. It was an R&B hit, but it passed unnoticed on the pop charts, as did its follow-up, "Framed," which was similar in style but a far more savage critique of the American judicial system. The protagonist, this time—portrayed by Robin Bobby Nunn, who successfully mimicked Berry's slow, deliberate delivery—is falsely accused of holding up a liquor store and is tried and convicted for the crime. "I'm always blamed," complains the chorus, leaving unsaid the obvious "because I'm black."

Of the remaining handful of Robins' recordings on Spark, two stand out. "Whadaya Want?" is an infectious jump tune, its style a throwback to the forties, sporting a laundry list lyric of what the singer doesn't want. What he *does* want is "a little girl to love," which, as intoned by Carl Gardner in a mocking tenor, pokes fun at any notion of true romance. For the Robins, and the Coasters, romance is more a matter of raging hormones than heartfelt passion. Sex is at once tantalizing and terrifying. In "I Must Be Dreaming," an encounter with a young beauty at a club is just too good to be true for, as the members of the quartet boom in unison, "Love's never been this good to me before." In real life, Leiber and Stoller are telling us, nothing is ever as good as it is in a movie or a pop song—a liberating notion and the foundation for much of the comic appeal of their subsequent songs.

The idea that a beautiful woman only brings trouble is dramatically illustrated in the Robins' next and final single for Leiber and Stoller, the masterful "At Smokey Joe's Cafe," which marked a turning point for both the songwriters and the group. Leiber's convoluted lyric is one of his cleverest yet, with some neat internal rhymes, and Carl Gardner is superb as the hapless fool who makes the serious mistake of falling for the girl of the ill-tempered Smokey Joe. Every element of the record comes together beautifully. The opening musical hook, with the full group chanting the song's title, is galvanizing, as is the piercing sax break by Gil

Bernal that cuts through the smoky air of the low-life dive that serves as the setting. The sax breaks, whether played by Bernal or King Curtis, would become another character in each Leiber and Stoller playlet, commenting on the action or establishing the proper mood, whether comic, sultry, or menacing.

"Smokey Joe's Cafe" was the Robins' first and only pop hit, going to #79 on the *Billboard* charts in 1955. It is not surprising that Leiber and Stoller chose it for the title of their recent long-running Broadway revue. It was the song that brought them to the attention of Atlantic Records, the premier R&B label on the East Coast. Atlantic made Leiber and Stoller a unique deal, unheard of at that time. They signed them to a contract as independent producers, selling their masters to Atlantic's new subsidiary label, Atco. The Robins' manager balked at the deal, however, and the impending move to the East Coast. Fortunately, Leiber and Stoller were able to coax Carl Gardner and bass man Bobby Nunn to leave the group and go with them. The two singers brought aboard friends Billy Guy, a baritone, and Leon Hughes, a tenor, to fill out a new group, the Coasters, named by Lester Sill for the West Coast they would soon be leaving. Spark Records folded, the Coasters were born, and the Robins, without the songs of Leiber and Stoller, quickly faded into obscurity, although they continued to record for various labels until 1961.

The Coasters' first release was "Down in Mexico," covering much the same exotic territory as "Smokey Joe's." Stoller's impeccable instrumentation, always at the service of the song, includes thumping congas for a south-of-the-border flavor, and Carl Gardner's intonation is as ripe as ever, giving a lift to such words as "Mex-i-ca-li." Equally good was the flip side, "Turtle Dovin'," the first of a string of songs dealing with sex. Here Gardner's vocalizing is truly lascivious, echoed by the hot twang of Ralph "Waldo" Hamilton's bluesy guitar.

Sex was also the focus of their next single, "One Kiss Led to Another," but in a more comic mode. The narrative has Gardner visiting his girl while she baby-sits; they become completely immobilized by their smooching. The punctuating kisses during the chorus is the kind of masterful touch that show Leiber and Stoller were as good at producing records as they were at writing them. The flip side was a fine version of the standard "Brazil," which proved the Coasters could have made a good living as a more traditional doo-wop group. Their occasional ballads are all the more distinctive because the lead is usually sung by bass man Bobby Nunn. "One Kiss" gave the Coasters their first pop charter, weighing in at #73. It was also the first Leiber and Stoller number that clearly appealed to the culture of white teens as well as black ones.

For the next year or so the group was so busy with touring and their relocation to the East Coast that they never saw the inside of a recording studio. But when they did finally produce their next single in March 1957, it became the biggest double-sided hit of their career. In "Searchin'," a guy on the trail of a lost love sees himself as a detective and Leiber had a field day fitting the names of his favorite fictional private eyes into the lyric. The irresistible musical hooks were provided by a rollicking piano played by Mike Stoller and the chorus "Gonna find her." "Searchin'" went to #3 and remained on *Billboard's* Hot One Hundred for 22 weeks. The flip, "Young Blood" (#8), is one of those rare occasions when Leiber and Stoller took on a third collaborator, Doc Pomus. It remains the Coasters most explicit foray into sexual fantasy, with Carl Gardner's outlandish delivery lending a lascivious suggestiveness to such lines as "What's your name?" which is repeated to great comic effect by each group member. This time the girl is indeed forbidden fruit: "young blood" is slang for an underage girl. The siren call of sex is so strong that our boys follow her home, where they are confronted by the girl's suspicious father, played by Bobby Nunn.

On their next single, "Idol with the Golden Head" (#67), Leiber mixes a Saturday afternoon serial adventure with a down-home country setting to produce a lyric that oozes with surreal humor. The idol oracle directs its owner to the doings of Big Foot Mae, one of Leiber's most delicious characters. Their next two Coasters' releases didn't chart, although one side, "What's the Secret of Your Success?," is one of the team's wittiest satires, with Billy Guy interviewing a rich cat who seems to have it all. Bobby Nunn's tag line is a succinct summary of the Coasters' rather bleak but realistic outlook on life: "Some cats got it and some cats ain't."

Their next hit was their biggest and one of their briefest. "Yakety Yak" runs two minutes, but it doesn't need another second to get across its point: parental nagging. The sax break by King Curtis is justifiably one of the most famous in rock 'n' roll, a yakety, stuttering bridge that Curtis originated but was carefully blueprinted by Mike Stoller. The record shot to #1 and turned the Coasters from a black comedy act into the high spokesmen for American teens in the fifties. The B side, "Zing! Went the Strings of My Heart," was another superb upbeat version of a standard, featuring Will "Dub" Jones, who replaced Bobby Nunn when he quit the group, and Cornell Gunter, who replaced Leon Hughes about the same time.

Nineteen-fifty-nine was a banner year for the Coasters. They placed three songs in the top ten, the first and foremost being "Charlie Brown" (#2) the national anthem for class clowns. The B-side, "Three Cool Cats," used humor to undercut the macho posturing of young males, describing a trio of would-be studs looking to score while "dividing up a nickel candy bar." The song was a favorite of the Beatles, who recorded it early in their career, along with "Besame Mucho," another Coaster hit from 1960. "Along Came Jones" (#9) took its inspiration from the still relatively young media of television and the all-pervasive western shoot-'em-ups of the era. As they did so often, Leiber and Stoller used the Coasters' comic timing to great effect as Carl Gardner describes each twist and turn of the melodramatic plot with the rest of the group gasping, "And then?" each time a step higher, until the tension is broken when Dub Jones clears his throat to make room for the chorus. Leiber and Stoller, who seemed incapable of producing an inferior B-side, tossed off "That Is Rock and Roll," which in its lighthearted way is as fine an homage to the genre as "It Will Stand" by the Showmen and "Rock 'n' Roll Is Here to Stay" by Danny and the Juniors. "Poison Ivy" (#7) is one of the team's finest statements on the torments of teenage libido, subtly hiding the real subject matter under the ruse of a skin rash. ("You can look but you better not touch.")

Despite their move into the pop mainstream, Leiber and Stoller had not sold out their social consciences. "What About Us?" released in 1960, is as bold a statement against racial and economic injustice as they ever delivered. As always the message is dressed up in bright musical hooks and comic delivery, which led some listeners, including *Billboard*'s reviewer, to miss the point. He described the song as "a complaint about a friend who has everything." A similar message is just as potent, if more artfully crafted, on the A-side of the disk in "Run Red Run," (#36). Ostensibly about a homicidal monkey who turns the tables on Red, his human master, it is actually a comic allegory of racial revenge, frighteningly prophetic of the violence that was to explode in America's black ghettos only a few years later.

Equally fascinating is the unjustly forgotten "Shoppin' for Clothes" (#85, 1960), which Leiber and Stoller adapted from the novelty "Clothes Line," written by Kent Harris and performed by Boogaloo and His Gallant Crew. In the playlet (Leiber and Stoller have all but dispensed with the song) customer Billy Guy comes under the mesmerizing spell of smooth-talking clothier Dub Jones, who tries to sell him the perfect suit. The hypnotic mood is further accented by a very jazzy sax interlude from King Curtis and a haunting, wordless background chorus. When Guy flunks the credit test, his humiliation is complete. "That," says Jones, getting in the last word, "is a suit you'll never own."

The early sixties saw a gradual falling off of the Coasters' consistently high level of work. "Little Egypt" (#21, 1961), about a belly dancer who ends up a housewife with a houseful of clinging kids, was as funny as anything Leiber and Stoller had written for the group. However, other writers were now composing for the Coasters with mixed results. Billy Guy's "Wake Me, Shake Me" (#51, 1960) and Bobby Darin's "Wait a Minute" (#37, 1961) were both fair imitations of Leiber and Stoller songs, but lacked their comic spark. "(Ain't That) Just Like Me," again coauthored by Billy Guy with Earl Carroll, who had recently joined the group from the Cadillacs, attempted a newer, hipper style for the Coasters, evoking several nursery rhymes in the lyric. It failed to chart, but was a hit for the British group the Searchers a few years later.

The British Invasion and changing musical styles made the Coasters' humor seem old-fashioned, but Leiber and Stoller were not ready to throw in the towel yet. In 1967 they resurrected the group with an album of fresh contemporary material. "Soul Pad," later released as a single, took the Coasters downtown to Greenwich Village to join the psychedelic crowd. Even better was the flip side, "Down Home Girl," written by Leiber and Artie Butler. The orchestration was topnotch (Phil Ramone was the engineer on the album) and Leiber's lyrics have never been sharper, telling the tale of a Southern black girl trying to pass for a city sophisticate.

Perhaps the epitome of the Coasters' work with Leiber and Stoller was "D.W. Washburn," a revival-thumping ode to an unrepentant reprobate who just wants to be left alone. The humanity that shines through the humor makes this one of the group's finest moments. In the end, D. W. thanks the good people for trying to help him but explains "I'm D. W. Washburn/And I believe I've got it made." Sadly, none of these sides found a hearing with the public, except "D. W. Washburn," which ended up as a minor hit for, of all people, the Monkees. The Coasters last charting record in late 1971 was, ironically, "Love Potion Number Nine" (#76), one of the few Coasters' tunes that wasn't originally done by the Coasters. Leiber and Stoller gave it to the Clovers, who had a hit with it back in 1959.

Today, several "Coasters" groups perform their greatest hits at clubs and concerts across America. Like the Drifters and other classic rock groups, they have become a national franchise. The original recordings, however, made with such skill and love, live on. And so do Carl Gardner, Billy Guy, Dub Jones, and other members from the glory days. Bobby Nunn died of a heart attack in 1986 and Cornell Gunter was shot to death while sitting in his car at a stoplight in Las Vegas in 1990.

The Coasters and Leiber and Stoller represent a unique collaboration in American popular music. At no other time have white and black artists melded so perfectly to produce a body of work of such enduring and universal appeal.

Sons of Coasters

The phenomenal success of the Coasters in 1958-59 led a number of black vocal groups to imitate their comic style. The Cadillacs, one of the pioneer R&B groups, had formed in 1953 and their influence went far beyond their biggest pop hit, "Speedo" (#17, 1956). They worked stylish and intricate choreography into their act, setting a standard that other vocal groups aspired to but rarely attained.

In 1959 the Cadillacs recorded a comic novelty, "Peek-A-Boo," that was a Coasters' sound-a-like, right down to the tag line, "Peek-a-boo, I'm watching you," delivered by bass man Bobby Phillips. It became the second-biggest hit of their career, rising to #28. Two more novelties followed, "Jay Walker" and "Please Mr. Johnson." The latter was well produced but the humor of a bunch of black kids pleading for a job in a white man's candy store seemed rather pointless. Neither tune made the pop charts, but both are preserved in the rock film *Go, Johnny, Go* (1959), complete with the Cadillacs' great choreography.

The Clovers had been around since 1946, when they got together in Washington, D.C., and were one of the biggest-selling black groups of the early fifties. They placed nineteen singles on the R&B charts from 1951 to 1955, but were best known to the general public for their two pop hits, the warm ballad "Devil or Angel" and the jump tune "Love, Love, Love." By 1959 the group seemed at the end of a long career, recording for United Artists. Fortunately for them, Leiber and Stoller were working at United Artists at the same time on a free-lance basis. Their latest composition, "Love Potion Number Nine," was about a guy who buys an aphrodisiac to change his luck with girls, only to end up kissing a cop. The song had the Coasters written all over it, but, instead, the duo gave it to the Clovers, who had the biggest pop hit of their career with it (#23). Five years later, the Searchers from England had their biggest hit in the States with their sinuous guitar version.

The most successful group to follow in the footsteps of the Coasters was the Olympics from Compton, California, formed under the leadership of Walter Ward at Centennial High School in 1954. First known as Walter Ward and the Challengers, they languished in obscurity until befriended by ballad singer and king maker of L.A. R&B, Jesse Belvin, who helped them get an agent and a contract with Demon Records of Hollywood.

In the 1958-59 television season there were a total of twenty-two westerns on the air, a fact that did not escape the attention of songwriter Fred Smith, son of the group's agent, John Criner. He cowrote a novelty song on the subject called, somewhat erroneously, "Western Movies." The song, very much in the Coasters' style, told about a guy whose girl spends all her time watching westerns on TV, ten of which found their way into the lyrics. Walter Ward's sandpaper baritone had little of the comic expressiveness of Carl Gardner or Billy Guy, but the material was timely, the lyrics amusing ("*Broken Arrow* has broken my heart"), and there was plenty of gunfire at the start and finish, taken from an old scratchy sound effects record.

"Western Movies" became one of the top novelty records of the year, shooting all the way to #8, and the Olympics were immediately established as the second-most-popular novelty act in rock. "Western Movies," in fact, may have influenced Leiber and Stoller to write their own TV satire, "Along Came Jones," for the Coasters the following year.

"(I Wanna) Dance With the Teacher" (#71), took the Olympics further into Coasters' teen territory. The emphasis on dancing in the title was telling, for most of their subsequent records would focus more on dancing than novelty. This might have been a smart career move, since black novelty was losing its appeal in the sixties and many black vocal groups were cashing in on the new dance craze. Even the Coasters tried their hand at the form in 1962 with "Teach Me How to Shimmy" and "The Climb," which Leiber and Stoller originally called "The Slime," their editorial comment on teen dances.

The Olympics moved to the Arvee label in 1960 and had a string of pop hits, only one of which reached the top forty, the strange but tantalizing "The Bounce" (#40, 1963). Interestingly, although their sound was very "black," few of their singles made the R&B charts, perhaps because the dances they sang about appealed more to white teenagers. Two of their best dance singles, "Shimmy Like Kate" (#42) and "Dance by the Light of the Moon" (#47), both from 1960, were imaginative reworkings of the old tunes "I Wish I Could Shimmy Like My Sister

Among the imitators of the Coasters, none were more successful than the Olympics, although many of their hits were more dance oriented than novelty. Here they get the drop on the record-buying public with their first and biggest hit, "Western Movies."

Kate" and "Buffalo Gals." "Dancin' Holiday" (#86, 1963), their follow-up to "The Bounce," was actually adapted from a Franz Liszt rhapsody!

But if the Olympics borrowed from other sources, they themselves were borrowed from and not always kindly. Their "Big Boy Pete" (1959, #50), a memorable novelty about a tough dude in the Stagger Lee mode, was lifted note for note by the Northwestern garage band the Kingsmen to become "The Jolly Green Giant" (see Chapter 4). "(Baby) Hully Gully" (#72, 1960), their first dance hit, was recycled by their own label, Arvee, and recorded by the Marathons (aka the Jayhawks and the Vibrations) as "Peanut Butter" (#20, 1961). Actually, the Olympics were supposed to record the novelty song but were on tour at the time. Arvee enlisted the Vibrations, then under contract to Checker, and gave them a new name to prevent legal problems. Checker, however, found out about the ruse, and in revenge released "Peanut Butter" on its Argo sub-sidiary with the Vibrations, listing them on the label pointedly as the "Vibrations named by Others as MARATHONS." Of course, the teen audience didn't care who they were, they just found "Peanut Butter" a funny record you could dance to, and the Arvee version became the hit.

Perhaps the unkindest cut of all was when Felix Cavaliere happened to hear the Olympics' song "Good Lovin'" on his car radio and later recorded his own version with his group the Young Rascals. The Olympics' version peaked at #81 in 1965. The Rascals' version went to #1.

For all their problems and limitations (the group had three baritones, no bass man, and usually backed leader Ward in ragged unison) the Olympics had a longevity that nearly matched the Coasters, recording from the late fifties to the early seventies. Like the Coasters, they were able to adapt to changing times and some of their mid-sixties singles, such as "Baby, Do the Philly Dog" (#63), are solid soul rockers with an exciting Motown beat.

Other groups spent years as backup singers before finding in novelty their moment in the sun. The Rivingtons had worked and recorded under half a dozen names since the mid-fifties. They had their greatest exposure as the Sharps, backing Thurston Harrison on the rock classic "Little Bitty Pretty One" and then providing the background rebel yells and whoops on the hit instrumentals of guitarist Duane Eddy. In 1961 they became the Rivingtons, named after the New York boulevard where Adam Ross and Jack Levy, their new managers, grew up.

Group member Rocky Wilson, Jr., was serving a thirty-day sentence for his part in a fight in a liquor store when someone whispered the cryptic words "Papa-Oom-Mow-Mow" in his ear as he lay in his cell bunk. He stored the strange phrase in his memory bank and later took it back to his group mates. "That's the funniest word I ever heard," responded lead singer Carl White, coming up with the first line of what would prove one of the most influential novelty songs of the 1960s. The strange "dit-dit-dit" chorus evolved because the group didn't have the money to pay for horns on the recording session.

"Papa-Oom-Mow-Mow" was released on Liberty Records in the summer of 1962 and peaked at #48. The logical sequel, "Mama-Oom-Mow-Mow," "bubbled under" at #106, but the group bounced back the following spring with the similarly sounding "The Bird's the Word" (#52), which proved to be the last word from the Rivingtons. The next year, however, both their hits were fused together by a wild surf band from Minneapolis, the Trashmen (see Chapter 4), who had a colossal hit that proved an eventual windfall for the Rivingtons. Their catchy phrase was now a household word and they continued to tour the country into the early '90s.

The Halos were another in-demand back-up group who memorably filled in the background doo-wop on Curtis Lee's "Pretty Little Angel Eyes" and Gene Pitney's second hit, "Every Breath I Take," both produced by a young Phil Spector. The group's bass man, Arthur Crier, wrote a lament for brow-beaten husbands, called "Nag." The comic number was enlivened by a strong dance beat and the speeded-up voice of a harridan wife. It went to #25 in the summer of 1961, a few months after another ode to matrimonial problems, "Mother-in-Law" by Ernie K-Doe, ruled the charts at #1.

Wild and Crazy Guys

The West Coast, home of the Robins, Coasters, and Olympics, and New York, home of groups like the Cadillacs and the Halos, were not the only centers for black novelty music. New Orleans, with its relaxed rhythms and live-and-let live philosophy, was a hotbed for colorful and eccentric musicians from Professor Longhair to Huey "Piano" Smith and the Clowns.

The biggest purveyor of New Orleans novelty was Minit Records, founded in 1960 and managed by Allen Toussaint, whose talents as a songwriter, producer, pianist, and bandleader were astonishing. He produced the semi-novelty "Ooh Poo Pah Doo" for Jesse Hill and Lee Dorsey's string of hits beginning with "Ya Ya" (see next section).

Toussaint's biggest success in the novelty field, however, was "Mother-in-Law" by the irascible Ernie K-Doe. Son of a local Baptist preacher, Ernest Kador, Jr., began singing in the church choir at age seven. He first recorded under his real name in 1955. When he signed with Minit in 1961, owner Joe Banashak changed the hard to pronounce Kador to K-Doe. According to legend, composer Toussaint rejected "Mother-in-Law" as an unworthy effort and threw it in a wastebasket, where K-Doe retrieved it and insisted on recording the song. The tune struck a personal chord: K-Doe's mother-in-law had moved in and was wreaking havoc in a marriage that he later referred to as "nineteen years of pure sorrow."

With its infectious back beat and the irresistible hook of bass man Benny Spellman's singing of the title, "Mother-in-Law" sped to #1 on

One of the reasons Ernie K-Doe's version of Allen Toussaint's "Mother-in-Law" was such a tremendous hit may have been the personal conviction of the singer. Ernie's relationship with his own mother-in-law at the time was strained to say the least. Here he promotes his doubled-sided follow-up hit. (Photo courtesy of Showtime Archives, Toronto)

both the pop and the R&B charts, one of only a handful of novelty songs to achieve this distinction. Its popularity can be gauged by the spate of answer songs it inspired, including two "Son-in-Law" songs by the Blossoms and Laurie Brown. As for Ernie K-Doe, he came back with two more tantalizing Toussaint-produced novelties. "Te-Ta-Te-Ta-Ta" (#53) was another slice of childish nonsense from Toussaint's imagination, while "A Certain Girl" (#71) was a coy hymn to an unnamed beauty and contained the memorable chorus, "What's her name?" Ernie's reply: "Can't tell ya." Today the outrageous K-Doe remains a fixture on the New Orleans musical scene, appearing regularly at festivals and fêtes.

Another colorful Crescent City character is Bobby Marchan, who had been head clown in Huey Smith's legendary group the Clowns. It was Marchan who sang lead on the Clowns' twin classics "Rockin' Pneumonia and Boogie Woogie Flu" and "Don't You Just Know It," which gave the world the infectious jungle call and response that began with the immortal words "Uhn-uhn-uhn-uhn." Part of the Clowns' vaudeville-like act was dressing up in skirts and dancing. This posed no problem for Marchan, who had been working steadily as a female impersonator since the early '50s in his native Ohio. When he first moved to New Orleans in 1954, he became a star of the all-drag Powder Box Revue at the Tijuana Club.

In 1960 Marchan went solo, signing with Fire Records. One of his first releases was a cover of "There's Something on Your Mind," a bluesy ballad written by Rocky Wilson of the Rivingtons and a hit the previous year for veteran sax man Big Jay McNeeley and his vocalist Little Sonny Warner. Marchan sang the ballad straight on the first side of the single but on the flip side, Part 2, things began to get very strange. It opens with Marchan delivering an impassioned sermon about somebody else "rockin' your cradle," at which point he launches into a chorus of "Something on Your Mind." That's no sooner over than he returns to his sermon, only now events take a darker turn. He proceeds to buy a pistol at a pawnshop, break in on his adulterous lover and his best friend, and shoot him dead. He's about to forgive her when the story deftly turns into black comedy and another of his best friends comes through the door. ("This really makes you blow your top.") Marchan shoots the girl and immediately regrets it. She dies in his arms singing the main melody.

Interestingly, Marchan had lifted the chilling monologue from an obscure 1949 recording, "I'll Get Along Somehow" by his idol, blues singer Larry Darnell. Marchan's bizarre novelty gave pop audiences a rare glimpse of the darker side of ghetto life and it went #31 pop (#1 R&B). Despite years of recording, Marchan never had another pop hit. He continued his career as a female impersonator, managed other acts such as New Orleans' Higher Ground, and even hosted his own MTV program, "The Cutting Edge!" unfortunately not in drag.

If love drove Bobby Marchan to murder, it drove Bobby Hendricks to utter madness. Another Ohio boy, Hendricks moved to New York in the

Bobby Marchan made his mark in New Orleans music as lead singer for Huey Smith and the Clowns before striking out on his own with the bizarre "There's Something on Your Mind, Part 2." He later returned to his first love—female impersonation.

mid-fifties, where he was briefly a member of the Drifters, singing lead on their 1958 recording of Leiber and Stoller's "Drip Drop." He signed as a solo with New York's Sue Records later that year. His self-written dance number, "Itchy Twitchy Feeling," with the Coasters singing backup, went to #25 on the pop charts. Nearly two years passed before he had his second and last charter, the memorable "Psycho" (#72, 1960; not to be confused with country singer Jack Kittell's 1975 song of the same title about a mass murderer). The novelty, cowritten by Clyde McPhatter, whose high tenor Hendricks remarkably resembled, is set in a psychiatrist's office where the practically catatonic Hendricks is ending his last session with an unctuous shrink played by New York deejay Dr. Jive. As the psychiatrist reviews the unhappy love affair that brought Hendricks to him, the singer picks up the last word of each speech and repeats it in a kind of pig Latin that foreshadows Shirley Ellis's "The Name Game." Despite his assurance that "Everything's gonna be alright," Hendricks is still singing his catatonic chant as the psychiatrist ushers him out with "Good-bye, young man, good-bye." A most original and disturbing record.

By the mid-sixties soul humor in pop music and culture had lost much of its earthiness and relevance. Moms Mabley, queen of bawdy black humor, had her only charting single with a touching rendition of Dion's "Abraham, Martin and John" (#35, 1969). Redd Foxx, the father of blue records, became a TV star in the tame black sitcom *Sanford and Son*. And Pigmeat Markham, whose career started in Southern medicine shows in the second decade of the century, was appearing regularly on TV's *Rowan and Martin's Laugh-In*. Markham's journey from minstrel show to television was an extraordinary one. In minstrel tradition, this black comedian wore blackface until World War II. When he stopped wearing the makeup many fans were aghast to learn that he wasn't white!

Markham's famous vaudeville sketch "Here Comes the Judge" was such a hit on *The Ed Sullivan Show* that he reprised it on *Laugh-In,* and the title became one of the show's most popular catchphrases. Inevitably it was turned into a record, in which Markham gives an amazing rap performance, twenty years before the style became popular. Unfortunately, the record is marred by a couple of corny vaudeville turns. The wide exposure from television took the single to #19, but a cover by Motown artist Shorty Long went all the way to #8. Long's version was a slick slice of Motown that bore little resemblance to Markham's original.

A native of Birmingham, Alabama, Long was an effective novelty artist in his own right. He came to Motown in 1964, recording the self-penned "Devil with the Blue Dress" on the company's new Soul label. A classic slow rocker, the song languished until Mitch Ryder and the Detroit Wheels energized the beat two years later in a hit medley with Little Richard's "Good Golly Miss Molly." Long himself finally made the charts with two minor hits, "Function at the Junction" and "Night Fo' Last," before striking gold with "Here Comes the Judge" in June 1968. Two more versions of this popular song charted, "Here Comes Da Judge" by the Buena Vistas (#81) and "Here Come the Judge" by the Magistrates (#54), who were actually three of the Dovells. Within a year of becoming Motown's first and only hit novelty artist, Shorty Long drowned with a friend when their fishing boat collided with a freighter in Ontario, Canada. Pigmeat Markham died at age seventy-seven on December 13, 1981.

Kid Stuff

The games and rhymes of childhood hold a continuing fascination for teens and adults. The hypnotic spell of Mother Goose and the Brothers Grimm does not dim with age. These ambiguous, often cryptic tales of childish folly, talking animals, and just plain nonsense continue to haunt us far beyond the age of innocence.

While this world of fancy has been plumbed successfully by white recording artists from the Big Bopper to the bubbly blather of the 1910 Fruitgum Company ("Simon Says," "1,2,3 Red Light"), it is black artists who have captured it most memorably.★ And it comes as no surprise. White kids playing hopscotch are no match for black girls playing double dutch with a pair of intertwining jump ropes. It's obvious who takes their games more seriously.

The same New Orleans gumbo that dished up Ernie K-Doe and his mother-in-law also produced Lee Dorsey's "Ya Ya" (#7, 1961), which he

---

★*Two exceptions are Henson Cargill's "Skip a Rope" (#25, 1967) and Harry Chapin's "Cat's in the Cradle" (#1, 1974), two of the most trenchant commentaries in pop music on childish innocence corrupted by an adult world.*

based on a rhyme he heard children chanting in a playground. "Ya ya" was a girl and "la la" was, we assume, the car in which he was waiting for her. The song's easy, joyful mood is darkened by the fear that "I don't think she's coming."

Dorsey was a prizefighter known as "Kid Chocolate" before he met Allen Toussaint at a party.(In his early days at Minit, Toussaint had tried his hand at his own kiddie tune, "Twiddle Winks," which he recorded with another singer under the name Allen and Allen.) Toussaint convinced Dorsey to abandon the ring for the recording studio. After "Ya Ya" the pair produced "Do-Re-Mi" (#27), another childlike tune with adult intentions and the memorable tag line "Forget about the do and think about me." Under Toussaint's skillful direction, Dorsey would move on to more adult matters ("Get Out of My Life, Woman" and "Working in the Coal Mine") but he always maintained a playful side.

Another boxer turned R&B artist was David Walker (aka Bunker Hill) who was a national contender and Archie Moore's sparring partner. Walker gave up boxing for gospel music, becoming a member of the Mighty Clouds of Joy. Tempted to go secular, Walker recorded the outrageous "Hide and Go Seek" under the management of Link Wray's brother Ray Vernon. He used his unlikely pseudonym to hide his secular singing from his gospel brethren.

Backed only by a thumping drumbeat and a chorus of game players that make the party goers on Gary "U.S." Bonds's records sound downright decorous, "Hide and Go Seek" is a wild, improvised romp that sounds like a cross between a Saturday night gospel meeting and a house party. While lines like "Will you put down that thing you got in your hand" gave radio stations pause, Hill himself tried to show a little restraint. When a rhyme led him to the word "hell" he announced, "I ain't gonna say that!" Nonetheless, he was not invited back by the Mighty Clouds of Joy.

Few R&B artists have enjoyed the longevity of Rufus Thomas, who started out in 1936 in the Rabbit Foot Minstrel Show and ended up doing the funky chicken in the 1970s. His first notable record was "Bear Cat," a male answer to Big Mama Thornton's "Hound Dog" and the first hit record from Sam Phillips's Sun Records. In 1960 Rufus's duet with daughter Carla, "Cause I Love You," would be the first hit of Memphis's struggling Satellite Records, which would later change its name to Stax.

"Walking the Dog" (#10, 1963) was the biggest of Thomas's four "dog" songs, based on a dance he'd seen a woman do during a performance. While the dog was an appealing dance in Thomas's gutsy vocal, it was the nursery rhymes embroidering the lyric that undoubtedly helped make it an R&B classic, recorded by more than a hundred other bands.

The "Loop De Loop" (#4, 1963) was a more obscure dance based on the children's game of the same name and sung by Johnny Thunder, whose follow-up, "Ring Around the Rosey" failed to entice. But a permutation of that same game, "Sally, Go 'Round the Roses" (#2, 1963) sung by the girl group the Jaynetts, was as dark and haunting as any Mother Goose nursery rhyme. The mysterious lyrics, the aching lead vocal by Ada Ray, and the ominous keyboard vamp all contributed to one of the most disturbing pop songs of the early '60s. The familiar tale of a love betrayed is given a menacing spin as the child's game evokes a kind of madness that threatens to engulf the unfortunate Sally. It is not surprising that the Jaynetts were never heard from again. Where could they go from here?

In contrast, Inez Foxx played it straight, adding only a rock beat and a gospel fervor to the folk lullaby "Mockingbird." The echoing vocal of her brother Charlie, who also wrote this version, gave it a unique sound that hoisted it into the top ten. The duo returned a few months later with the similar-sounding "Hi Diddle Diddle" (#98) before turning their considerable talent to more adult fare. Charlie Foxx died in 1998.

Adolescent game players found their true champion in a West Indian-born soul singer named Shirley Ellis, who, with her manager and writing partner Lincoln Chase, created a new and exciting sound of big brass and pounding drums in 1964 with "The Nitty Gritty" (#8). Although it had nothing to do with childhood matters, Ellis claimed to have first heard the phrase in a nursery rhyme. A year later she gave youngsters a new game in the infectious, if somewhat puerile, "The Name Game" (#3), complete with detailed instructions. (Remember banana fana fo?) The long instrumental coda, cut from the single, was the most exciting advance in soul music since Stax's Memphis Horns and Motown's Funk Brothers.

Her follow-up, "The Clapping Song" (#8), was equally engaging and employed two traditional children's rhymes punctuated by slaps and claps while Shirley once again gave complete instructions for this intri-

Shirley Ellis poses against a backdrop of some of the names she twisted around so ingeniously in "The Name Game." Part of her success was due to her producer and writing partner Lincoln Chase, who created the exciting and exotic orchestral settings of many of her records. (Photo courtesy of Showtime Archives, Toronto)

cate game of patty cake. The song was her only hit in Great Britain and was revived there in 1978. It was successfully covered in 1982 by, of all people, Pia Zadora. After all this, Ellis's last game song, "The Puzzle Song" (#78), was something of a letdown (where was the puzzle?). Still, it had an intriguing inverted melody and the irresistible beat of an African talking drum.

When it came to new sounds, nobody in the early sixties could top Phil Spector. While establishing his wall of sound, Spector took time out to create a nostalgic piece of late doo-wop, "Puddin' 'N' Tain" (1963, #43), based on the familiar children's rhyme. The chant is a girl's teasing response to a boy who asks her name. (For the record, her real name was Betty.) The song was sung by the Alley Cats, led by Bobby Sheen, who was one-third of Spector's group Bob B. Soxx and the Blue Jeans. The exotic percussive opening bears a striking resemblance to Spector's earlier "Pretty Little Angel Eyes," but is very different from the recordings Spector was producing at the same time with the Crystals and, a little later, with the Ronettes.

3 Parody, the Sincerest Form of Flattery

"My records are not released . . . they escape."—*Stan Freberg*

"You're looking into Tiffany's most elegant show window, and in the window is a black velvet pillow, and right in the middle of the pillow is an onion. That's me."—*Allan Sherman*

"I'm kind of a pop culture Cuisinart."— *"Weird Al" Yankovic*

Parody—the humorous or satirical imitation of a piece of literature or music—has had a checkered past in popular music. In the last sixty years there have been only four masters of the form: Spike Jones in the '40s, Stan Freberg in the '50s, Allan Sherman in the '60s, and "Weird Al" Yankovic in the '80s and '90s. (The '70s was its own parody.) Besides these gentlemen, and Homer and Jethro and Ben Colder (aka Sheb Wooley) in the country field, successful parodies of pop and rock have been few and far between. Neither Freberg nor Sherman were particularly sympathetic to contemporary rock music and until Yankovic came along in the early '80s, there were few satirists with a strong point of view toward the music other than distaste. That's too bad, for there has been much to make fun of in both the lyrics and music of rock 'n' roll. But then good musical parody is hard to come by in the best or worst of circumstances.

Stan Freberg Presents American Popular Music

When Stan Freberg burst on the rather staid musical scene in early 1951 with the outrageous "John and Marsha," a new era in comedy and the novelty record was born. Although "John and Marsha" mercilessly parodied radio and television soap operas, most of Freberg's subsequent work would satirize popular music in all its curious manifestations. Just as Spike Jones and his City Slickers skewered the romantic crooner and lush orchestras of the '30s and '40s, so Freberg would lambaste the Hit Parade of the '50s. Today many rock critics have taken Freberg to task for hating rock 'n' roll, forgetting that he mercilessly satirized every other form of pop music from calypso to country and western.

Stanley Victor Freberg was born in Los Angeles on August 7, 1926, the only son of a Baptist minister, who named him for British explorer Henry Stanley. As a boy, Freberg fell in love with radio, which he has referred to as "my first library." A champion debater in high school, he decided to forgo college and went to Hollywood after graduation. His ability to mimic and impersonate was his meal ticket and he alternated between the cartoon studios of Warner Bros., where he matched wits and voices with Mel Blanc, and radio, where he worked as a "celebrity impersonator." His impersonations became more far-ranging when he was hired by country and western band leader Cliffie Stone for his early morning radio program *Coffee Time at Harmony Homestead*. When Freberg couldn't find people in the street at the show's early hour to invite into the studio for an on-air coffee and a chat, he began playing them himself, employing a myriad of vocal disguises. It was a talent that would prove invaluable when he began making his classic novelty records.

After a stretch in the army's Special Services during World War II, Freberg returned to cartoon voice work and in the late '40s teamed up with Warner's animator Bob Clampett and voice-over colleague Daws Butler to create early television's wittiest puppet show, *Time for Beany*, which appealed to adults as well as kids. (Albert Einstein was a big fan.) The program ran every weekday for five years, winning three Emmys and a Peabody Award. Freberg's talents as a puppeteer may be over-shadowed by his subsequent work in records, but no less a luminary than the late Jim Henson has named him as his only influence.

Freberg first performed "John and Marsha" as a comedy routine while traveling with Red Fox and His Musical Hounds, a minor-league Spike Jones-type band. Cliffie Stone took Freberg's demo of "John and Marsha" to Capitol Records, which quickly signed him to a recording contract. The record consisted of a pair of lovers (both played by Freberg) repeating each other's names in every emotion imaginable, while insipid strings played in the background. A meeting of Capitol Records execu-

Stan Freberg was a nondiscriminating parodist who took on all comers, from Lawrence Welk to rock 'n' roll. Here he sounds a gong to start a TV special, The Chun King Chow Mein Hour. *Chun King was one of Freberg's many business clients whose sales were boosted by his humorous ad campaigns. Madison Avenue's gain, unfortunately, was the recording industry's loss. (Archive Photos)*

tives almost killed the record's release. One of them couldn't understand why all the two characters said were their names. The company soon came to appreciate Freberg's offbeat humor, or at least his salability, when the single sold 250,000 copies in two weeks and peaked at #21 on the pop charts.

Freberg's next release, a choral version of "I've Got You Under My Skin" (#11), was intended as a parody of the Weavers' call-and-response hit version of the folk song "On Top of Old Smokey." But it also satirized the lush vocal groups of the fifties. As leader Stan forgot the words of the Cole Porter lyric, the singers dutifully repeated whatever he said. This kind of accidental studio mayhem would become a Freberg trademark. Interestingly, Freberg's brand of parody rarely involved changing the lyrics of the song he was lampooning. His satirical sting lay more in the way he pushed the musical style over the edge or in the escalating conflicts between producers, engineers, and recording artists.

"Try" (#15, 1952), where he did change the lyrics, was a devastating parody of Johnny Ray's overwrought singing technique ("You too can be unhappy if you taa-ryyy"), while his "C'est Si Bon" (#13, 1954) gave the same treatment to Eartha Kitt's high-intensity warbling. His biggest hit of the rock era, "Yellow Rose of Texas" (#16,1955), doesn't so much poke fun at Mitch Miller as it does at the Lone Star State, with Freberg playing a Texas martinet who is confounded at every turn by a runaway snare drummer (Alvin Stoller) who keeps drowning out the chorus. Even better is his dead-on reconstruction (deconstruction?) of Les Paul and Mary Ford's ground-breaking multitrack recordings, in "The World Is Waiting for the Sun," where Paul's electronic wizardry goes on overload and explodes like an atomic bomb.

Just as juicy is Freberg's extended send-up of *The Lawrence Welk Show,* "Wun'erful, Wun'erful" (#32, 1957), where even the record label is funny (Side uh-one and uh-two). Freberg's parody of Welk's perky champagne music and his repertory company of bland, cardboard singers and musicians (may my mother-in-law forgive me) is priceless. The climax, with the Aragon Ballroom floating out to sea from the Santa Monica Pier on an ocean of bubbles is as surreal an aural picture as Freberg ever painted. His desperate cry, "Turn off the bubble machine!" has become a favorite catchphrase for Freberg fans.

But it was the emergence of rock 'n' roll that raised Freberg's hackles the highest. His attack on Elvis with his witty version of "Heartbreak Hotel" (1956, #79) justifiably takes on the overuse of echo by Presley and the other graduates of the Sun school of rockabilly. He was less on target with his attacks on doo-wop. In his version of "Sh-Boom," he plays a record producer urging group members to mumble more, when in fact the Chords' enunciation in their rock classic is crystal clear, especially compared with many of the rock artists to come after them. And Freberg's putdown of the monotone piano accompaniment on "The Great Pretender" seems petty and beside the point in light of the Platters' vocal sublimity.

The biggest hit of Freberg's career, and his only #1 record, was not a musical parody, but a clever takeoff of the second-highest-rated program of the 1953-54 television season, *Dragnet.* "St. George and the Dragonet" was the first of Freberg's mini-radio dramas, starring his stock company of comic voices including June Foray, the voice of Bullwinkle's Rocket J. Squirrel, and Daws Butler, the man behind Huckleberry Hound and Quick Draw McGraw.

Dragnet star and producer Jack Webb was one of the few targets of Freberg's satire who was amused by the results, and even allowed him to borrow the NBC Orchestra to play the famous Dragnet theme that opened the record. The retelling of the St. George tale using Webb's understated narrative style was ingenious. ("This legend is true. Only the needle has been changed to protect the record.") The sequel, "Little Blue Riding Hood" (#9, 1953), was also pretty good, but inspiration started to flag in "Christmas Dragnet (Part I and II)" which dealt with a Scrooge-like giant whose heart is finally warmed up by Sergeant Joe Wednesday.

Partly because of his failure to find a foothold in a changing marketplace dominated by rock music, his continuing nemesis, Freberg decided in 1960 to abandon novelty songs for advertising. For the next couple of decades he provided some of the freshest and funniest radio and television commercials for products as diverse as Kaiser aluminum foil and Chun King chow mein. Along the way he picked up twenty-one Clios, the Oscar of the advertising world. He did not entirely abandon recording, however. In 1961 he produced his most lavish production, a concept album on American history entitled *Stan Freberg Presents the United States of America—Part I: The Early Years.* For this "ambitious vaudevillian musical comedy," as he has called it, he gathered his stock company of familiar voices. The result was a mixed bag of corny jokes, silly anachronisms, and some truly funny sketches. Freberg's humor is typically most on target when music is at the heart of the satire, as when a hip jazz flute player pops up during the Revolutionary War to mess up "Yankee Doodle." The musical numbers show Freberg to be a clever songwriter in the traditional Broadway musical comedy style, as in the ambitious "It's a Round Round World" number from the Columbus sketch. It's not surprising to learn that he envisioned the project for the Broadway stage, and for years worked on a production with producer David Merrick. Freberg's relationship with the mercurial Merrick and its disastrous end is memorably recounted in Freberg's autobiography *It Only Hurts When I Laugh.*

In 1996 Freberg released the long-anticipated sequel to the first volume of his history, *The Middle Years,* on Rhino Records. Despite typically great production values and another fine cast of voices (this time including David Ogden Stiers, Lorenzo Music, and Tyne Daly), the album is a major disappointment. Freberg's satirical sword has lost its edge and most of the sketches are flat and surprisingly unfunny. In one sketch involving Stephen Foster, Freberg crams a dozen titles of Foster's songs into the dialogue in a belabored joke that goes nowhere. In "Abe Lincoln in Analysis," the sixteenth president's desire to become a vaudevillian has little comic or historical point.

Stan Freberg, for all his crotchety curmudgeonly ways is, at his best, a brilliant parodist. The man they call the Father of the Funny Commercial is, more importantly, one of the Granddaddies of the Modern Novelty Record, which in his gleeful hands has been a means of poking fun at the vaudeville that is American popular culture.

A Nice Jewish Boy from Chicago

An amateur is a person who pursues a craft for the pure love of it rather than financial gain. Allan Sherman, parodist par excellence, was an ideal amateur, singing his songs at parties for friends and celebrities in a voice one critic called "pure nasal Brooklynese." The very badness of it was warm, appealing, and familiar, as was Sherman's middle-class Jewishness, which he mercilessly parodied in his best material. But when the

Looking like the befuddled man-child he was, Allan Sherman zoomed to stardom with three million-selling comedy albums in a row. His clever Jewish parodies of traditional and popular songs made him one of the most beloved figures of early sixties' pop culture. But not everyone approved of his work. When composer Richard Rodgers heard his "There Is Nothing Like a Dame" transformed by Sherman into "There Is Nothing Like a Lox," Rodgers called him "a destroyer." (Photofest)

amateur turned professional, success destroyed the fragile talent of this funny fat man and the laughter turned to sadness.

He was born Allan Copelon on November 30, 1924, in Chicago. His father, Percy, was not a doctor, lawyer, or businessman, but a race car driver and auto mechanic, originally from Birmingham, Alabama. For a time he ran the largest automotive garage in Chicago. Allan's mother, Rose (whose maiden name, Sherman, he later adopted), was a more identifiable character, a free-spirited woman who divorced his father when Allan was six and took him through a progression of different homes, cities, and husbands. His grandparents in Chicago were the one anchor in his life. They took him regularly to the Yiddish theater, fostering a lifelong love of performing and of all things Jewish.

In 1941 he entered the University of Illinois, where he wrote a humor and gossip column for the daily campus paper. He left school for the army in late 1942, but was discharged within six months for asthmatic allergies that would plague him later in life. He returned to college, found a girlfriend, Delores Chackes (whom he later married), and was expelled for trespassing with her and another couple into a closed sorority house they had entered to play the phonograph. It was a ludicrous scenario right out of his sly satire of campus unrest in the '60s, "The Rebel."

Already writing parodies of show tunes (his takeoff of *Oklahoma* was performed at the university), Sherman tried out his material in a Chicago show biz bar called Gibby's, whose patrons included the actor Edmond O'Brien. O'Brien and other professionals encouraged him to try his luck in New York, which he did. But there was little demand for his parodies in the Big Apple and Sherman turned his talents to gag writing for the new medium of television. He wrote material for some of the best of the early variety shows, including *Cavalcade of Stars* and *Broadway Open House*. In 1951 he and friend Howard Merrill created the game show *I've Got a Secret* and sold it to Goodson-Todman Productions for one dollar with a promise of $125 weekly to split between them when the show hit the air. Seven years later the company sold the popular show to CBS for just under $3,000,000.

Throughout the fifties Sherman worked steadily as a producer for *I've Got a Secret* as well as a writer for comedy specials for stars like Victor Borge and Phil Silvers. These outside activities eventually led Goodson-Todman to fire him from *Secret,* but he soon created another hit game show for CBS, *Your Surprise Package.* The show was produced in Hollywood and Sherman moved to California, a move that would change his life forever.

In Hollywood, the Shermans' next-door neighbor was Harpo Marx, who was famous for throwing big parties. When Sherman arrived one evening and sang some of his parodies, he became a prized guest at various Hollywood gatherings. His songs earned him the admiration of such seasoned pros as Milton Berle, George Burns, and Jack Benny.

The year 1962 was the turning point in Sherman's career. *Your Surprise Package* was cancelled by CBS and he was unceremoniously fired as producer of Steve Allen's new late-night variety show for Westinghouse before it reached the air. Desperate for cash, Sherman took his song parodies to Capitol and Warner Bros. Records looking for a record deal. Power agent Bullets Durgom got him a contract with Warners, but producer Mike Maitland was convinced that his show tune parodies would lead to a nightmare of litigation, since the songs were all copyrighted. He suggested that Sherman write new parodies using the tunes of old folk songs in the public domain, to keep costs down and cash in on the then current folk revival. This decision, in retrospect, was serendipitous. The contrast between the quaint, familiar folk melodies and Sherman's wry, contemporary Jewish lyrics gave the parodies the creative spark that would make them memorable and hysterically funny.

Sherman got to work and in three weeks produced enough new material for an album. *My Son, the Folk Singer* was released in October 1962 and within a month sold 65,000 copies. It shot to #1 on the *Billboard* album charts and remained on the charts for a year, eventually selling over a million and a half copies—the fastest-selling LP in record history to that time.

My Son, the Folk Singer remains a landmark in American comedy. Sherman's sheer inventiveness is astonishing, ranging from cowboy songs ("The Streets of Miami") to early English folk tunes ("Sir Greenbaum's Madrigal") to calypso ("My Zelda," who unlike Matilda, runs off with the tailor). The most daring number was "The Ballad of Harry Lewis" sung to "The Battle Hymn of the Republic," about a cloth cutter who perishes in a factory fire in the garment district. It includes the justly renowned pun "He was trampling through the warehouse where the drapes of Roth are stored." Equally entertaining was "Shticks and Stones," a medley of brief parodies that showcased Sherman's talents better than many longer numbers.

The most endearing track on the album was "Sarah Jackman" ("Frerer Jacques"), a distinctly Jewish boy-girl duet with Christine Nelson, who later put out her own Shermanish album along with a rash of other copycats. As evidence of the impact Sherman was making on American society, President Kennedy was overheard singing "Sarah Jackman" in the lobby of a New York hotel.

After eighteen years in show business, Allan Sherman was an "overnight success." And success was sweet. Unemployed in September, on New Year's Eve he was playing Carnegie Hall to a packed house. A *Billboard* review of his performance there on December 28, 1962, described him as "a rather stout elf on stage" but praised his "universal appeal" and "the cleverest lyric material since the heyday of W. S. Gilbert."

To prove the point, on his next album, *My Son, the Celebrity,* Sherman adapted two Gilbert and Sullivan numbers, "Tit-willow," which became the very funny "The Bronx Bird Watcher," and "When I Was a Lad" which leaned a little too much on Gilbert for its comic inspiration. Warners rushed out the album a month after *My Son, the Folk Singer,* and the results are spotty, with Sherman starting to move away from strictly Jewish material. This might have seemed a good idea at the time, but without the ethnic focus, many of his parodies were less pointed and funny, leading to such one-joke songs as "Mexican Hat Dance" and "Won't You Come Home, Disraeli?" ("Bill Bailey"). Two gems, both Jewish, but also satirizing American consumerism at midcentury, are "Al 'N Yetta" ("Alouette") about two TV addicts, and "Harvey and Sheila," sung to "Hava Nagila," that recounts the rise of a young couple through an alphabet soup of middle-class success (PhD, RCA, PTA, and the like).

My Son, the Nut, from early 1963, saw a further decline in Sherman's material, where too often his ingratiating voice and not the lyrics carried the day. High points of the album were a Shermanish retelling of the French Revolution ("You Went the Wrong Way, Old King Louie"), the self-mocking monologue "Hail to Thee, Fat Person," and "Hello Muddah, Hello Fadduh!" a young boy's lament from summer camp set to the classical strains of Ponchielli's "Dance of the Hours" from the opera *La Gioconda.*

This last number became his most popular song and made the classical piece forever identified with Sherman as much as the William Tell Overture is with the Lone Ranger. Interestingly, there is hardly a Jewish reference in the song, only the boy's Brooklyn accent possibly betraying his ethnic background. The humor is thoroughly grounded in reality, no more so than the final twist when the sun comes out at Camp Granada and the youngster sings, "Gee, that's better,/ Muddah, Fadduh, kindly disregard this letter."

"Hello Muddah, Hello Fadduh!" was released as a single and zoomed to #2 on the singles charts, matching the success of Sherman's albums. Its appeal transcended national differences and it was the top record in South Africa, Australia, New Zealand, even Hong Kong. It won Sherman the year's Grammy for Best Comedy Performance, which he had been edged out of the previous year by Vaughn Meader's *First Family* album. The man who described himself as the "world's worst singer" was playing to packed houses in Las Vegas, the Hollywood Bowl, and New York's famed Copacabana and appearing regularly on national television. In August 1963 he hosted the *Tonight Show* for a week for the vacationing Johnny Carson.

But Allan Sherman's fall was nearly as meteoritic as his rise. His two 1964 albums were disappointing and failed to reach the top twenty. As he strove to find new material to parody, his comic ideas became increasingly precious and trite. The childlike charms of "Sarah Jackman" and "Hello Muddah, Hello Fadduh!" gave way to the middle-age crankiness of "Pop Hates the Beatles." Further albums were even less enthralling, although there were glimmers of the old Allan in the originals "Lotsa of Luck" and "Good Advice," and the parody "Crazy Downtown" (#39, 1965), his only other top forty single, which turns Petula Clark's celebratory hit into a comic lament for worried parents waiting up for their wayward teenagers.

Fame and fortune had caused the once disarmingly honest Sherman to compromise himself. When NBC executives warned him to can the ethnic Jewish humor in his first comedy special, *Allan Sherman's Funnyland,* he complied and bombed with what one critic called "a disappointing hour of half-hearted Shermania."

The funny fat man lost fifty pounds, grew a beard, and divorced his wife. His last comedy album, *Togetherness* (1967), was filled with such feeble efforts as "Westchester Haddassah" ("Winchester Cathedral") and for the second time he failed to reach even the lowest end of the charts. Now middle-aged, Sherman was a late bloomer during the "Summer of Love." He wrote a flop Broadway show, *The Fig Leaves Are Falling,* about his broken marriage, and then penned a curious book on the sexual revolution called *The Rape of the A.P.E. (American Puritan Ethic)* published by Playboy Press.

Once again overweight, broke, and in poor health, Sherman died suddenly in November 1973 from respiratory failure while entertaining friends at his Los Angeles home. He was forty-nine.

Allan Sherman might have had a longer and happier life if he had contained his performances to Hollywood parties and never entered a recording studio. But then the world never would have had the pleasure of knowing Harvey and Sheila, Harry Lewis, Sarah Jackman, and Camp Granada.

Ben Colder: Sheb Wooley No. 2

In 1962 Sheb Wooley, the man who wrote and sang "The Purple People Eater," was slated to record a western tune "Don't Go Near the Indians" for his label, MGM. Wooley was busy filming his second season on the popular TV western series *Rawhide,* and he turned down the record. It was offered instead to movie cowboy and western singer Rex Allen, who had a top twenty hit with the song on Mercury.

"Don't Go Near the Indians" was a ballad about an adopted Indian boy who mistakenly falls in love with his own sister. Under its sentimental surface the song made an ugly racist statement against Native Americans. Wooley, who had a keen sense of humor, saw that "Indians" was ripe for parody and wrote "Don't Go Near the Eskimos," transferring the story to the frozen north where the hero, whose father works at a weather station, falls for an Eskimo girl with the coldest nose in Alaska.

MGM liked the spoof, but because Wooley was not known for parodies (although he had sung nearly every other kind of song in his long stint at the label) they suggested he use a pseudonym. He came up with three, all reflecting the song's far north setting—Ben Freezin, Klon Dyke and Ben Colder. The record label chose the third and thus one of the most prolific parodists in pop and country music was born.

"Don't Go Near the Eskimos" rose to #62 on the pop charts, telling MGM that there was a definite market for this kind of satire. In 1963 Colder returned to the charts with equally clever takeoffs of two of the biggest country crossover hits of the year, Bobby Bare's "Detroit City" and Bill Anderson's "Still." "Detroit City No. 2" (#90) mocked everything on the original from the opening twangy bass guitar hook to Bare's yearning for his old Southern home ("I don't want to go home"). And why should he when he's the "number one washer crammer in the whole shock absorber division" of the Detroit assembly line?

"Still No. 2" (#98) mocked the earnestness of Bill Anderson's midsong monologue ("I've lost count of the hours and I've lost track of the time. And you know why, darling? I lost my watch.") In the end Colder is searching for another kind of "still" in which to drown his sorrows, revealing a character trait that would unfortunately dominate most of his subsequent recordings—that of a unredeemed, dim-witted drunk.

The drunken routine quickly became boorish and predictable and took most of the edge off the parodies. For example, in "Hello Walls No. 2," a spoof of the Faron Young 1961 hit, Colder is bumping into walls and floors after a drinking spree. "Fifteen Beers Ago" finds him with a full bladder waiting in a long line at the men's room in a local bar. His last appearance on the pop charts was a tepid takeoff of Jeannie C. Riley's #1 hit of 1968, "Harper Valley PTA."

While his success in the pop market tapered off in the late sixties, Ben Colder continued to be popular in the country market and was voted the Country Music Association Comedian of the Year in 1968. The following year he joined the cast of *Hee-Haw,* CBS's country-style answer to *Laugh-In*. In concert Wooley would delight audiences by coming out for half of the program in his shabby Colder persona, then in the other half as himself. The act was so convincing that some audience members believed Wooley and Colder were two different performers!

In the 1990s Colder continued to spoof "the big ones," as one of his album titles puts it. His "Shaky Breaky Car," a takeoff of Billy Ray Cyrus's "Achy Breaky Heart," is one of those rare occasions when the emphasis isn't on alcohol and women. Although he has shown little of the wit of Allan Sherman or even Homer and Jethro, Ben Colder managed, especially in his early days, to deflate the silly sentiments of many a countrypolitan ballad and displayed another side of a multitalented and often underappreciated singer, songwriter, and actor—Sheb Wooley No. 1.

Parody Goes Preppy

The Four Preps were once called the Pat Boone of male harmony groups. But beneath the clean-cut, collegiate image lurked an anarchic spirit that eventually asserted itself. "I'd always been a free spirit, very irreverent and extroverted." confessed Bruce Bellard, one of the group's founding members in a 1990 *Goldmine* interview.

The Preps' journey from pop to parody began in a church choir in 1956, where the four students from Hollywood High School (Bellard, Ed Cobb, Glen Larson, and Marvin Ingraham) would practice their four-part harmony. Even then they were performing parodies, but at the time they never thought of trying to record them.

Their performance at a UCLA dance was taped by a friend who sent it to manager Mel Shauer. He was impressed and got the group a long-term contract with Capitol Records, making the Preps, at age sixteen, the youngest vocal group to that time to be signed to a major record label. Almost immediately they had a modest hit with the misty ballad "Dreamy Eyes" (#56), a much bigger hit later for teen idol Johnny Tillotson. It was another year before the Preps had another hit, their biggest, the Bellard–Larson penned "26 Miles" (#2, 1958) that started a teen exodus to Santa Catalina, "the isle of romance." More ballads followed—the Kingston Trio-influenced "Big Man," "Lazy Summer Night," and "Cinderella," from the soundtrack of the first *Gidget* movie.

Then the Four Preps started to veer into new and novel territory. "Down by the Station" (#13, 1960) was a cute and clever adaptation of the traditional children's song that told the tale of a commuting Lothario who gets his comeuppance. Their next single, "Got a Girl" (#24), was more satirical, as they gently chided their competition, the teen idols Fabian, Bobby Rydell, and company, who had captured the heart of their girlfriends. Around the same time Ed Cobb and the group's pianist and arranger, Lincoln Mayorga, moonlighted as the instrumental rock group the Piltdown Men and charted with the novelty "Brontosaurus Stomp" (#75). The Piltdown Men had no further hits stateside but caught on in Great Britain, where they scored three top twenty hits over the next year and a half, all with a caveman theme.

Meanwhile Bruce Bellard's love of mimicry led the Four Preps to incorporate a medley of parodies of other vocal groups into their live act. In what he called their "musicalette," they imagined that the groups

Not your garden-variety male harmony quartet, the Four Preps kick up their heels in the studio. Comedy was a part of their act from the beginning, although it didn't surface in their records until the early '60s, climaxing in the parody medleys "More Money for You and Me" and "The Big Draft." (Photofest)

joined the Peace Corps, just inaugurated by President Kennedy, leaving the Preps behind to make "More Money for You and Me" (#17, 1961). The medley was included on a live album, *The Four Preps on Campus*, recorded at North Hollywood High. Even though Capitol cut the single version by nearly two minutes, "More Money for You and Me" remains a clever and witty spoof of six vocal groups. Among the best of the parodies are takeoffs of the Kingston Trio, who end up in Cuba as prisoners of Castro, and Dion and the Belmonts, including the delicious image of the Belmonts stealing hubcaps in the parking lot while Dion croons "A Teenager in . . . Jail?" They also turned the tables on one of their own, the Four Freshmen, explaining, "They can't afford to gradu-ate,/They're making too much dough."

A year later they released another medley, "The Big Draft" (#61), that sent more groups away, this time into the armed service. (This disk may well contain the first mention of South Vietnam on a pop record.) At the time, the Preps were all serving in the National Guard and were on active duty in 1961 during the Berlin crisis. The medley included another poke at Dion, with the Preps doing a very credible imitation of the Del Satins on "Runaround Sue." But in their version Dion warns listeners about Uncle Sam: "He goes . . . after little boys." There were also neat takeoffs on the hypervocalizing of Dick and Deedee trying to get over not a mountain but the Berlin Wall, and the Marcels, who developed heartburn on top of "Heartaches" from the army stew.

The medley format the Preps pioneered was imitated by a British quintet, the Barron Knights, who had several top ten successes in their homeland with similar records, the last in 1966. The British were apparently a more appreciative audience for parody than Americans. The Barron Knights were still recording parodies as late as 1979, when "The Topical Song," their takeoff on Supertramps' "The Logical Song," was their first and only hit in the States.

The more traditional style of the Four Preps and other American harmony groups was imitated by another British group, the Bachelors. Ironically, the Preps covered the Bachelors' first British hit, "Charmaine." Both versions stiffed in the States and the Bachelors came over a year later in 1964, riding the coattails of the Beatles to fame and fortune.

In response to the British Invasion, the Four Preps expressed the disdain of hundreds of American artists left out in the cold with the satirical "A Letter to the Beatles" (#85, 1964). The record is actually a more pointed attack on the merchandising of rock stars than on the Beatles personally. But the lawyers representing the Fab Four were not amused and pressured Capitol, which was also the Beatles' label in America, to pull the record from circulation. It was the Preps' last-charting single. Their final single, two years later, was a rousing version of Phil Ochs's "Draft Dodger Rag," which brought their involvement with the armed services full circle. From the National Guard to dodging the draft, the Preps were keeping up with the times.

After their breakup in 1967, group members went on to successful individual careers. Ed Cobb turned to songwriting and producing, scoring with such diverse fare as Brenda Holloway's "Every Little Bit Hurts" and the Standells' "Dirty Water." Bellard became a television scriptwriter for such series as *McCloud,* which happened to be produced by Glen Larson. In 1988 Bellard and Cobb reformed the Preps, teaming up with David Sommerville of the Diamonds and Jim Pike of the Lettermen. In a varied and colorful career, the Four Preps proved that novelty can bloom in the most unlikely of places.

Parade of Parodists

Notwithstanding the artists previously considered in this chapter, most parodies in the pop and rock market have come and gone without leaving a trace. Who remembers such ethnic spoofs as the Lovin' Cohens' "Noshville Katz" ("He runs a kosher deli") or "Cholley-Oop" by the Hong Kong White Sox? Who but the hard-core novelty collector would seek out "50 Ways to Beat Your Lover" by Guy Gilbert or "Mrs. Green You've Got an Ugly Daughter" by Kenneth Young?

Among the one-hit wonders in the parody genre, most benefited substantially from the success of the originals. "Small Sad Sam" (#21, 1962) was a parody of Jimmy Dean's monster hit "Big Bad John." While John saves a crew of miners from a cave-in, sacrificing himself in the process, Sam saves himself by climbing out of a plunging elevator over the heads of his fellow passengers. As sung by veteran Cleveland deejay Phil McLean, "Sam" was mildly amusing, but probably would have benefited from a more earnest delivery, say by Jimmy Dean himself. A gay parody, "Big Bruce," by Steve Greenburg, grazed the Hot One Hundred at #97 in 1969.

Then there was the curious case of Senator Bobby's "Wild Thing" (#20, 1967), which managed to parody both Bobby Kennedy and the rock classic by the Troggs. Chip Taylor, the song's composer, wanted to do a version by Senator Everett Dirksen, who recently had a spoken-word hit with the ultra-patriotic "Gallant Men." When Dirksen wasn't available, Taylor hired comic Bill Minkin to impersonate him. Minkin, singing over the original demo track for the Troggs, recorded his Dirksen version on one side and a Bobby Kennedy version on the other. The Kennedy version, with the sound engineer interjecting words of encouragement ("A little more Boston soul, Senator"), became the hit. A follow-up single with Kennedy and Dirksen doing a duet of Donovan's "Mellow Yellow" barely scraped the charts at #99, proving that nonpartisan party politics doesn't work, at least in the recording studio.

One of the funniest parodies of the sixties was "Leader of the Laundromat" (#19, 1964) by the Detergents, a dead-on spoof of the Shangri-Las #1 girl group death rock song "Leader of the Pack." Written by Paul Vance and Lee Pockriss, who had learned a thing or two about novelty songs since they wrote "Itsy Bitsy Teenie Weenie Yellow Polkadot Bikini," "Laundromat" effectively mocks the melodramatic style of the Shangri-Las' mini-dramas, from its opening "guy talk" to the famous ending with those pretentious piano chords. ("Who's that playing on the piano?" "I don't know.")

The head Detergent was Ron Dante from Staten Island, a veteran demo singer for such Aldon Music staff songwriters as Carole King and Burt Bacharach. The group recorded a string of further parodies and novelty songs, including another Shangri-Las' takeoff, "I Can Never Eat Home Anymore." But only their immediate follow-up, "Double-O Seven" (#89), made the charts. It was a garden-variety spoof on the James Bond films and the Detergents had the chutzpa to repeat their first hit's tag line. After the group split up in early 1967 Dante moved from novelty to bubblegum, becoming one half of the Archies. When last heard from, he was working with Barry Manilow and producing hit jingles, proving that his moment in novelty heaven was, indeed, a fluke.

Although not really a parody, the last word on death rock spoofs was the totally outrageous "I Want My Baby Back" (#92, 1965) by Jimmy Cross. Jimmy's girl is dispatched when their jalopy collides head-on with the Leader of the Pack's motorcycle on a wet roadway. ("Over there was

my baby, and over there was my baby, and way over there was my baby!")
The record ends with a crazed Cross digging up his baby's grave ("Hot
dang! Pay dirt!") and indulging in a little necrophilia, which got the disk
banned on many radio stations. Aside from being one of the funniest and
most outrageous 45s ever to hit the charts, the record gets an A for sound
effects, with a car crash that tops the destruction heard on both the
"Leader" records. Unfortunately, little else was heard from Cross, who
later became a successful producer of the Jefferson Starship. He died of
a heart attack in 1978 at the age of thirty-nine. May he rest in pieces.

The death of civilization itself was augured in "Deteriorata" (#91,
1972), the National Lampoon's hilarious send up of "Desiderata," an
insufferable inspirational tract pompously read by TV talk host Les
Crane. Jackson Beck doles out such sage nuggets as "Rotate your tires.
. . . Whenever possible, put people on hold," while Melissa Manchester
leads the backup chorus with "You are a fluke of the universe, you have
no right to be here." It all ends with the cheery news that "the world
continues to deteriorate. . . . Give up."

By the mid-seventies, with Stan Freberg long gone to Madison
Avenue, Allan Sherman dead, and Tom Lehrer still teaching full time at
Harvard, it seemed like pop music had pretty much given up on parody.
But then in the eighties along came a kooky accordion player from Los
Angeles to jump-start the genre.

Weird Al

How does a precocious teenager with a gift for parody get the opportunity to be heard? In the late seventies the one bright spot in the world
of novelty music was not a record producer or company executive, but
a deejay named Barry Hansen, better known to the audience of his
nationally syndicated radio show as Dr. Demento, whose specialty was
novelty music in all its bewildering variety. In 1976 sixteen-year-old
Alfred Yankovic of Los Angeles recorded two novelty songs in his
friend's bedroom and sent the cassette to the good doctor. Hansen was
impressed with the quality and played both songs ("Belvedere Cruisin'"
and "School Cafeteria") on his program.

Encouraged by this response, Yankovic kept up a correspondence with
Demento and continued writing parodies while attending California

Polytechnic State University in San Luis Obispo. One of them was "My Bologna," a takeoff of the Knack's "My Sharona," which he recorded in a campus bathroom. By happy coincidence the Knack came to Al's college and he had the opportunity to play his parody for them. They were delighted and introduced him to an executive at their label, Capitol, which released his original bathroom recording.

The most successful novelty artist of the '80s and '90s, "Weird Al" Yankovic got his start sending homemade cassettes of his parodies to the Dr. Demento radio show. The good doctor liked the material and gave it an airing. Yankovic's career took off a few years later when "Eat It," his spoof of Michael Jackson's "Beat It," became a top twenty hit. (Photofest)

Eventually he made an album that included the early material he sent to Demento as well as an ingenious spoof of Toni Basil's hit "Mickey," entitled "Ricky," that also lampooned the sitcom humor of *I Love Lucy* (remember Ricky Ricardo?) with great support from Tress MacNeille as Lucy. The album took off and "Ricky" became a minor hit single (#63, 1983).

An avid baby boomer, Weird Al (which he started calling himself while a deejay at his college radio station) scored the following year with another double-edged parody, "I Lost on Jeopardy" (#81, 1984) that spoofed both Greg Kihn's "Jeopardy" and the perennial TV game show, even including a guest appearance by smooth-talking announcer Don Pardo, who tells him everything he didn't win. ("But that's not all. You made yourself look like a jerk in front of millions of people.")

Sandwiched between these two singles was Yankovic's biggest hit to date, a takeoff of Michael Jackson's phenomenal "Beat It." "Eat It" transferred Jackson's fake macho attitude into the frustrations of a parent who's had his fill of a child who just won't eat. The premise was a clever one and although the song was mostly a laundry list of food, it worked and rode all the way to #12.

Over the next two years Yankovic had a few more modest hits, the brightest being a parody of Madonna's "Like a Virgin." The gallows humor of "Like a Surgeon" was guaranteed to get few laughs from the AMA but it also had its share of good lines like the clincher "I can hear your hearbeat/For the very last time" followed by a medical flatline.

But like Allan Sherman two decades before him, Yankovic's very pro-lificness brought down the level of his satire, which seemed stuck on the adolescent humor of songs about food and old television shows (witness *The Food Album* and *The TV Album*). By the time he recorded "Fat," another Michael Jackson takeoff ("Bad"), most older listeners were fed up with his food fetish and were ready for some low-caloric, higher-nutritional satire.

When he actually got back to making fun of the music itself and the artists who made it, his stock took an upswing and so did record sales. "Smells Like Nirvana" (#35, 1992), Al's first top forty single since "Eat It," is a sly and devastating spoof on one of the super groups of the nineties and their dense lyrics and depressive style. ("Well, I'm yelling and we're playing,/But I don't know what I'm saying.") Not only did lead singer Kurt Cobain approve of Al's parody of "Smells Like Teen Spirit," but he felt it showed that the group had made the big time.

Nearly as hilarious was his transformation of Coolio's angst-ridden home boys of "Gangsta's Paradise," to the "technologically impaired" boys in black of "Amish Paradise" (#53, 1996), one of the best parodies of rap music to date. Such crazy juxtapositions are truly weird and often memorable. Who else would think of turning Tommy James and the Shondells' bubblegummy "I Think We're Alone Now" into a paean to gene splitting, "I Think I'm a Clone Now"?

In light of the growing difficulty of finding songs in the '90s to parody that everyone recognizes, Yankovic has been turning increasingly to writing original novelty songs, some of which have proven to be his best work. The gleeful nihilism of "Christmas at Ground Zero," the burnt-out torch song "One More Minute," and the cheery nerdiness of "Everything You Know Is Wrong" have a satirical edge that has been missing from many of his parodies. His 1999 album, *Running with Scissors,* includes a satire of the never-ending *Star Wars* saga, set to Don McLean's "American Pie."

Yankovic's talent for packaging his songs in videos, many of which he has directed himself, has been impressive. *Rolling Stone* named his video of "Smells Like Nirvana" one of the 100 best music videos of all time. His elaborate production on the "Amish Paradise" video won him a Grammy in 1996.

Weird Al's energy and enthusiasm is infectious and even when the parody is less than brilliant, the production values are rarely less than first-rate (love that accordion). It's easy to criticize the only artist who has had the talent and chutzpa to build a career in novelty songs in the past two decades and has managed to survive at it nearly that long. It will be interesting to see what direction Al's "weirdness" takes in the years ahead.

The struggle to find common songs that we, as a community of listeners, can respond to, is a daunting challenge for any contemporary parodist. Like all humor, parody thrives on a single, common culture, a group of people who can laugh together at things they share. Our twenty-first-century technology may be putting the world at our fingertips, but it is also compartmentalizing that world to the point where there may be little left that we can enjoy together. The day may not be far off when everyone will be walking around playing his or her own private radio station on a Walkman. And that's no laughing matter.

④ Monsters, Madmen, and Other One-Hit Weirdos

> "The first and only time I sang the song in front of a live audience, I felt I was being laughed at. That was very hard for me to take."—*Jerry Samuels (aka Napoleon XIV) on "They're Coming to Take Me Away, Ha-Haaa"*

> "It is the worst song I have ever heard."
> —*Dan Sullivan, music critic of the* Minneapolis Tribune, *reviewing "Surfin' Bird" by the Trashmen*

> "I'm just a novelty-type guy doing weirdo bloody comedy."
> —*Rolf Harris*

In their desperate search for a hit record, novelty artists have turned to movies, television, American history, the musical past, and even the funny pages for inspiration. If they were lucky the result was a hit record, after which their luck usually ran out. As everyone knows, most novelty artists are one-hit wonders, although you will find in this jam-packed chapter some exceptions to the rule. But whether one-, two-, or three-hit wonders, these weirdos made music that—for better or worse—continues to haunt our collective consciousness.

Monster's Holiday

Just before Thanksgiving 1950, a novelty song called "The Thing" charted. It was a harmless little tune sung by bandleader and novelty meister Phil Harris about a fellow who finds a box on the beach that contains, well, a thing. We never learn exactly what the "thing" is, but nobody wants it and they are constantly telling our hero to "Get out of here with that (knock, knock, knock) and don't come back no more!" It was a silly song for a silly time and it shot to #1 on the Hit Parade.*

Within a year of Harris's "The Thing" a movie was released with the same title. Only this thing didn't come out of a box but from outer space. It had a head like a carrot and it liked to kill people and drink their blood. *The Thing* helped usher in a new era in movie horror in which monsters no longer came out of coffins or mad doctor's laboratories, but from alien worlds. Science fiction horror movies were the rage in the 1950s, spurred on by the UFO craze and renewed interest in life on other planets.

One of the big creature features of 1958 was *The Blob,* in which a young Steve McQueen battled an ectoplasmic monster from another world. The theme song was a curious quasi-instrumental with a "Tequila"-like beat and a tricky sax riff. The vocal sections were bright and cheerful descriptions of the physical properties of the Blob, which sounded like some kind of harmless cartoon character. "The Blob" (#33) was sung appropriately by the Five Blobs, who were actually one "Bernie Nee" whose voice was overdubbed five times. The composer was a young man named Burt Bacharach who would, in time, write better songs for better movies.

The alien creatures of the '50s continued to find favor in the '60s. *The Outer Limits,* a sci-fi TV anthology series, debuted in September 1963 with its full share of creepy beings from other planets. A few weeks earlier the "Martian Hop" (#16) by the Ran-Dells entered the charts. Three cousins from Villas and Cape May, New Jersey, the Ran-Dells were led by Steven Rappaport, a keen student of electronic music. Although Rappaport employed electronic sounds to enhance the record, no high-speed technology was used on the crazy Martian doo-wop vocals, which were sung in falsetto and bass.

In "Mr. Spaceman" (#36, 1966), an early example of country rock, the Byrds pleaded with a friendly alien to take them along "for a ride." Dr. West's Medicine Show and Junk Band took an even more laid-back

---

A very similar novelty record, "Close the Door" by New York disk jockey Jim Lowe, appeared in 1955. Lowe's "things" were more aggressive than Harris's and invaded people's homes. Instead of a knock they were identified by a squeaking sound. Lowe would go on to greater fame the following year trying to get inside "The Green Door," the biggest novelty record of 1956.

approach to an alien invasion in "The Eggplant That Ate Chicago" (#52, 1966). Lead singer and group founder Norman Greenbaum soared to a more spiritual plane four years later with his first and biggest solo hit, "Spirit in the Sky." But the final word on weird aliens must go to Brownsville Station, whose "Martian Boogie" (#59, 1977) recounts a chance encounter with a little green man in a greasy spoon who shares a cigarette with an earthling, giving him a high that is out of this world (Martian-juana?). It was the popular rock trio's last charting single and they went out in style.

At the same time that monsters like the Blob were invading drive-in movies across the nation, their predecessors, the classic Hollywood monsters of the '30s, were making a comeback on the new medium of television. Strapped for income as television cut into their audience, many Hollywood studios sold off their old film libraries to the enemy, giving local TV stations fresh fodder to fill out their programming schedule. A new generation of young viewers were introduced to Frankenstein, Dracula, and the Mummy, each of whom would have their own hit record over the next few years.

Old horror movies became a staple of late-night television and dozens of *Shock Theaters* sprang up on local television, hosted by station employees dressed up in Halloween costumes. They would introduce the evening's feature and then crop up during the commercial breaks, usually with unscripted patter. Their appearances were often more eagerly anticipated by viewers than the movie was.

Among the most popular of these late-night ghouls was Roland, a cadaverous undertaker on WCAU-TV in Philadelphia, played by station announcer John Zacherle. Zacherle would seem to have been a strange choice for the job, for as a child he wasn't allowed to see horror movies. He later graduated from the University of Pennsylvania with a B.A. in English literature and went on to serve honorably in the army during World War II, leaving with the rank of major. After the war Zacherle pursued a career in acting. It was a stint as an undertaker on an afternoon kids' cowboy show on WCAU that got him selected to host *Shock Theater*.

Zacherle's ghoulish sense of humor quickly made him a local celebrity and he soon had his own fan club. Once he asked listeners to send him three human hairs for a pillow and received 23,000 replies. Among his legions of fans was Bernie Lowe, producer of Cameo Records, who would watch the show with his daughter. Lowe approached Zacherle with the idea of cutting a record of him reciting some of his grisly limericks, backed by rock music. The TV host didn't quite see the point, but agreed to make the record with Cameo's house band, Dave Appel and His Applejacks, providing the accompaniment.

"Dinner with Drac" was definitely a gruesome bite. Zacherle's description of his meal with the infamous Count was distinctly unappetizing and included some ghoulish etiquette ("Igor, the scalpels go on the left with the pitchforks!") Lines about dining on the veins of a mummy named Betty got the record banned in Britain, where horror was no laughing matter, but stateside the disk peaked at #6. Zacherle became a national celebrity, hosting Halloween parties on *American Bandstand* and soon leaving Philly for the bright lights of New York, where he became

Zacherle appears to be concocting a ghoulish cocktail for his "Dinner with Drac." The twisted novelty was his only hit record, but he remained a favorite fixture on late-night television for years to come, introducing hoary old horror films and often interrupting them with his gruesome antics. (Photofest)

"Zacherly" on WABC-TV's *Shock Theater*. His career as a recording artist proved less fruitful, and further monster disks on Cameo and other labels went straight to the grooveyard. He continued to make appearances into the early 1990s and in 1996 released a new CD, *Dead Man's Ball,* which proves you can't keep a good ghoul down.

Hard on the heels of Zacherle's success, a voice-over specialist and a would-be songwriter collaborated on the "Dracula Cha Cha," which disappeared without leaving a bloodstain. A year later, however, the same team of Bob McFadden and Dor struck pay dirt with "The Mummy" (#39, 1959), a rather silly playlet about a Casper Milquetoast-type ancient Egyptian (McFadden) in search of a copy of "Kookie, Kookie, Lend Me Your Comb" (Novelty feeding off novelty). Everyone he meets runs away screaming until he happens upon a nonplussed beatnik (Dor), whose response to "Aren't you afraid of me?" is "Oh, yeah. Like, help."

The duo never had another hit, but both went on to bigger things. McFadden became a familiar voice on several '60s TV cartoon shows, creating Milton the Monster and Cool McCool. Dor, whose real name was Rod McKuen, continued to write songs and had a minor hit with one of the worst twist novelties, "Oliver Twist." After that, he turned his modest talents to poetry with far greater success.

The most renowned of all monster novelties was created by an aspiring actor who happened to do a very good impersonation of Boris Karloff. Bobby Pickett was born in Somerville, Massachusetts, where he grew up watching Saturday matinee horror movies at the theater his father managed. After a stint in the Signal Corps in Korea, Pickett moved to Hollywood. While looking for acting work, he formed a vocal group with an old friend from home, Lenny Capizzi. They called themselves the Cordials, and the highlight of their stage act was when Pickett used his Karloff voice for the monologue in the song "Little Darlin'."

Capizzi convinced Pickett they should write an original song for his Karloff voice. Since 1962 was the year of crazy dances, they came up with one for monsters. Pickett wanted to call the finished song "Monster Twist," but Capizzi won out with "Monster Mashed Potatoes," later shortened to "Monster Mash." Gary Paxton, who knew a good novelty song when he heard one, agreed to produce the record. He added dragging chains, bubbling brew noises, and a creaking coffin (actually a rusty nail being pulled slowly from a board), and added the indispensable backup chorus, the Crypt-Kickers, who included himself, his partner John McCrae (later of Ronnie and the Daytonas), and Leon Russell on piano.

"Monster Mash" was turned down by four major record labels, so Paxton put it out on his own Garpax label and eventually linked up with London Records, which readily agreed to distribute the single. The hook-laden dance tune, boosted by Pickett's gleeful impersonation of the most famous voice in monster film land, made the "Monster Mash," as Boris would say, "a graveyard smash." By Halloween 1962 it was #1. The good-natured Karloff was amused and sang the song on

Looking very preppie and most unmonsterlike, Bobby "Boris" Pickett had wanted to be an actor, but his best performance was playing Boris Karloff in the novelty classic "Monster Mash." Karloff himself sang the tune on several television programs but complained that Pickett gave him a lisp he never had. (Archive Photos)

several television shows, although he protested that he didn't lisp. The stuffy British censors banned the song as "offensive," although it became a hit there in 1973, the same year it returned to the top ten in the U.S., an unprecedented event for a novelty song.*

Pickett and Paxton returned to the charts three months later with a surprisingly good seasonal follow-up, "Monster's Holiday," which went all the way to #30 (see Chapter 9). Further monster releases didn't do so well and Pickett was eager to shed his lisp and show that he could sing as himself. In 1963 he scored a minor hit with "Graduation Day" on Garpax, but further non-novelties eluded the charts. In the '70s he teamed up with L.A. deejay Bob Hudson of Hudson and Landry (see Chapter 6) and later Peter Ferrera, who produced TV comedy specials for Jonathan Winters. Together the two wrote a wicked parody of TV's "Star Trek." Unfortunately, Pickett was working in Los Angeles when Ferrera recorded the piece and although he is listed on the label, Pickett makes no appearance in "Star Drek," which become a favorite number on the syndicated Dr. Demento radio program.

Bobby "Boris" Pickett never really succeeded at removing the "Boris" from his name. Being forever connected with his monster hit may have frustrated his career, but then how many other recording artists can lay claim to a song that is to Halloween what "Rudolph the Red-Nosed Reindeer" is to Christmas?

Novelty songs about Martians and monsters are one thing, but one about a madman? One day in 1966 recording engineer and sometime song-writer Jerry Samuels booked an hour and a half of studio time to try out a strange idea for a song that had been percolating in his brain for some time. He came out ninety minutes later with perhaps the strangest novelty song ever to reach the pop charts.

Nine years earlier, Samuels had spent eight months in a psychiatric hospital and apparently the experience had made a deep impression on him. The tune he recorded, "They're Coming to Take Me Away, Ha, Haaa," was the monologue of a madman who explains how he was driven insane by the inattentions of his pet dog (shades of Son of Sam). More disturbing than the lyrics themselves was the pitch of Samuels's voice, which rose higher and higher, reaching a feverish peak of com-

---

*It had returned to the charts earlier in 1970, checking in at #91.

plete dementia. It took Samuels, by his own account, nine months to perfect the recording technique whereby he was able to change the speed of his voice while keeping the tempo of the music unchanged. In the process he achieved the most original technological advance in the squeaky voice department since David Seville brought the Witch Doctor to life eight years earlier. The spiraling madness of that voice was the aural equivalent of an EC horror comic from the '50s, a truly frightening caricature. Of course, like the horror comics, it was also funny. "I knew it wouldn't offend mental patients," Samuels said in an interview with Wayne Jancik. "I would have laughed at it if I had heard it when I was in the hospital."

Mental-health professionals disagreed strenuously. When Warner Bros. released the single under the nom de disque Napoleon XIV (Samuels chose XIV because he liked how the Roman numerals looked), public outcry was so strong that the record was pulled from the playlists of radio stations across the country. But word spread quickly, and even without airplay, the record shot up the charts. In under a week it sold 500,000 copies, the fastest-selling disk in Warner Bros.' history. The flip side was another outrageous tour de force, the same song recorded backwards, "Aah-Ah, Yawa Em Ekat Ot Gnimoc Er'yeht."

Napoleon XIV poses on his only album cover with the invisible pooch who drove him to insanity. His alter ego, Jerry Samuels, has never released his photograph without the mask, only adding to the mystique of one of the most bizarre novelty songs of all time. (Photo courtesy of Showtime Archives, Toronto)

The single peaked at #3 and Warners rushed out an LP using material by outside writers. One of the first pop novelty concept albums, *They're Coming to Take Me Away, Ha, Haaa* had some predictable gimmick tracks, including a bizarre dance called "Doin' the Napoleon" (guess where you put your hand!) and an answer song, "I'm Happy They Took You Away, Ha-Haa!" by Josephine XV. But there were also some fascinating variations on the madness theme, including "The Place Where the Nuts Hunt the Squirrels," "Marching Off to Bedlam," and "I Live in a Split Level Head," in which Samuels overdubs his voice and the two voices overlap in a schizoid cacophony that writer Ronald L. Smith has called "a rap record for psychopaths." "I'm in Love With My Little Red Tricycle" was, in its quiet way, just as disturbing as the title track, with no background music except a celesta and the finger bell on the tricycle. It was issued as Napoleon's follow-up single, but was pulled from distribution before it could chart.

Unable to complete a second album, which he believed would be his masterpiece, Samuels dropped out in true '60s fashion and made his living selling custom-made roach clips and other pot paraphernalia. In the mid-'70s he settled down in Philadelphia and hit the piano bar circuit. By the 1980s he had found his true vocation—playing and singing in nursing homes! What would Napoleon say about that?

In 1986 Rhino Records rereleased his long-out-of-print album in honor of its twentieth anniversary. Ten years later, with Samuels's cooperation, they brought out a CD, *The Second Coming,* that included all the original album's tracks as well as material from the lost second album and more recent compositions. Unfortunately, the new stuff is generally puerile, often sounding like songs Tom Lehrer would have tossed into the wastebasket. A sequel, "They're Coming to Get Me Again, Ha-Haaa!" is a mere retread of the original, whose power to make us both laugh and shiver has not diminished in over three decades. In a genre filled with colorful, madcap characters, Napoleon XIV remains the maddest of them all.

The Trashmen were hardly mad, but they sounded like they were taking speed the day they recorded their perennial garage rock classic, "Surfin' Bird" (#4), in late 1963. The Trashmen were an anomaly—a surfing band from Minneapolis, where the nearest water was the Mississippi River and a bunch of lakes. Like many surfing and garage bands of the day, the Trashmen took their material wherever they found it, from old Buddy Holly songs to R&B to Dick Dale instrumentals. They had particular fun with a medley of two songs by the Rivingtons (see Chapter 2), "Papa-Oom-Mow-Mow" and "The Bird's the Word," although the Trashmen claim they didn't hear the Rivingtons' version until much later. The medley was the highlight of their stage act and a local deejay dubbed the manic-paced medley "Surfin' Bird." The group recorded it on the Soma label in the fall of 1963 and soon their regional hit turned into a national blockbuster, peaking at #4.

The Trashmen were high on the heap when their first album came out featuring their eccentric takes on two songs by the Rivingtons, "Papa-Oom-Mow-Mow" and "The Bird's the Word." The Soma label had a knack for finding offbeat groups. They also recorded the Fendermen and the Castaways of "Liar, Liar" fame. (Photofest)

By the time they released a well-received album, the Trashmen found themselves being sued by the Rivingtons for recording their songs without permission or a share of the royalties. The suit was settled out of court and the Rivingtons were recognized as the song's co-composers on all further copies. "Bird Dance Beat," the follow-up, sung again by drummer Steve Wahrer in his raspiest voice, went to #30 and was a #1 hit in several Latin American countries. But the Trashmen apparently hadn't learned their lesson. Another single, the instrumental "Bird Bath," supposedly by group member Dal Winslow, was a rip-off of "Church Key," written and recorded by another surf group, the Revels. This time the music publisher sued the group and they re-recorded the song as "Bad News" (which it was), giving credit to the original composers.

The Trashmen continued to tour and record for several more years, transforming themselves into a more sedate country rock group by 1967. Steve Wahrer formed the New Trashmen a few years later, but teamed up again with his original band mates in the 1980s. Wahrer died, ironically, of throat cancer, on January 21, 1989, at age forty-seven. The remaining Trashmen continue to perform their primal classic to this day, when the spirit moves them.

Another Minneapolis surf band was the Novas, whose sole hit, "The Crusher" (#88, 1965), was less manic than "Surfin' Bird" but just as wild. Lead vocalist Bob Nolan gave a gravel-voiced impersonation of Milwaukee wrestler Reggie "The Crusher" Lisowski. The song was a parody of current dances and included the eye-gouge, the hammerlock, and the crusher, with graphic instructions. The single has the distinction of being one of the most sought-after 45s in *Goldmine's Rock 'n' Roll Record 45 RPM Record Price Guide,* pulling in $75 in near-mint condition. Too bad my copy has all those scratches.

But enough of madmen and monsters. Let's head for the wide open spaces, where the buffalo roam and where novelty records are as thick as sage brush. Better make that loco weed.

Way, Way Out West

The American West has held a firm grip on the national imagination since the publication of the first Western dime novel. In the 1940s and 1950s singing cowboys like Gene Autry and Roy Rogers straddled the media of radio, movies, and television as easily as they straddled their

Larry Verne is so pleased with his number-one hit song, "Mr. Custer," that he's busting his britches. The song's composers picked him out of a photography darkroom to record the song because they liked his Southern drawl. (Photo courtesy of Showtime Archives, Toronto)

favorite horses. In 1957 eight of the top twenty television program were Westerns. The next year their number rose to eleven, with seven Westerns in the top ten. A number of novelty artists heeded the call to "go West" and got a hit record or two for their troubles.

Perhaps no historic event in the American West has been more revisited by writers, filmmakers, and artists than Custer's Last Stand at the Little Big Horn on June 25, 1876. Songwriters Al DeLong, Fred Darian, and Joseph Van Winkle had the clever idea in 1960 of viewing the massacre from the perspective of one of Custer's soldiers who sees what's coming and pleads with the general to give him the afternoon off. Larry Verne happened to work in a photographer's studio down the hall from the office of DeLong and Darian in southern California. The trio found Verne's thick Southern drawl qualified the nonsinger to record their novelty song, "Mr. Custer."

Verne's scraggly pleadings and silly mutterings ("Hey, Charlie, duck yer head! You're a little bit late on that one, Charlie. Wheew! I bet that smarts.") were enhanced by a hearty chorus of calvary men, a strumming guitar, whooping Indians, and swooshing arrows. Despite the funny premise, the demo was turned down by every label the songwriters played it for. A shorter version (the original ran four and a half minutes) was finally picked up by Era Records and the rest, as they say, is history. "Mr. Custer" was the biggest-selling novelty record in a bumper year for novelty, going all the way to #1.

Verne and his songwriters struck a second time with the similarly formatted "Mr. Livingstone," in which Verne was cast as Stanley. The Indians were replaced by African natives, but the premise lacked the gallows humor of its predecessor and it stalled at #75. Further singles, including "The Coward That Won the West" and "Return of Mr. Custer," were as immovable as Sitting Bull. Verne, who had previously worked as a stuntman on such Western television series as *Rin Tin Tin* and *Range Rider,* soon went into the movie set construction business, where he did very well for thirty-five years. His last job before retiring was on Steven Spielberg's *Lost World.*

As funny in its way as "Mr. Custer," but largely forgotten, is Sonny Gianotta's "The Last Blast of the Blasted Bugler" (1962). An "Eastern" more than a Western, it recreates the climax of Rudyard Kipling's classic adventure ballad "Gunga Din." As Din the water boy warns the British troops of an ambush by Indian rebels with his bugle call, he is literally shot to pieces by enemy gunfire. He continues to blow his bugle, however, with greater and greater difficulty, finally expiring like a bull elephant in heat. Sick, sick, sick, but funny, funny, funny. This rare novelty record is told almost entirely through music and sound effects.

Phil Humphrey and Jim Sundquist, better known as the Fendermen after the guitars they played, could have soldiered alongside Larry Verne, having the same rustic, redneck sense of humor. Their sole hit, "Mule Skinner Blues" (#5, 1960), was written in 1931 by the father of country music, Jimmie Rodgers. Their version is notable for its irrepressible laughter, whoops, and tight guitar work. After the duo split in 1966, Sundquist went on to play with country bands, while Humphrey, who did all the hollering, rode into the sunset for parts unknown.

Western parodies on disk predate Frankie Laine's "Blazing Saddles," from the Mel Brooks film of the same name, by more than a decade. Murray Kellum made a goofy cowboy in "Long Tall Texan" (#51, 1963), although the country singer actually grew up in Plain, Texas. Allan Sherman gave us a distinctly Jewish showdown in front of the Fountainebleau Hotel in "The Streets of Miami," his parody of "The Streets of Laredo" from his first album *My Son The Folk Singer*. A much funnier Jewish gunslinger appeared in Frank Gallop's "The Ballad of Irving" (#34, 1966). "Irving," which took its inspiration from Lorne Greene's hit "Ringo," was all the funnier because Gallop and his pompous WASP announcer voice played entirely against type. "Butterfingers" Irving, "the 142nd fastest gun in the West" eventually guns himself down in front of the Frontier Deli. Gallop's television credits ranged from the sepulchral host of *Lights Out,* one of television's first horror anthologies, to the announcer of *The Perry Como Show.*

Far less funny is another "Ringo" parody, "Gringo" (1964), by El Clod (aka Marty Cooper). The record is full of unfunny Hispanic stereotypes, including spicy tacos that do in the hero quicker than a blazing six gun. This and other El Clod releases were coproduced by H. B. Barnum, who under the name Dudley had parodied Marty Robbins's monster Western hit "El Paso" as "El Pizza" in 1960. Seemingly infatuated with food, Cooper and Barnum finally hit the mark with "Peanut Butter," which they produced in 1961 for the Marathons (see Chapter 2).

Country artist Dave Dudley, who started the cycle of trucking songs with his classic "Six Days on the Road," did the same for the urban cowboy a few months later with the equally pungent "Cowboy Boots" (#95, 1963). The song's hero sees himself becoming as rich as Roy Rogers, if only he can get the proper wardrobe. The song predated the film *Urban Cowboy* and the craze for Western chic by nearly two decades.

But the last word in Western novelty should fittingly go to the king of the cowboys himself, Roy Rogers, who made the *Billboard* pop charts for the first and only time with the sentimental "Hoppy, Gene and Me" (#65, 1974). His touching tribute to the Hollywood cowboys who were role models for a generation of baby boomers shows that behind all the laughter there remains a lot of heartfelt affection for a West that still looms large in our imaginations.

See You in the Funny Papers

Comic strip and cartoon characters have been fertile ground in pop music at least as far back as "Barney Google" and his goo-goo-googley eyes. Warner Bros.' voice meister Mel Blanc had a million seller in the summer of 1948 with "Woody Woodpecker," whose voice he created while moonlighting for the Walter Lantz company. He hit the top ten a second time two and a half years later with "I Taut I Taw a Puddy Tat," playing both Sylvester and Tweety Bird.

The fifties were pretty bare of comics-inspired novelties, but the sixties got off to a fast start with a very funny song about a dour cave man named Alley Oop. Songwriter Dallas Frazier probably chose Vincent T. Hamlin's popular comic strip because of its prehistoric setting and the comic possibilities of the protagonist's name. Frazier's song might have gone unnoticed but for a chance meeting with another ambitious young man at 2 A.M. at a Hollywood gas station where Frazier worked. The motorist who stopped for a fill-up was Gary Paxton, arriving in Hollywood from Arizona, where he had found success as one half of Skip and Flip ("It Was I," "Cherry Pie"), one of the best boy duos of the late fifties. The two chatted for a while and Paxton promised to stay in touch and listen to some of Frazier's songs.

Paxton soon formed a partnership with Kim Fowley, another ambitious young producer. They landed a contract with tiny Lute Records and Paxton recorded a solo effort, the weirdly titled "You're Ruinin' My Gladness." His next single was to be Frazier's "Alley Oop," but there was a problem. Paxton was still officially under contract to Brent Records, who produced his Skip and Flip singles. So he issued "Alley Oop" under the name the Hollywood Argyles, in honor of the site of the recording studio, on the corner of Hollywood Boulevard and Argyle Avenue.

The people at Lute Records really outdid themselves in this publicity still for the Hollywood Argyles and their hit "Alley Oop." Presumably leader Gary Paxton is the caveman feeding the plastic dinosaur. "Alley Oop" was so popular in 1960 that two other groups had hit covers, Dante and the Evergreens and the Dyna-Sores. (Photo courtesy of Showtime Archives, Toronto)

The recording session of "Alley Oop" was a memorable one. Paxton and his motley chorus of backup singers, including his girlfriend and some pals, were drunk on hard cider, which may partly account for his strangely elastic lead vocal. Sounding very hip and very black, Paxton read Frazier's lyrics off a brown paper bag, wrapping his lips lovingly around words like "Die-na-saw-er." The chorus's monotone chant of "Al-ley Oop-op-op-op-op" gave the record a numbing, hypnotic effect and drummer Sandy Nelson, fresh from his big hit "Teen Beat," struck the top of a Coke bottle for a harder percussive sound. The sloppiness of it all made the song weirdly appealing and soon Alley Oop and his ugly club were ruling the charts at #1.

Another team of hungry young producers, Lou Adler and Herb Alpert, decided that "Alley Oop" was a tune worth covering. They called up a group, recorded them in the studio the next day, and had the record pressed the day after that. One day later the disk was spun on Dick Clark's *American Bandstand*.

Unlike the Hollywood Argyles, Dante and the Evergreens were a real group before they recorded "Alley Oop." Don Drowty (Dante) formed the quartet while in high school in Los Angeles. He faithfully recreated Paxton's greasy vocal while Adler and Alpert threw in some unnecessary comic sound effects—a "boing" spring and what is supposedly the cackle of a dinosaur. Their quick initiative paid off and Dante and the Evergreens' version of the song went to #15 in June. A third, all-black version by the Dyna-Sores on Rendezvous Records charted the same day. The Dyna-Sores were actually top session musicians Rene Hall (who sang lead), Ernie Freeman (piano), Earl Palmer (drums), and Plas Johnson, who got in some nice licks on his sax near the record's end.

Though a hot act on tour, Gary Paxton's Hollywood Argyles had the dubious distinction of being one of the few groups to reach #1 and never have another charting hit. Paxton went on to produce another chart-topping novelty, "Monster Mash," two years later and eventually abandoned the world of novelty for gospel music, becoming a born-again Christian in the 1980s. The hip cat who sang about a cave man was at one point romantically linked to Tammy Faye Bakker.

Dante and the Evergreens had one follow-up hit, "Time Machine" (#73), written by Barry Mann and Howard Greenfield, who were probably cashing in on the popularity of the hit film of H.G. Wells's science fiction story released that same year. The song, sung by Dante in his "Alley Oop" voice, is about a guy who wants to build a time machine so he can meet Cleopatra. Tuneful but not terribly novel, it has a clever fadeout, with Dante warning a snake to stay away from Cleo, then crying "Aww, too late!" Drowty eventually retired from recording, became a teacher, and now brings rock acts to schools nationwide through his charity American Music Project.

Another group to copy Paxton's hip vocal style successfully was the Ivy Three, so named because the trio formed at ivy-covered Adelphi College on Long Island in 1959. Their song "Yogi" (#8, 1960) was inspired by cartoon character Yogi Bear, a supporting player on William Hanna and Joseph Barbera's *The Huckleberry Hound Show*, one of the first television cartoon series. The novelty cleverly played off both the cartoon bear and the other more mystical type of yogi. Each chorus ended with a rousing "Hey, Boo-Boo!" referring to Yogi's faithful side-kick. (A year earlier rocking guitarist Boyd Bennett reached #73 with his Yogi Bear novelty instrumental, "Boogie Bear.") Although the Ivy Three were never heard from again, lead singer Charles Koppelman and group member Don Rubin formed a production company that produced hit records for the Lovin' Spoonful, Gary Lewis and the Playboys, and Petula Clark. In the '80s they cofounded SKB Records and discovered, among others, folk singer Tracy Chapman.

The Kingsmen, a premier garage band from the Pacific Northwest, had as sloppy a style as the Hollywood Argyles. This may have helped them turn an obscure little tune by Richard Berry about a sailor on leave into the most celebrated rock anthem of the sixties, "Louie, Louie." Lead singer Jack Ely's almost unintelligible reading of the innocent lyrics convinced millions of listeners that there was something lewd about the song. An investigation by the FBI followed. To be fair to the Kingsmen, all they were doing was what thousands of garage and surf bands were doing—playing around with an established song, giving it their own unique spin.

The Kingsmen moved into novelty territory in late 1965 with "The Jolly Green Giant" (#4), about the unhappy romance between the famed cartoon trademark for packaged vegetables and a giantess. Whether the Kingsmen got permission from Green Giant to use their trademark character is not known, but they certainly didn't get the okay to lift the song's melody from the Olympics' "Big Boy Pete." Later that year they had another hit with the first rock ode to an X-rated cartoon character,

Playboy's "Little Annie Fanny." When Gary Paxton heard "Annie Fanny" (#47) he surely wasn't amused. The melody was a rip-off of "Alley Oop."

Batman, one of the first comic book super heroes, achieved new popularity in the mid-sixties through the television series starring Adam West as the Caped Crusader. A rash of Batman records were released by such diverse recording artists as LaVerne Baker, Peggy Lee, and Jan and Dean (who devoted an entire album to him). But the most memorable Batman novelty was the spoken parody "Ratman and Bobin in the Clipper Caper" by the folk group the Brothers Four, who managed to also bring into their pastiche the Beatles, Dracula, and Lawrence Welk. Holy Champagne Music!

If Batman ruled on television in 1966, Charles Schulz's *Peanuts* was the reigning comic strip in the United States, if not the world. The *Peanuts* gang and their dog Snoopy proved to be a merchandiser's dream. Besides countless licensed products, there were *Peanuts* comic collections, TV specials, a hit Off-Broadway show, and even books of sayings from Charlie Brown. Of all the characters, Snoopy, the philosophical dog, was perhaps the most beloved. A canine with the richest fantasy life since Walter Mitty, he was fond of stretching out on the roof of his doghouse and imagining himself as a World War I flying ace locked in a deadly duel with the "Red Baron," Manfred Freiherr Von Richthofen (1892-1918) of Germany.

Just before Christmas 1966 the Royal Guardsmen, a rock sextet from Ocala, Florida, released "Snoopy vs. the Red Baron." The hook-laden, upbeat ballad, complete with interjections in German from the Red Baron (Snoopy is never heard from on the record) and the sounds of an aerial dogfight, became an airborne hit, flying to #2 and staying there for an entire month. Although it was a novelty, "Snoopy vs. the Red Baron" had the rousing patriotic fervor of such earlier martial hits as Jimmy Dean's "P.T. 109" and Johnny Horton's "Sink the Bismarck."

A few months later the Royal Guardsmen came back with the inevitable sequel, "The Return of the Red Baron," which began by explaining, rather illogically, that the Baron had parachuted out before his plane crashed and was back seeking vengeance on the dog who did him in. Surprisingly, the follow-up peaked at #15, the rare case of a novelty group achieving two solid hits in a row on the same theme. Emboldened by their success, the Royal Guardsmen resurrected Snoopy a third time with "Snoopy's Christmas" which charted on *Billboard*'s Christmas list three years running. In 1968 they ran "Snoopy for President" (#85) as an independent. ("Some wear the sign of the elephant, and some wear the sign of the mule, but we'll hold the sign of the beagle high, and love will shine right through.") In 1969, just in time for the moon landing, they sent Snoopy into space as "The Smallest Astronaut," which didn't chart, despite the rousing roll call of all the U.S. astronauts that closed the record.

The Royal Guardsmen were a crack band and had as many non-novelty hits as Snoopy songs. "Baby Let's Wait" (#35) was their biggest, but the most charming was "Airplane Song (My Airplane)" (#46), which could have been sung by a daydreaming Snoopy.

The Royal Guardsmen disbanded in 1970, the same year that an actual children's TV character had a hit of his own. *Sesame Street,* a product of the Children's Television Workshop on Public Television, was for the children of the '70s what *Howdy Doody* was for their parents. Ernie, one of the most popular of the Muppets, would sing about his favorite toy at bath time. "Rubber Duckie" (#15), actually sung by Muppet master Jim Henson, was released as a single on Columbia in the summer of 1970. Henson had another hit at decade's end, this time as his other alter ego, Kermit the Frog. "Rainbow Connection" (#25) had the added advantage of being heard on the soundtrack of the Muppets' first film, *The Muppet Movie,* in 1979.

The cartoon-comic connection was a powerful one in American novelty records in its golden age. Meanwhile, from across the sea, the British were exporting their own brand of novelty to our shores. While its roots also lay in pop culture, it was a very different culture.

London Calling

Humor and music have a long tradition in Great Britain, going at least as far back as the English music hall of the early 1900s, the British version of American vaudeville. Novelty songs were the hallmark of many top music hall performers, who delighted audiences year after year with their specialty numbers. Although the music hall tradition died a slower death than vaudeville, by the 1950s it was a worn-out relic of the past.

One of the new musical crazes at that time was Dixieland jazz, or, as the British public came to call it, trad (traditional) jazz. Introduced by

American servicemen during the war years, American jazz swept the British entertainment world in the late '40s and early '50s. One of its top interpreters was Chris Barber, whose eclectic tastes included not only jazz but American blues, rhythm and blues, and folk music. Out of Barber's large band grew a smaller ensemble that included banjo, guitar, bass, and the homely washboard and kazoo. This group included banjo-playing Scotsman Lonnie Donegan, whose musical tastes were as far-ranging as Barber's.

On the Barber band's first record for Decca in 1954, Donegan sang a 1930s folk song closely associated with one of his idols, American bluesman Leadbelly. "Rock Island Line" was a train song about a clever engineer who fools the toll man at a bridge by misrepresenting his cargo. Donegan's energetic vocal, backed by his banjo picking, made "Rock Island Line" one of the most unlikely song hits of 1956 and a breath of fresh air in the staid atmosphere of British pop music. A headline in England's *Melody Maker* called Donegan "The Scots–Born Irish Hill-Billy From London." "A few months ago his chief claim to fame was as a banjo player," went the article, "one of that curious race who according to a guitarist friend, are responsible for every disaster from train crashes to tornadoes."

The phenomenal success of "Rock Island Line" led Donegan to leave the Barber band and form his own smaller "skiffle" band. With its free-wheeling nature, homemade instruments, and irreverent approach to music of all kinds, skiffle was a kind of fifties version of American sixties garage music. The first homegrown British popular music since music hall, skiffle took the country by storm and sent thousands of British youth raiding their mothers' kitchens for washboards. Skiffle groups like the Vipers and Johnny Duncan and the Bluegrass Boys had hits of their own, but Donegan was, and remained, "King of Skiffle," touring the United States and taking "Rock Island Line" to #8 on the American charts.

For his next hit record, Donegan traveled further back into the musical past, recording Ernest Hare and Billy Jones's 1924 novelty "Does the Spearmint Lose Its Flavor on the Bedpost Overnight?" He changed spearmint to the more contemporary "chewing gum" and threw in some improvised lyrics and banter with his skiffle mates. The added excitement of a live performance in Oxford took "Chewing

Lonnie Donegan was crowned the king of skiffle, England's home-made folk-jazz music of the fifties. Donegan had two big hits in the United States, five years apart. He made his first appearance stateside during the inter-mission of a Harlem Globetrotters' exhibition game. (Photofest)

Gum" to #3 in 1958. When the record was released in the United States the following March, it flopped. Two years later a Boston deejay got hold of a copy of the original and began playing it. The response from the public was overwhelming. "Chewing Gum" was rereleased on Dot Records and went to #5 in August 1961. By then Donegan's star had started to dim back home, although he remained popular for years to come and inspired two Liverpool lads, John Lennon and Paul McCartney, to form their own skiffle group. Skiffle's irrepressible energy fueled the Mersey beat, whose creators traded in their washboards for electric guitars.

If Charlie Drake had been born a few decades earlier, he would undoubtedly have been a music hall headliner. Instead the London-born comic and singer found success in the media of radio and television. Short of stature, with a shock of red hair and a Cockney accent you could cut with a kitchen knife, Drake became an unlikely rock star in 1958. His cover of Bobby Darin's first hit "Splish Splash" outsold the original in Britain and he later successfully covered both the ballad "Volare" and the Larry Verne novelty "Mr. Custer."

If Drake's Cockney accent seemed out of place at the Little Bighorn, it was just as strange coming from the mouth of an Australian aborigine. Yet this didn't put off the public from his original composition, "My Boomerang Won't Come Back." A hit at home, it was bought by United Artists and released in the States in early 1962. The unique sound of the digareedoo, an aborigine instrument, and a clever story line about a hapless aborigine made this infectious comic ballad from the bush a hit in America too, rising to #21. Part of the song's appeal is due to the excellent production by George Martin who, before he took on the Beatles, was considered the king of British comedy records. (Peter Sellers was another client.) Drake had no further novelty hits in America and eventually abandoned recording for acting. He continues to enliven the British stage and television with his comic antics.

"My Boomerang Won't Come Back" is less well remembered today than it should be because it was overshadowed the following year by another Australian-based novelty, written and sung by a bona fide Aussie. Rolf Harris is a truly Renaissance man who, since arriving in England at age twenty-two, has become a much-loved national treasure. A painter, sculptor, singer, musician and published author, Rolf first came to public attention as a cartoonist and storyteller on a British television kiddie show. Soon after, his paintings were given an exhibition at London's Royal Academy of Art. For all his success, Harris was homesick for Australia and became a frequent patron at the Down Under Club for expatriates. The camaraderie at the club inspired him to write a song about his homeland, patterned after the current calypso craze.

"I tried to bring in as many Australian animal slang terms and nicknames as possible," he told Stu Fink in an interview for *Goldmine*. The song, "Tie Me Kangaroo Down, Sport," was the comic last will and testament of a dying Australian stockman. The mesmerizing "wobble board," heard so prominently in "Kangaroo," was not an authentic aborigine instrument but Harris's own invention. He accidentally created it when he placed a still-wet portrait board of Masonite on a stove to dry

Rolf Harris remains England's favorite Australian. Besides making some fine novelty records, he has also excelled as a cartoonist, musician, painter, sculptor, and storyteller. He first recorded his classic "Tie Me Kangaroo Down, Sport" in his bathroom. (Photo courtesy of Showtime Archives, Toronto)

and flapped it in the air to cool it off. The strange wobbling noises intrigued him and he turned it into a musical instrument. Masonite sold 55,000 wobble boards as "Tie Me Kangaroo Down, Sport" reached the upper end of the British charts. When the record first hit the States nearly three years later, a *Billboard* ad optimistically referred to the wobble board as "the biggest craze since the hula-hoop." It may not have been that, but the novelty song was a huge hit, going to #3. It elicited such answer novelties as "Tie My Surfing Board Down, Sport" and "Tie My Hunting Dog Down, Jed" by Arthur "Guitar Boogie" Smith, which Harris himself would later record.

Further hits eluded Harris in America. "Sun Arise," his fascinating take on an authentic aborigine chant released several months before "Kangaroo," only went to #61, and a cheery ode to addition, "Nick Teen and Al K. Hall," barely grazed the bottom of the charts for a week in late 1963. In England, however, his popularity continued to grow. He became good friends with an up-and-coming band called the Beatles, who joined him in singing "Tie Me Kangaroo" at their live 1963 Christmas Show, which Harris emceed. In 1969 his version of the antiwar song "Two Little Boys," an old music hall standard, became the top single of the year and as late as 1993 he had a top ten hit with his wobble board parody of Led Zeppelin's "Stairway to Heaven."

As much an institution in England as he is in his homeland, Harris modestly refers to himself as "just a novelty-type guy doing weirdo bloody comedy." The public disagrees. In a 1992 poll a thousand Londoners were asked to identify a famous painter. Harris received 38 percent of the votes, beating out Michelangelo and Rembrandt. Not bad for an Aussie, eh, sport?

Harris's invasion of England was nothing compared to the invasion of America by dozen of British bands in 1964. The "new sound" of the Beatles and other beat groups was originally derived from such American sources as blues, R&B, and the girl groups. But it wasn't long before the "invaders" were doing distinctly British material, some of which looked back fondly to, of all things, the British music hall.

Herman's Hermits, a band far more popular in America than back home, had their first #1 hit in the U.S. with the beguiling "Mrs. Brown You've Got a Lovely Daughter," whose lyrics and plunkety guitar line were distinctly evocative of old-fashioned variety. Their next #1 single three months later was authentic music hall, the novelty "I'm Henry VIII, I Am," first made popular by performer Harry Champion back in 1911. Ironically, the silly tune was considered "too British" for English audiences and was never released as a single in their homeland. It remains one of the Hermits' brighter moments on disk, even if they never bothered to learn more than one chorus of the song ("Second verse, same as the first!")

Their last foray into their musical roots took place in the spring of 1966 when they resurrected the breezy and likable "Leaning on the Lamp Post" from the 1920s British musical *Me and My Gal*. When the musical became a surprising Broadway hit in the 1980s, many theater-goers were surprised to hear a Herman Hermits' song in the score.

Another sixties British group that rediscovered their roots was the dapper duo of Peter and Gordon, who in late 1966 forsook the ballads of Lennon and McCartney for novelty songs with a decidedly music hall beat. "Lady Godiva" (#6) was a clever updating of the good lady from Coventry by composer Mike Leander. Godiva winds up cutting her long hair and making X-rated movies for her director boyfriend, all of which somehow managed to pass the usually strict and humorless British censors. They followed it with the similarly tongue-in-cheek "Knight in Rusty Armour" (#15) and the more demure "Sunday for Tea" (#31). The duo had their last-charting single in June 1967 with the theme song of the Michael Winner comedy heist film *The Jokers*. After that they split and Peter (Asher) went on to become one of the most successful producer-managers of the 1970s, guiding the careers of Linda Ronstadt and James Taylor.

Meanwhile, the retro-musical bandwagon of the sixties continued to roll forward with a monster hit from a man who sang (horrors!) into a megaphone.

Back to the Twenties

The old saw "Everything old is new again" applies as much to music as it does to every other aspect of popular culture. Nothing is more certain than that what is outré one moment will sooner or later come back into fashion, from ragtime to disco (yes, even disco). If, for example, an argument can be made that the "Swinging Sixties" were no more than the Roaring Twenties revisited, it may rest on the phenomenal success of the New Vaudeville Band in late 1966.

British composer and record producer Geoff Stephens had a love for British pop of the 1920s and '30s that might have been considered unseemly at the very moment when London, thanks to the Beatles and a revitalized youth culture, was the hippest place on the planet. But the very ferment and excitement of the sixties made youth look back fondly on the last outbreak of uninhibited fun—the twenties, and its music.

"Winchester Cathedral," as sung by Stephens with studio musicians (there was no "band"), sounded like it was lifted right off an old, scratchy 78 from his record collection, right down to the "o-vee-o-dees." But Stephens had actually written it himself, inspired by a calendar photo of the famed medieval cathedral that hung on the wall of his office cubicle in London. True to the spirit of Rudy Vallee, who ended up covering the song himself, Stephens sang it through a megaphone. "Winchester Cathedral" was the second-biggest-selling record of 1966 in America and incongruously received a Grammy for "Best Rock and Roll Recording." The hummable tune made it a singer's dream and it was covered four hundred times over the next four years. Capitalizing on his newfound fame, Stephens quickly pulled together a group of seven musicians to perform on tour as the New Vaudeville Band, led by Tristram, Seventh Earl of Cricklewood (aka Alan Klein). Strangely enough, the band was a hit in Las Vegas and played the Aladdin Hotel for a year.

After the obligatory follow-up ("Peek-A-Boo," #7 in the U.K.), Stephens continued to tour the band for several years, while continuing to write songs for other artists, including more contemporary pablum pop like "Smile a Little Smile for Me" for Flying Machine and the Wayne Newton tear-jerker "Daddy Don't You Walk So Fast."

The biggest retro-musical star in the '60s firmament, however, was an American whose eccentricities, both vocal and personal, endeared him for a time to a nation. With his long scraggly hair, trilling falsetto, Dickensian manners, and tiny ukelele, Tiny Tim was a novelty act with a capital "N." But even novelty acts have to pay their dues and Tim paid his in spades.

He was born Herbert Khaury on April 12, 1930, in New York City. A high-school dropout, he competed in amateur talent shows for years, carrying his ukelele around in a shopping bag and supporting himself with menial jobs. In 1953 he found Jesus and, shortly thereafter, the falsetto singing style that would become his trademark.

"Not only was it easier on my throat, but I found that I was thrilling myself as well," he said. Audiences were hardly thrilled by Khaury, laughing and booing at his interpretations of classic pop evergreens. He played the role of an albino freak (with white pancake) named Larry Love, the Singing Canary, at Hubert's Museum in Times Square. A frequent performer in Greenwich Village and New Jersey, he didn't land his first paying gig until 1962, at the appropriately named Cafe Bizarre in the Village.

A year later his manager, whose specialty was midget acts, named him Tiny Tim. Better venues got him more publicity and Tim's genuine affection for the old-time songs he sang shined through all the artifice. What had been freakish in the fifties had, by the mid-sixties, become

With his long hair and his genuine eccentricities, Tiny Tim was one of the most beloved of novelty artists, and a hero to the flower children of the late '60s. (Photofest)

intriguing and even commercial. Tim had stayed the same, but the times had changed. He was booked on *The Merv Griffin Show* and landed a small bit in an underground movie directed by Peter Yarrow, of Peter, Paul and Mary fame. It was Yarrow who invited Mo Ostin of Reprise Records, the label started by Frank Sinatra, to hear Tim at the Scene, a disco club. Ostin was charmed and signed Tim immediately.

An album, *God Bless Tiny Tim,* was produced by Richard Perry and sold 200,000 copies. A single from it, "Tip-Toe Thru' the Tulips With Me," last seen on the pop charts in 1929, rose to #17. "Tulips" was the perfect vehicle for this strange man with the high-pitched voice. It was enchantingly quaint, yet also progressive, expressing a hippie philosophy that was peaceful and slightly absurd in a very sixties' way. The Singing Canary had become the darling of the smart set, a regular on *The Tonight Show,* which garnered its highest ratings ever on the evening of December 18, 1969, when Tim married seventeen-year-old Victoria May Budinger (his adored "Miss Vicky") in front of a TV audience of 21.4 million households.

But like those tulips, fame was fleeting for Tiny Tim. Within a year of his popularity peaking he was a has-been. His third Reprise album *For All My Little Friends* in 1969 was a failure and the label dropped him in 1971. He returned to the smaller venues he had haunted for years, barely skipping a beat, as if the world fame had simply been a brief aberration. "In this business you take what you can get," he said philosophically.

In 1977, the same year he divorced Miss Vicky, Tim recorded two songs on an Edison cylinder at the Edison Museum in Bellard, Illinois, which he considered one of the highlights of his career. After a quiet period he was "rediscovered" in the 1980s by a new generation of listeners and returned to touring and recording, including the well-received LPs *Girl* and *The Impotent Troubadour.* Between engagements he acted in the slasher film *Blood Harvest* (1986) and then spent eight months with a traveling tent circus.

On September 30, 1996, while opening his act at a ukulele concert in Greenfield, Massachusetts, he suffered a heart attack and fell off the stage. Eight days later he suffered a second attack and died. At his funeral, attended by four hundred people including many long time fans, Tiny Tim was buried with his ukulele across his chest, his stuffed rabbit by his side, and six tulips in his coffin. His third wife, Susan

Khaury, said at the funeral, "He really tried to be a good person." Few people would dispute that statement.

Whether Tiny Tim was a "bad" singer remains debatable. There is little doubt, however, that Elva Miller (aka Mrs. Miller), by nature or design, was an awful vocalist. After seven years of vocal lessons, this housewife from Missouri yearned for the limelight. Her privately made recordings caught the ear of a Capitol Records executive and in early 1966 the label put out the archly titled album *Mrs. Miller's Greatest Hits.* Although all the cuts were covers of other people's hits, the album struck the public's funny bone and two cuts became a double-sided hit, her cracked versions of Petula Clark's "Downtown" (#82) and The Toys' semi-classical "A Lover's Concerto" (#95).

Mrs. Miller was, it must be admitted, entertaining. Whether she deliberately forgot lyrics midsong or lost her tempo is questionable, but her enthusiastic amateurism sounded sincere and she did some very nice bird calls. Her moment in the spotlight was predictably brief and she returned, unscathed by success, to her home and family.★

Mrs. Miller's semi-operatic numbers backed by a male chorus were reminiscent of the 1930s, but the delightful "I Love Onions" (#63, 1966) sung in a breathy voice by Susan Christie, sister of singer Lou Christie, was another slice of twenties' fun, heightened by a kazoo accompaniment and a male chorus singing into megaphones. Unlike her more famous brother, lightning didn't strike again for Miss Christie. Maybe it was all those onions that kept the record-buying public away from her subsequent releases.

No one went further in re-creating the retro-sound than comedian-impressionist Guy Marks, whose "Loving You Has Made Me Bananas" (#51, 1968) is a loving if slightly demented parody of the distinctive remote dance band radio broadcasts of the '20s and '30s. It opens with a loquacious commentator coming to you "from the Hotel Sheets in downtown Plunketville" with "the sweetest music this side of the Monongahela River."

★*Mrs. Miller was not the first "bad" singer to hit the big time. She was preceded more than a decade earlier by the more exotic but equally off-key songbird Leona Anderson. A favorite of TV comedian Ernie Kovacs, her signature songs "Fish" and "Rats in My Room" were recorded for posterity on Tony Burrello's Horrible Records.*

There was no way bandleader Benny Bell's "Shaving Cream" would have made it onto the airwaves back in 1946 when it was originally recorded. Bell, born Ben Samberg, led a double life as a songwriter and vocalist from the 1920s through the 1940s, creating Jewish novelty songs starring "Pincus the Peddler" as well as bawdy, risqué party numbers that were popular on jukeboxes. One of the most outrageous was "Shaving Cream," in which each stanza ends in a never-quite-mentioned four-letter word for feces. What undoubtedly made the record so appealing to novelty deejay Dr. Demento, who rediscovered it on his weekly syndicated program, was the corny ballroom orchestral backing and vocalist Paul Wynn's straight delivery that made the lyrics—which grew increasingly naughty—all the funnier. (Bell recorded the song himself after Wynn's version, but reissued the original in the '70s "as a gesture of friendship.")

Rereleased on Vanguard, "Shaving Cream" took off after a New York disk jockey warned the listening audience before playing it with these words: "If you have children in the room, or if you are particularly sensitive to a dangerously naughty record, you should leave the room or switch stations immediately." Few did, and "Shaving Cream" went to #30 on the charts in 1975, twenty-nine years after it was first recorded. The more sexually suggestive follow-up, "Everybody Wants My Fanny" from 1949, flopped, proving that toilet humor sells better than anal sex. Benny Bell died at age 93 on July 6, 1999.

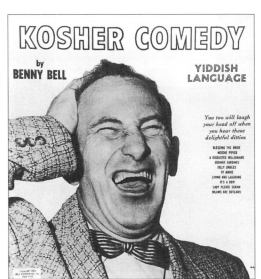

Benny Bell and his sometimes risqué records had been completely forgotten by the time deejay Dr. Demento rediscovered "Shaving Cream," his ode to a favorite four-letter word. This album features Bell's more legitimate material: Jewish novelty songs. (From the collection of Ronald L. Smith)

But when it came to low, bawdy humor nobody could beat the British, as another Benny—Benny Hill—proved when his half-hour comedy show became a huge hit in the States in the late 1970s. The theme song for *The Benny Hill Show* was perhaps the last pop throwback novelty of the decade of love, the aggressively nonsensical "Gimme Dat Ding" (#9, 1970). The honky-tonk ditty was recorded by the British duo of Roger Greenaway and Tony Burrows, who called themselves the Pipkins, and was originally written, believe it or not, for a British children's television program.

From Bobby Pickett to the Pipkins, the novelty market of the '50s and '60s was strewn with the corpses of one-hit wonders, perhaps leading us to believe that a career in novelty music is an oxymoron. But the next chapter presents two distinctive artists who are outstanding exceptions to the rule.

⑤ Ray Stevens and Roger Miller: Kings of Sixties Novelty

> "If all you have on your plate is black-eyed peas, I like black-eyed peas, but damn, I'd like a little corn on that too every now and then."—*Ray Stevens*

> "I always took a great deal of pride in being original. When somebody said, 'My God, where did that come from,' that was the big payoff for me."—*Roger Miller*

The label "novelty song" has always been a bit pejorative. It denotes a piece of music that amuses for a moment in time and then is tossed out like yesterday's newspaper. But the best of so-called "novelty" music is something quite different—it expresses a comic point of view that is universal in its appeal. Ray Stevens and Roger Miller, whose work brightened the latter years of novelty's golden age, created such enduring music—some of which happens to be funny and some of it dead serious. Though Miller was the greater artist, both deserve a special niche in the Novelty Hall of Fame, a genre they both defined and transcended.

Both men were from the South and their music and songs reflect their country roots as well as a deep love for rhythm and blues and rock. Miller began, and largely remained, a country artist. Stevens flitted between rock and country over his long career. Both men were irrepressible, overgrown children in the recording studio and in Miller's case, in his personal life too. Both were true originals, bringing something new and fresh to a field that was often tired and predictable.

Funny Man

Perhaps no recording artist in the rock era has been more closely identified with novelty music than Ray Stevens. And no artist has struggled more mightily to escape the novelty label, nor been so successful.

He was born Harold Ray Ragsdale on January 24, 1939, in Clarkdale, Georgia, where his father was a cost engineer. As a boy he loved both country and western and rhythm and blues with a passion. In high school in Albany, Georgia, he and several classmates formed an R&B band. At fifteen Stevens got a job as a weekend disk jockey on a local radio station. At about the same time the family moved to Atlanta and Ray submitted some songs he had written to Prep Records, a subsidiary of Capitol. Prep was impressed enough to offer him a recording contract. His first release, "Silver Bracelet," was a local hit in 1957, as was his third, "Chickie Chickie Wah Wah," a rhythm number put out on the Capitol label the following year.

After two more releases flopped, Capitol dropped the young singer and he moved to NRC (National Recording Corporation), where he recorded "Sergeant Preston of the Yukon," a spoof of the old fictional Mountie made popular on radio and in the comics. "Sergeant Preston" owed a lot to both the Coasters, whom Stevens idolized, and Gary Paxton's elastic vocal style on "Alley Oop." But Stevens's loquacious delivery, which at times resembled a Southern door-to-door salesman on a jag, was all his own. So was his uncanny talent for imitating animals, in this case, Preston's lead husky, King.

The song began to take off, selling 200,000 copies, when the record company got an irate letter from King Features Syndicate, threatening to sue because Stevens had not gotten permission to use their trademark character. The single was quickly withdrawn and Stevens learned a valuable lesson. In the colorful gallery of comic heroes and heroines he would bring to life in the years ahead, nearly all of them would come from his own imagination.

Nineteen-sixty-one was a critical year in the career of Ray Stevens. He graduated from Georgia State University with a degree in music theory, moved to Nashville, and went to work for Mercury Records as an assistant A&R (Artist and Repertory) man at $50 a week. He also made his own records, hitting the top forty with his first release. "Jeremiah Peabody's Poly Unsaturated Quick Dissolving Fast Action

Pleasant Tasting Green and Purple Pills" (#35) remains the longest title of any song to chart in the rock era and only a fast talker like Steven could wrap his mouth around it with such ease. The rhythm track and chorus was again reminiscent of the Coasters. But Stevens's enthusiastic huckster was an original and the satire of American advertising at the dawn of the decade was funny and pointed.

After a second single, "Scratch My Back," fizzled, he hit his stride with the classic "Ahab the Arab" (#5). "Ahab" was basically the same tune as "Sergeant Preston" with new lyrics. It tells the improbable tale of Ahab, "sheik of the burning sands," and his affair with the harem girl Fatima "of the seven veils." Along the way Stevens portrays both Fatima (who lets loose with one of the most infectious laughs on wax) and Clyde, Ahab's trusty camel. Few listeners may have ever heard a camel wail, but Stevens's imitation was utterly convincing. The juxtaposition of the exotic setting, countless pop culture references, and Stevens's Southern pitchman delivery was hilarious. ("There she was, friends and neighbors, laying there in all her radiant beauty . . . sipping on a ROC coca-cola, listening to her transistor, watching the Grand Ole Opry, and reading MAD Magazine, while she hums 'Does Your Chewing Gum Lose Its Flavor.'")

"Ahab" was one of the biggest novelty hits of 1962 and the die was cast for Ray Stevens. His next three releases didn't approach the popularity of "Ahab," but each was memorable in its own way. "Further More" (#91) was the garrulous complaint of a rejected lover set to a waltz beat that included a scat singing intro and closing that preceded Roger Miller's "Dang Me" by almost two years. "Santa Claus is Watching You" (#45) was a slightly dark holiday novelty with Clyde the Camel making a cameo appearance as one of Santa's reindeer. The melodramatic Orbison-like ballad "Funny Man" (#81) was an early manifestation of Stevens's serious aspirations as a songwriter and singer.

Stevens finally broke back into the top twenty again with "Harry the Hairy Ape" (#17, 1963), which is "Ahab" again with new lyrics. While Stevens's ape imitation is a winner, the song lacks the comic inventiveness of "Ahab." Perhaps the funniest moment is when Stevens, in a high-pitched voice, points out a hole in the plot when a deejay plays a record that Harry never made ("What record?" "Shut up!"). "Speed Ball" (#55), about a reckless motorcyclist, was still another retread of "Ahab." It was clear that the singer, like Speed Ball, was running out of gas. Further novelty songs about such kooky characters as "Butch Barbarian," "Bubble Gum the Balloon Dancer," and "Mr. Baker the Undertaker" ("who never sends a card that says, 'Get Well Soon'") failed to chart. The British Invasion of 1964 hurt the market for novelty songs, along with most other genres of American rock, and Stevens wisely downshifted his recording career and concentrated on production work. He did some first-rate producing and arranging for such mainstream artists as Patti Page, Brenda Lee, and Brook Benton.

In 1966 he signed with Monument, a label that favored country artists, with the agreement that he would be allowed to record both novelty and

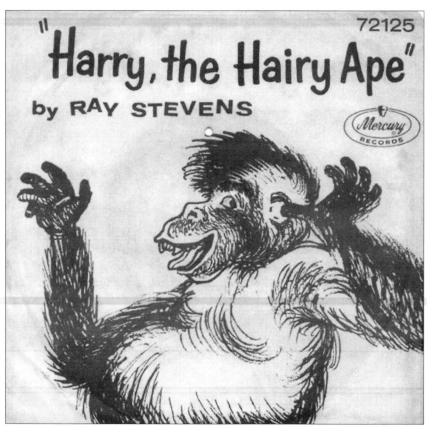

"Harry, the Hairy Ape" was just one of Ray Stevens's memorably zany creations, which also included "Ahab the Arab" and "Gitarzan" and his jungle band. Mercury clearly put its money into the recordings rather than the artwork on their picture sleeves. (From the collection of Don McLaughlin)

serious songs. "Freddie Feelgood (And His Funky Little Five Piece Band)" (#91, 1966), was a tour de force, with motor-mouth Stevens, energized by a brass section and a live audience, playing all the instruments in the band. It was followed in 1968 by "Unwind" (#52) and "Mr. Businessman" (#28), contemporary up-tempo ballads containing a typical late-sixties social message. There was a particularly strong moral tone to "Mr. Businessman" that may have been partially attributed to his having recently been burned in a business deal.

Just as it looked like Ray Stevens the funny man was taking a back seat to the serious singer, he finished out the decade with his biggest novelty hit since "Ahab," the hilarious "Gitarzan" (#8, 1969), based on an idea given to him by bandleader and arranger Bill Justis. The plot line was basically "Harry the Hairy Ape" again, with Tarzan and his jungle band hitting it big as entertainers. Stevens topped himself by playing Tarzan, Jane, and his monkey and then bringing them together in a crazy trio. How Stevens pulled off that feat before a supposedly "live" audience remains a mystery. The pounding brass arrangement, used earlier in "Freddie Feelgood," helped make "Gitarzan" not only one of the funniest novelties of the decade, but also one of the rockingest. Stevens followed it with his version of the Coasters' classic "Along Came Jones" (#27), which fit him like a glove. His last hit single for Monument was another serious side, Kris Kristofferson's "Sunday Mornin' Comin' Down" (#81).

Roger Miller, who was already on the downswing of a spectacular recording career, introduced Stevens to Andy Williams, who signed Stevens to his new label, Barnaby, in 1969. Williams handed Stevens the hosting job for his TV show's summer replacement variety series and the comic singer wrote a song for the show's theme and his first Barnaby release.

"Everything Is Beautiful" is the kind of bathetic ballad that makes one wish Stevens had stuck with novelty. The opening chorus of "Jesus Loves the Little Children," sung by his two daughters at their Nashville elementary school, is the sort of sentimental ploy the old Ray Stevens would have satirized mercilessly. But the early '70s was the right time for this kind of overblown peace-and-love ballad, and it zoomed to #1, Stevens's first chart topper.

After another relatively fallow period in the early seventies, Stevens returned to top form with the biggest hit of his career, the novelty

By the early seventies Ray Stevens had broken free of novelty with a string of successful contemporary serious songs. By the eighties he was back in novelty to stay, promoting a best-selling video of his favorite funny songs. (Photo courtesy of Showtime Archives, Toronto)

"The Streak" (#1, 1974). He got the idea while on a transcontinental flight when he read an article in a news magazine about the streaking fad (young men running naked in public), and he wrote the song within a few days. "The Streak" was the most elaborate of his comic playlets, opened by an "on the spot" reporter who follows the appearances of the streaker from a downtown supermarket to a high school basketball game. In the zany supporting cast are a Middle American couple, Ethel and Earl; Earl spends the record trying to protect his wife from the sight of the naked runner. ("Don't look, Eth-ull! It was too late.") The comic payoff comes when Ethel, to Earl's great chagrin, goes over to the enemy. ("Eth-ull, is that *you*?") Although the streak craze vanished quickly, Stevens's record, one of his best novelties, continues to draw laughs.

His last major hit the following year was a fresh and offbeat bluegrass version of "Misty" (#14) arranged for steel guitars, banjos, and fiddles. It won him his second Grammy for Best Arrangement. Two years later he took another standard, "In the Mood" (#40, 1977), and, in what may be his zaniest record to date, clucked the tune as a chorus of chickens and billed himself as the Henhouse Five Plus Too. Stevens ended the decade, his third as a recording artist, with a dead-on spoof of the artist he himself came dangerously close to emulating at the beginning of the seventies, "I Need Your Help Barry Manilow" (#49, 1979).

By the mid-eighties, his days as a hit maker over, Stevens resigned himself once again to being a full-time novelty artist and signed with MCA Records. Since then he has produced a string of albums of varying quality. But while much of his material is less than satisfying, he has still shown flashes of his wild wit in a memorable song like "Mississippi Squirrel Revival," which pokes fun at charismatic Southern religion.

For all his criticism of businessmen, Stevens has proven to have a pretty good head for business himself, direct-marketing his songs on a multi-million-selling video on late-night television and performing to sell-out crowds at his own theater in the country music mecca of Branson, Missouri, in the early nineties.

Ray Stevens's output is large and erratic. His "serious" songs suffer from some of the same glibness that make many of his novelty songs less than memorable. One wishes he'd slow down the frenetic pace and find a really funny idea to latch onto. Yet at his best he is one of rock's funniest funny men and his trio of novelty classics—"Ahab the Arab,"

"Gitarzan," and "The Streak"—are as funny today as when he recorded them. Ray Stevens has persisted in a career that has had its full share of ups and downs, and he has ultimately prevailed.

King of the Road

Roger Miller's first big country hit record was "When Two Worlds Collide." The song was a fairly conventional country ballad and gave little indication of what was to come from this gifted singer-songwriter. But the title could well symbolize Miller's amazing career, which drew on the world of country and the world of pop. (Some would add a third world, jazz.) In the songs of Roger Miller the sparks that would fly when these worlds collided were memorable indeed and gave a new meaning to the term *novelty.*

The road to fame was not an easy one for the man who became "King of the Road." He was born Roger Dean Miller on January 2, 1936, in Fort Worth, Texas. Youngest of three sons, his father died when he was barely a year old, and his sickly mother, rather than put her sons in an orphanage, parceled them out to her late husband's three brothers. Roger ended up in Erick, Oklahoma, on a hardscrabble farm with Uncle Elmer and Aunt Amelia.

Life on the farm was grim. Young Roger didn't live in a house with electricity or a telephone until he was in his teens. He grew to hate farm life and longed for something better. "Something better" was represented by cowboy actor and rising recording artist Sheb Wooley, who married Miller's cousin, Elmer's daughter. Wooley would bring his guitar to the Miller home and sing and play, giving Roger his first real exposure to music. When he was eleven, Wooley gave him a fiddle and he learned to play it.

Miller's formal education ended after eighth grade and the youth took to the road, wandering around Oklahoma and Texas and working as a ranch hand, a rodeo rider, and a dehorner of cattle. These experiences would help him to empathize with the world's dispossessed and later inspired his most famous song.

The army proved to be his ticket out of an aimless life. He served in the Special Services during the Korean War, playing guitar, drums, and fiddle in a country band. Miller's sergeant was Horace J. "Happy" Burns, whose brother happened to be Jethro Burns, one half of the country comedy duo Homer and Jethro. Recognizing Miller's raw talent, Sergeant Burns helped get him an audition with his brother's good friend Chet Atkins, who was head of production for RCA Records in Nashville.

Miller's audition for Atkins was, in his own words, "a disaster." He had forgotten his guitar and had to borrow Atkins's. Despite this failure he decided to stay in the country music capital and got a job as a bellhop in the Andrew Jackson Hotel. He wrote some impressive songs but couldn't find a recording company that would let him record them. "I'd sing songs for people and they'd say that would be good for someone else," Miller recalled years later.

The budding songwriter supplemented his income by taking a job playing fiddle in country comedienne Minnie Pearl's band. In 1957 Jimmy Dean recorded his song "Happy Child," but his own career continued to stagnate. In disgust, he and his wife, Barbara, moved to Amarillo, Texas, where he got a job as a fire fighter. This job only lasted until he slept through an alarm and was fired. He returned to Nashville and got a job playing in country star Ray Price's band, the Cherokee Cowboys. Price recorded his song "Invitation to the Blues" and took it to #1 on the *Billboard* country charts in 1958. Soon Miller's songs were being recorded by Ernest Tubb ("Half a Mind"), Faron Young ("That's the Way I Feel"), and Porter Wagner ("Dear Lonesome"). Miller recorded two singles himself for Decca but both stiffed.

In 1960 RCA, the label that had earlier rejected him, signed him up. Miller's very first single for RCA exhibited the hallmarks of his still evolving style. "You Don't Want My Love" was an odd number—an upbeat, rhythmically complex tune about a rejected lover for whom nature's beauty and happiness is a depressant. Its blend of the comical and the sad was something new in country music. So was the strange, jazzlike scat singing that Miller improvised between choruses. In its review *Billboard* called the song "an unusual side . . . [with] good sales potential." It went to #14 on the country charts. Retitled "In the Summertime," the song appeared five years later on Miller's second Smash album, *The Return of Roger Miller*.

Over the next three years Miller's unique style would continue to evolve, as he experimented with sounds, rhythms, and lyrics. On "Fair Swiss Maiden" (later a pop hit for Del Shannon) and "Trouble on the

Turnpike," he played with rock doo-wop, eventually abandoning it for his more personalized country jazz scat singing. He would perfect smooth but heartfelt country ballads such as "Sorry Willie," about the breakup of his friend Willie Nelson's first marriage, and "Lock, Stock and Teardrops," written for Patsy Cline, who died in a plane crash before she could record it. "I Know Who It Is (And I'm Gonna Tell on Him)" was an exuberant gospel rave-up, foreshadowing some of the best numbers from his Broadway show, *Big River.* "Hitch-Hiker" was a poignant character study, a dress rehearsal for "King of the Road."

Miller's last RCA session in November 1963 produced "It Happened Just That Way," which recalled the hard times of his childhood, filtered through a playful imagination. It was fresh, original, and vintage Miller, but the public wasn't buying. Guest spots on the *Tonight Show,* the *Jimmy Dean Show,* and a regular spot on *Merv Griffin* had given Miller valuable exposure, but his career still failed to catch fire.

Desperate and disillusioned, he made a deal with Smash, a subsidiary of Mercury Records, to record eighteen sides at $100 a side, a dozen of which would fill an album of novelty songs. He bought a used Chevy with the money and moved his family to California, where he took acting lessons with hopes of landing movie roles in Hollywood. He never got to audition. The Smash album, originally titled *Roger and Out* and retitled *Dang Me,* was selling, and the title number, which Miller claimed to have written in four minutes in a Phoenix motel room, was a blockbuster, soaring to #7 on the *Billboard* pop charts and #1 country.

"Dang Me," for all of us baby boomers listening to AM radio in 1964, was a revelation—in its way, as revolutionary a sound as the Beatles. Here was a novelty song that was part country, part pop, and part jazz, with crazy scat singing the likes of which had never been heard before on a pop record. The song was truly funny, voiced by a character who hated his irresponsible behavior but seemed unable to do anything to change it. The guilt and dark humor that runs through "Dang Me" like a black thread were traits that would permeate much of Roger Miller's best work.

"Chug A Lug" (#9), the follow-up, chronicled an adolescent's first experiences with alcohol that rang true for every kid who tried to buy a six-pack with a fake I.D. The striking bass guitar accompaniment was another Miller exercise in what he liked to call "depressive jazz." His next single, "Do-Wacka-Do" (#31, 1965), was an amusing expression of career envy, something that Miller must have keenly experienced in his first years in Nashville but was now observing from the other side of success.

"Armed with a catchy ditty . . . and flanked by his honey-haired bride of a few days, artist-composer Roger Miller provided a dramatic climax for the NARAS [National Academy of Recording Arts & Science] dinner . . . last week," began a *Billboard* report on the 1964 Grammy Awards. Miller won five out of six Grammys in the C&W category, only missing the one for Best Pop Vocal by a Female. Emcee Ralph Emery ended the dinner by quipping, "Thank you, folks, for coming to the Roger Miller awards dinner."

For all his wacky humor and carefree ways, there was a dark side to Roger Miller that can be glimpsed in this publicity shot, as well as in such songs as "One Dyin' and a Buryin'," the ultimate death-wish song. (Photofest)

But there were even greater things to come. In 1965 Miller produced his biggest hit and signature song, a tribute to the footloose hobo life he once knew. "King of the Road" is a full-bodied character study—laconic, lyrical, and propelled by an irresistible finger-snapping beat that is pure pop. The images are terse, compact, and unforgettable. The portrait of the tramp is affectionate but devoid of sentimentality. The same character who knows the names of every child in town also knows "every lock that ain't locked when no one's around."

With "King of the Road" Roger Miller became the literal king of country crossover music. The single eventually sold 2.5 million copies and sparked a spate of answer records, including Jody Miller's (no relation) delightful "Queen of the House" (#12 pop).

The 1965 Grammy Awards was another love feast for Roger Miller. "King of the Road" took five awards—for best Rock and Roll single (beating out "Yesterday" by the Beatles), best male vocal performance, best Country and Western single, best C&W song, and best C&W male vocal performance. The album *The Return of Roger Miller* won best C&W album, bringing Miller's Grammy total for the year to six, a record that would remain unbroken until Michael Jackson won eight Grammys in 1983 for his *Thriller* LP.

Miller's popularity was at its peak and so pervasive that he could release a non-novelty love song—the beguiling and melancholy "Engine, Engine Number 9"—and take it into the top ten. Even more of a departure was "One Dyin' and a Buryin'" (#34), as striking and haunting a musical portrait of a suicidal lover as has ever graced the pop charts. When Miller sings the tag line "I want to be free," it is with the dead honesty of a man who sees death not as a bitter ending but as a blessed release from the woes of love and life. As in all his songs, there is a large chunk of himself in the lyric. "Depression rides him like a monkey," said his friend novelist William Price Fox.

Miller finished out the landmark year of 1965 with two more delicious novelties—"Kansas City Star" (#31), a deft character study of a TV kiddie show host content to be the big frog in a little pond, and "England Swings" (#8), his loving tribute to the land of the Beatles and Big Ben that shrewdly returned him to the top ten on both sides of the Atlantic at the height of the British Invasion.

The king of the road was king of the hill, but fame had gone to his head, bringing out the "wild child" that his friends and family knew all too well. Like the wastrel in "Dang Me," Miller grew reckless, abused alcohol, experimented with drugs, and brought on the wreck of his second marriage. This last event inspired his thoughtful meditation on marriage and divorce, "Husbands and Wives" (#26, 1966), which, while not one of his biggest hits, has proven a favorite with singers from Willie Nelson to Ringo Starr.

And the hits kept coming. "You Can't Roller Skate in a Buffalo Herd" (#40) was as silly and nonsensical as anything he had previously penned, but contained a nugget of Millerean wisdom underneath the foolery, namely "You can be happy if you've a mind to."

But happiness seemed to elude Roger Miller. Success fit him uncomfortably and the guilt he felt as a wayward husband and absentee father wore heavily on him. And his creativity was starting to flag. An unremarkable, upbeat version of "Heartbreak Hotel" stalled at #84 and the original "Walking in the Sunshine" (#37, 1967) was tuneful but lacked the depth and humor of his best material. His last pop top forty single, "Little Green Apples" (#39, 1968), was tellingly not a Miller original, but a Bobby Russell composition. While Miller's version was memorable, it was overshadowed by O. C. Smith's version, which went to #2.

Miller's fortunes fluctuated in the 1970s. His biggest success now wasn't a record but a hotel he designed and built in Nashville, aptly called King of the Road. It remained a city landmark for years, spawning a hotel chain, until mismanagement took it into bankruptcy years later. The songs he wrote and performed as the narrator of the Disney animated feature *Robin Hood* (1973) were prime Roger, but the film itself was poorly received. He left Smash and wandered from label to label in search of that elusive hit that would put him back on top. The brightest spot in his life was his third and final marriage, to Mary Arnold, who sang backup for friend Kenny Rogers in the First Edition.

It seemed Roger Miller's career was all but over when he made an album, *Old Friends,* consisting of old and new songs with longtime friend and fellow outlaw Willie Nelson in 1982 for Columbia. The title single, on which the duo were joined by Ray Price, became a top twenty hit on the country charts and put Miller back in circulation. He began playing gigs again and appeared at the Lone Star Cafe in New York City. Among the fans who flocked around him one night after his set was Broadway producer Rocco Landesman, who suggested that the singer would be right to write the score for the musical version of Mark

Twain's *Huckleberry Finn* he was producing. Miller's reaction was that Landesman must be on drugs, but then he read Twain's novel for the first time and saw his own childhood in its pages. Few songwriters could better relate to bad boy Huck, his drunken, haunted father, and the runaway slave Jim.

Disney's animated **Robin Hood,** *for which he wrote and sang several songs as the rooster minstrel Alan a Dale, was Roger Miller's first foray into classic children's literature. The second came twelve years later in the Broadway musical* **Big River,** *an adaptation of Mark Twain's* **Huckleberry Finn.** *(Photofest)*

Big River, as the show came to be called, proved a Broadway smash in 1985 and the sweetest triumph of Miller's career, winning seven Tony Awards. The score is a valentine of Americana, filled with raucous humor and a gospel fervor in such memorable numbers as "Muddy Water" and "Waitin' for the Light to Shine."

The triumph was marred by shadows, however: Roger Miller had been diagnosed with cancer. He fought the illness for seven years before finally succumbing on October 25, 1992 in Los Angeles at age fifty-six. As he once said, "I never plan to be old, but I do plan to be *rich!*" He was rich indeed—in word, song, and soul. To the end, Roger Miller remained an original. As singer Roy Clark said at a tribute dinner to him in 1989, "When they made him they broke the gyroscope."

6 Bring on the Comics!

> "We were just regular guys. Actually, the truth of the matter is we belonged to the YMCA all during those years we toured."—*Cheech Marin*

> "Well, excuuuuuuuse me!"—*Steve Martin*

Comedy has existed on disk since the days of vaudeville headliners Webber and Fields, but it wasn't until the year 1960 that comedy became big business in the recording industry. That year Bob Newhart and Shelly Berman, two of a new generation of intellectual stand-up comics, released their first albums. Berman's *Inside Shelly Berman* was the first comedy album to sell a million copies and Newhart's *The Button Down Mind* won the Grammy for the Album of the Year, the first time a comedy album was ever chosen for this award. The sequel, *The Button Down Mind Strikes Back,* received the award for Best Comedy Performance and Newhart himself was voted the Best New Artist.

Other young comedians joined the rush to the recording studio. None made a more spectacular splash then Vaughn Meader, whose *The First Family,* released in 1962, was a gentle satire of President John F. Kennedy and his extended family. The album broke new ground for comedy records and was conceived as a series of short sketches recorded in the studio with a number of actors. Most prominent was Vaughn Meader as J.F.K.; overnight Meader went from unknown comic on TV's *Talent Scouts* to a household name. *The First Family* stayed on the *Billboard* LP charts for nearly a year, with twelve weeks in the #1 position. It eventually sold four million copies and remains the best-selling comedy album of all time.

Then came November 22, 1963. The tragic death of President John F. Kennedy destroyed the career of the comic most closely associated with him. When a 1962 Grammy Awards TV special was held a week after the assassination, Vaughn Meader was not allowed to appear on the program, even though *The First Family* had won the Album of the Year Award.

Comedy albums, however, continued to sell throughout the sixties and into the seventies, making recording stars out of comics as diverse as Bill Cosby and Cheech and Chong.

Shtick on 45

While albums were hot, hit comedy singles were a rare commodity during the golden age of novelty. Built on usually lengthy monologues or elaborate sketches, comedy seemed more suited to the LP format. Besides this, comedy was usually spoken and spoken records rarely appeared on the charts, even in the novelty category. Despite this, a select handful of comics have managed to hit the singles' charts with their shtick.

There were comedians on the charts before Eddie Lawrence (born Ed Eisler), but he was one of the first mainstream comics to turn his attention primarily to making records. His "The Old Philosopher" (#34, 1956) was a rich character whose laundry list of outrageous woes would have given Job pause. Each chorus of bad luck ended with a folksy "Is that what's bothering you, brother?" as the musical ensemble the Sentimental Four played "Beautiful Dreamer" in the background. Then Lawrence broke into a spirited if cliché-ridden pep talk to a brass band accompaniment ending with the catchphrase "You'll never give up, never give up, that ship!"

Although Lawrence never hit the singles' charts again, he remained popular for years with a string of comedy albums, most of them built around the character of the Old Philosopher. There was "The Old Philosopher on the Range," "The Old Philosopher at Home," "Son of the Old Philosopher," "The Lawyer's Philosopher," and even "The Deejay's Philosopher" ("You say here it is January and the old payola hasn't come through yet?").

But Lawrence was far from a one-note comic. He created a host of colorful characters on his albums. Tracks like "No Business," delivered in his best pitchman voice, took a funny but pitiless view of the multitudes who vainly pursue a career in show business. On tracks like "The Good Old Days" and "Lord Bellyacher" he created an unforgettable grouch who sat at a bar complaining about everything from calypso to Cinemascope in a free-flowing monologue that showed Lawrence's playwrighting skills (he cowrote the Broadway show *Kelly* in the early 1960s). A versatile talent, Lawrence is also a trained artist who in his younger days studied for five years in Paris with abstract artist Fernand Léger. After years out of the limelight he returned in 1994 with his first CD, *The Jazzy Old Philosopher,* which updated his act for a new generation of fans.

Eddie Lawrence, "The Old Philosopher," poses with one of his paintings, a portrait of his friend actor Jason Robards. Besides being one of the first comics to concentrate primarily on making records, Lawrence has also pursued careers as an author, playwright, actor, and painter. (From the collection of Ronald L. Smith)

Monologues of a very different kind were the specialty of a twenty-eight-year-old North Carolinian whose country-bumpkin interpretation of America's second favorite sport became a top ten hit in 1954. "What It Was, Was Football (1 & 2)" by Andy Griffith was released on a local label in his home state and sold so well that Capitol Records picked it up for national distribution. The following year Griffith had another hit with his country-boy interpretation of the sexy, suggestive lyrics of "Make Yourself Comfortable" (#26) sung by Jean Wilson.

In Elia Kazan's film *A Face in the Crowd* (1957), Griffith revealed a surprising dramatic side to his talent as a ruthless country hustler who rises to prominence through radio, records, and television. A few years later he settled down into sitcom celebrity as the sheriff of the little town of Mayberry on the long-running TV series *The Andy Griffith Show.*

Jim Backus was another familiar face on television, most notably as millionaire Thurston Howell III, one of the seven castaways on *Gilligan's Island* (1964-67). But back in 1958 he was best known as the voice of

UPA's nearsighted cartoon character Mister Magoo, whose whimsical laughter permeates "Delicious!" (#40). With every sip of champagne, Backus and his lady companion get giddier and giddier while a small combo plays sedate cocktail music in the background. (His companion is labeled only as "Friend" on the record label, and some pressings of the Jubilee single misspelled "Backus" as "Bakus.") Not a bad laughing record, but it pales when compared to Steve Allen's "Impossible," in which the comedian's giggle fits demolish his trumpet solo; Spike Jones's parody of Patti Page's "I Went to Your Wedding;" and the delirious Christmas novelty "Jingle Bells (Laughing All the Way)," by the mysterious St. Nick.

A less gregarious couple is found in "Ambrose (Part Five)" by Linda Laurie (#52, 1959), who delivered an amusing one-sided conversation in her best Brooklynese during a stroll through a subway tunnel with her morose boyfriend, Ambrose. "Why can't we walk in the park like other boys and girls?" she complains, to which he gruffly responds "Just keep walking!" This strange single ends in midsentence, making one wonder what happened in Part Six. (Were they both demolished by a subway train?) Laurie had no more charting novelties but years later she reemerged as a successful songwriter, providing Helen Reddy with two of her best character songs, "Delta Dawn" and "Leave Me Alone (Ruby Red Dress)."

Laurie came naturally by her New York accent, but nightclub comic Buddy Hackett created his popular Chinese waiter character out of whole cloth. In 1956 Hackett reprised the character in "Chinese Rock and Egg Roll" (#87), in which he complained about the corroding effects "lock and loll" were having on his restaurant business. Hackett's energy was infectious even if the routine was stale and more than a little offensive.

More endearing was the Hispanic character José Jimenez, the creation of comic Bill Dana, who was born William Szarthmony in Quincy, Massachusetts. Like Allan Sherman, Dana was primarily a comedy writer who performed at parties until his boss, Steve Allen, encouraged him to go professional with his Jimenez character on his television variety show.

In 1961, with the Mercury space program just under way, Dana released his second comedy album, *José Jimenez The Astronaut,* which consisted mostly of Don Hinckley interviewing José live at the Hungry i in San Francisco. It was not unlike the "Man in the Street" sketches

Dana was part of on the Allen show. The timing of the topical album was perfect and it sold extremely well. A six-minute single culled from the album, "The Astronaut (Parts 1 & 2)," climbed to #19 on the pop charts. While the jokes are amusing, it is José's gentle little boy character that remains appealing today. ("Mr. Jimenez, you must have some opinions on the race for space." "All right, I will. . . .") The controversy over the Hispanic stereotype forced Dana to abandon the character in 1970, complete with a mock funeral for José held in Los Angeles. Dana's career was pretty much buried with him.

If José seemed tongue-tied at times, it was nothing compared to the twisted phraseology demonstrated by night club comic and trumpeter Jack Ross in 1962's "Cinderella." In his retelling of the familiar fairy tale,

With his puppydog face and self-effacing manner, José Jimenez was a gentle, winning persona for comic Bill Dana. Jimenez was unofficially adopted as the eighth astronaut in the Mercury Seven Project after the release of his best-selling comedy album and single "The Astronaut." When Gus Grissom took his first flight into space, Alan Shepard comforted him with the words "José, don't cry too much." (Photofest)

Ross deftly switches the first letters of words to great comic effect. The Handsome Prince became "Pransome Hince," "Sleeping Beauty, "Beeping Sleauty," and "rubies and pearls," "pubies and rearls." The record, recorded live with raucous laughter, climbed to #16, making it one of the highest-charting spoken comedy singles of the rock era. Ross's only other charting single earlier that same year was "Hey José (Ching, Ching)" (#58), a novelty instrumental that had the same south-of-the-border sound that a year later would make Herb Alpert a very rich man.

They Can Sing, Too!

Surprisingly, more comedians have succeeded on the pop charts singing than cracking jokes. Some comics, such as Art Carney and Wally Cox, both of whom blossomed as television stars in the early '50s, began their show biz careers as singers. Carney sang as a novelty vocalist for Horace Heidt's orchestra for three and a half years on the road, and Cox's night-club comedy act included odd yodeling numbers along with witty monologues. He reprised his yodel to grand effect in the 1953 release "There Is a Tavern in the Town." The next year Carney brought his Ed Norton character from *The Honeymooners* to musical life in the obscure novelty "The Song of the Sewer."

Neither of these singles sold well, nor did the string of novelty songs Jerry Lewis recorded for Capitol from 1949 to 1954. Lewis's zany, child-like comic persona was perfectly captured in such specialty numbers as "Are You For Real"—which billed him as "Jerry Lewis (Child Star)"—"I Love a Murder Mystery," and the incredible verbal tour-de-force "I'm a Little Busybody," a classical takeoff based on a theme by Nicolo Paginini, which had to be edited manually nineteen times by the sound engineers in the days before multitrack recording.

A star of clubs, films, and television, Lewis had about given up on a recording career when his ten-year partnership with Dean Martin broke up in 1956. He headed for Las Vegas for a much-needed vacation with his wife and friends, when he received an urgent call from Judy Garland's husband, Sid Luft, to fill in for the ill singer at the Frontier Hotel. Lewis did an admirable job for an hour and then closed with Garland's signature tune, "Rock-A-Bye Your Baby to a Dixie Melody." The song brought down the house and the comic quickly recorded the number and three others at his own expense in the Capitol studios.

When Capitol refused to release the songs, he took his demos to Decca. The label had him record enough material to fill an album.

Released as a single in November 1956, "Rockabye" went to #10 on the pop charts in just three weeks. The loony comedian who couldn't land on the charts with a string of funny songs finally hit it big with a schmaltzy standard that made Al Jolson famous back in 1918. Lewis had only one more hit, another standard, "It All Depends on You," in early 1957 before returning to films and television full time. His distaste for rock 'n' roll is well known, although he seemed to take some paternal pride in the success of son Gary with his band, the Playboys, in the sixties.

Soupy Sales, rock star? Anything was possible in 1965 when a new dance craze seemed to surface every week. The TV kiddie show host and comic concocted one called "The Mouse," which he performs here before a delighted teen audience during a Good Friday rock show at New York's Paramount Theatre. (Photofest)

Comic Dick Shawn, who years later would play a singing Hitler in Mel Brooks's *The Producers,* had no compunction about singing rock 'n' roll in "Rockin' the Scales." Neither did Timmie ("Oh Yeah") Rogers, a black vaudeville and club comic. A headliner at New York's Apollo Theater and one of the first black stand-ups to break into white nightclubs in the '50s, Rogers's trademark was going wide-eyed and exclaiming, "Oh Yeah!" The catchphrase is conspicuously missing from his 1957 hit record, "Back to School Again" (#36), whose antischool lyrics (strange coming from a forty-two-year-old comic) and heavy stroll beat made it a hit with the *American Bandstand* crowd. Interestingly, Rogers's "Oh yeahs!" were appropriated the same year by singer Billy Williams on his much bigger hit "I'm Gonna Sit Right Down and Write Myself a Letter."

Another vaudeville-style comic who tapped into the rock market was the incorrigible Soupy Sales, whose 1960s kiddie television show seemed aimed as much at adults as at children (and so were the custard pies he flung with gleeful abandon). "The Mouse" (#76, 1965) was just another silly sixties' dance based on an animal, but when Soupy performed it on TV's *Shindig* with his hands behind his ears, his eyes squinched up, and his front teeth sticking out like a rodent, who could resist?

A more substantial musical mark was made by Bill Cosby, whose love of black music from jazz to soul is well known to viewers of his various hit television shows. After producing seven million-selling comedy albums, Cosby turned to singing and struck gold with his first single, an upbeat, funky version of Stevie Wonder's "Uptight," overlaid with the curious tale of a philosophical old man with a penchant for getting run over by trains. "Little Ole Man (Uptight—Everything's Alright)" (#4, 1967) was the first and biggest of five charting singles for Cosby, which included the funky medley of "I Can't Get No Satisfaction" and "Hold On, I'm Coming" in "Hooray for the Salvation Army Band" (#71, 1967). "Yes, Yes, Yes" (#46, 1976) from the album *Bill Cosby is Not Himself These days, Rat Own, Rat Own, Rat Own* was a choice parody of the bombastic vocalizing of Barry White, with Cos ruminating soulfully about a wife who cracks up his car and takes money out of his wallet. Since then he has sung straight R&B on the LP *At Last Bill Cosby Really Sings.* And he really can.

Bill Cosby first made his mark on comedy albums, but then proved a decent vocalist, having some fun with the Motown sound, disco, and the heavy-breathing technique of Barry White. (Photofest)

"Little Ole Man" had a serious message, and other comics, often in their twilight years, have achieved a potent poignancy singing serious songs. Veteran comedian Jimmy Durante touched the heart with his warm rendition of "September Song" (#51, 1963), while black comic Moms Mabley, the queen of bawd, gave a deeply affecting resonance to "Abraham, Martin and John" (#35, 1969) that Dion could only aspire to. George Burns, eternally young, sang in his wistful, pungent singspeak about how "I Wish I Was Eighteen Again" (#49, 1980) and immediately took the prize for the longest period between hit disks (his last one was back in 1933).

Walter Brennan may technically be more of a character actor than a comedian, but his best-known role was as the feisty, frisky Grandpa Amos McCoy on TV's first rural sitcom *The Real McCoys* (1957-63). He spoke his way through the weepy "Old Rivers" (#5, 1962),★ about an old farm worker and the boy who loved him, with strong support from the Johnny Mann Singers, a Floyd Cramer-like piano hook, and a full orchestra. By the end there wasn't a dry eye left in the house.

Red Skelton didn't sing "The Pledge of Allegiance" (#44, 1969) but he also went for the heart strings as he parsed the pledge in tribute to an old high school teacher. It was a patriotic response from a beloved figure of a simpler time to the counterculture of the sixties at the height of the Vietnam War.

There was nothing sentimental about Steve Martin, one of the first true rock 'n' roll comics. Starting out as an all-around entertainer at Disneyland, where a friend taught him to play the banjo, Martin went on to write TV comedy material for the Smothers Brothers and Sonny and Cher. His first experience as a stand-up was as the opening act for stoned-out rock groups in small California clubs in the mid-seventies.

"I was a total drug casualty," confesses Martin, who could not work in the chaos of the psychedelic scene. After "going straight" in his famous white suit and sticking an arrow through his head, he finally made the big time as a self-described "wild and crazy guy."

In 1978, at the peak of his popularity as a comic, Martin made his second album for Warner Bros., *A Wild and Crazy Guy,* which included the novelty song "King Tut" featuring the Toot Uncommons (#17,

---

★*A few years earlier Brennan had tried his hand at novelty in "Space Mice," a Chipmunks' clone.*

Before he became a "wild and crazy guy," Steve Martin worked for eight years at Disneyland, where he learned to play the banjo. His interest in "King Tut" went beyond his hit novelty single; Martin is actually a longtime serious art collector. (Photofest)

1978). Inspired by the then traveling exhibit of artifacts from Tut's tomb, the song became one of the biggest novelty hits of the '70s, benefiting from exposure on *Saturday Night Live.*

Another young comic whose career was furthered by *Saturday Night Live* was Billy Crystal, who was a regular on the show in 1984 and 1985. Unlike Martin, who basically played himself on stage, Crystal developed a colorful gallery of characters including dead-on impressions of Sammy Davis, Jr., and Argentinean actor Fernando Lamas. His catchphrase while playing Lamas was a flowery, highly insincere "You look marvelous." In the summer of 1985 Crystal released the album *Mahvelous!* from which a single "You Look Marvelous" (#58) emerged, set to a thumping disco beat.

Before bidding adieu to comic songbirds, it is fitting to mention one of the pioneer teams of screen comedy who sang some great novelty numbers in their films but never made the charts. This was partially righted in 1983 when a Chicago band called Jump 'N The Saddle recorded "The Curley Shuffle" in honor of the most beloved of the Three Stooges. The catchy song with a big-band beat went all the way to #15 and became one of the decade's biggest novelty songs.

The Three Stooges were known for gratuitous violence and an anarchical spirit. In the early seventies a new breed of rock-inspired, counterculture comics would bring their own brand of anarchy to the novelty record.

Booze, Drugs, and Rock 'n' Roll

By the late sixties the counterculture was a force to be reckoned with. The message "tune in, turn on, and drop out" was being heard across the land, and comics were not immune to its siren call. George Carlin, who started the decade portraying the Hippy, Dippy Weatherman on *The Ed Sullivan Show,* entered the seventies getting arrested on stage for spouting obscenities in a concert in Cincinnati. Carlin, like his idol Lenny Bruce, found an enthusiastic audience in the '60s generation, but not even he had the impact of two young ex-musicians who by the early '70s were being heralded as "the kings of rock comedy."

Richard "Cheech" Marin and Thomas Chong, better known as Cheech and Chong, drew their humor straight from the mean streets of

America at a time when "scoring" meant getting drugs and not women and marijuana was the drug of choice for hippies and straights alike.

Marin was born in the Watts section of Los Angeles into a Mexican-American family. His father, ironically, was an L.A. police officer. Chong, part Chinese, was raised in Vancouver, Canada, where his father ran a topless night club. Both joined rock bands while still in their teens. How they eventually met was also indicative of the times. To avoid the draft, Marin fled to Canada in the late '60s, where Chong was a member of a promising local band, Bobby Taylor and the Vancouvers. The two decided to form their own group. On the first gig they landed they "started off with comedy," Chong recalled for the *Los Angeles Times,* "and somehow never got around to playing."

Their sketch comedy, influenced by a comedy ensemble called the Committee, dealt with subjects previously considered taboo by most mainstream comics. They created two characters, hippie druggies who were perpetually looking for a score or having misadventures while high. After proving a hit in Vancouver, they moved to Los Angeles in search of wider fame. While performing at the Troubadour club, Cheech and Chong were seen by producer Lou Adler, who quickly signed them to record for his Ode label. Their first album, *Cheech and Chong* (1971), established their rambling, drug-induced style of black comedy that found humor in drug deals and overdoses. It went top ten and eventually earned them a gold record. A single, "Santa Claus and His Old Lady," was released at Christmas time that year and was modestly successful. Three more gold albums followed, but Cheech and Chong's often repetitive and witless humor advanced little beyond the fuzzy minds of their one-dimensional characters.

Their singles, however, which also sold well, were often more interesting, especially those that parodied current music styles. "Basketball Jones" (#15, 1973), a spoof of "Love Jones" by Bright Side of Darkness, dared to poke fun at inner-city black culture and its preoccupation with the hoop game. It sold well, undoubtedly helped by the presence of such guest artists as George Harrison, Carole King, Billy Preston, and Darlene Love.

"Sister Mary Elephant (Shud-Up!)" (#24), a satire of a visit from a drug education officer at an inner city parochial school, was an interminable one-joke sketch, but "Earache My Eye featuring Alice Bowie" (#9, 1974) was as sharp a satire on heavy metal as Green Jellö's "Three

Cheech and Chong were kings of '70s rock comedy who built their routines around drug deals and other counterculture activities. Today Cheech Marin (left) is a family entertainer who divides his time between animated voice-overs and live acting in films and as a regular on the TV series **Nash Bridges.** *(Photofest)*

Little Pigs." More parodies followed, including "Bloat On, featuring the Bloaters" (#41, 1978), a takeoff of the Floaters' "Float On."

By then, however, the enterprising duo, who lived lives far straighter than their material would suggest, had turned their attention away from recording to making movies. They starred in four hit films in a row, based largely on the hippie characters they had created in their records. When they tried to play "real" characters in the historical comedy *The Corsician Brothers,* the result was a disappointing flop.

Cheech and Chong signed up with MCA Records in 1985. Their album *Get Outta My Room* produced one of their best and most heart-felt parodies, "Born in East L.A." (#48), from Bruce Springsteen's "Born in the U.S.A." It was based on an actual incident involving a naturalized citizen who was deported unfairly by the INS (Immigration and Naturalization Service). Interestingly, Springsteen got his first professional gig opening for Cheech and Chong in York, Pennsylvania, years earlier.

After this, the duo broke up and went their separate ways. Chong has had little solo success, although his daughter Rae Dawn Chong has starred in a number of movies. His attempt to resuscitate the comedy team with auditions for a new "Cheech" in 1997 fizzled.

Cheech Marin, however, has gone on to considerable fame as a comic, street-wise sidekick in movies and television, most notably in the Don Johnson crime series *Nash Bridges*. He has even had a second career as a recording artist on children's records as "Cheech, the School Bus Driver," who, by the way, wouldn't be caught dead smoking a joint.

The new permissiveness of the '70s brought a number of other "sick" comic duos to the fore in the novelty field. One of the most successful, if not noteworthy, was Hudson and Landry. Deejay Ron Landry, whom I used to listen to as a kid on Hartford, Connecticut's WDRC, moved to Los Angeles in the '60s and teamed up with Bob Hudson on the morning show at KGBS. The pair's humorous banter and comedy skits quickly made their morning show number one in L.A.

In 1971 they began recording some of their comic bits for Dore Records. Their album covers featured gruesome deaths by hanging, car crashes, and so on. But there was little that was cutting edge about the humor of Hudson and Landry. Their sketches were only intermittently funny, although the crowd at the Pomano National Golf and Country Club, where they recorded their routines live, seemed to find them hysterical. "Top Forty D.J.s" was an amusing bit about two deejays meeting on the street, but "Ajax Liquor Store" (#43, 1971) was an all-too-obvious sketch about a drunk calling a liquor store with a large take-out order. It attempted to do for booze what Cheech and Chong had done for drugs.

When he and Landry split in 1976, Hudson went on to make more humorous records with a number of other partners, including Bobby "Boris" Pickett of "Monster Mash" fame, with diminishing returns.

While morning shows were one of the last refuges of personality deejays and outrageous comedy on radio, late-night television was exploding with a second golden age of live comedy in NBC's ground-breaking *Saturday Night Live,* which debuted in October 1975. Among the show's original cast members were John Belushi and Dan Aykroyd, who played a memorable gallery of crazy characters. Few of these were as popular as a pair of black-garbed musicians who had an infatuation with rhythm and blues music: Joliet "Jake" (Belushi) and Elwood (Aykroyd) Blues.

The Blues Brothers became so popular that in 1979, the year Belushi and Aykroyd left the show, they starred in a feature film based on the characters, directed by John Landis. If there is any merit to *The Blues Brothers,* it is not in the antics of the leading characters and a myriad of car chases, but in the cameo appearances of such R&B legends as Aretha Franklin, James Brown, Ray Charles, and Steve Cropper and Donald Dunn, one half of Booker T and the MGs, who were part of the Blues Brothers' band.

The movie was so successful that Belushi and Aykroyd went on tour as the Blues Brothers and placed four songs in the top forty, including their less-than-inspired versions of Sam and Dave's "Soul Man" and Johnnie Taylor's "Who's Making Love." Such chutzpa can be forgiven, however, for their bringing the Chips' classic novelty "Rubber Biscuit" (#37, 1979) to a wider audience, although their version pales alongside the original. The questionable run of the Blues Brothers ended with Belushi's death by drug overdose on March 5, 1982. A sequel movie released in 1997, starring Belushi's brother Jim, was a failure.

The Blues Brothers briefly made comics Dan Aykroyd (left) and John Belushi into hit recording stars, although the real oxygen in their music came from their backup band that included Paul Shafer, Steve Cropper, and Donald Dunn. (Photofest)

A less hip, if slightly funnier, pair of fictitious siblings were Bob and Doug McKenzie, the alter egos of comics Rick Moranis and Dave Thomas, who created their dumb stereotyped Canadians while members of *Second City TV* (aka *SCTV Network*), a late-night comedy show that rivaled *Saturday Night Live*. The sting of the stereotypes was lessened by the fact that both Moranis and Thomas are Canadian.

The McKenzies' often witless humor rivaled the Blues Brothers for idiocy. Their feature film *Strange Brew* (1983) produced their sole hit, "Take Off," featuring a vocal by Gary Lee of the group Rush that sounds like an advertising plug for the Canadian Tourist Bureau with Bob and Doug kibitzing in the foreground. Although amusing, the song is not as funny as their version of "The Twelve Days of Christmas" (see Chapter 9), first heard on their album *Great White North*.

Like the comedy duos before them, the McKenzie Brothers quickly wore out their one-joke humor and disappeared. Freedom of subject matter did not guarantee great comedy nor novelty records. While attempting to find humor in the social and political world of the '70s, most of these artists only further reinforced the stereotypes they were supposedly poking fun at. The adolescent nature of much of the humor that came from the National Lampoon-Saturday Night Live nexus, particularly in the movies they created, was depressing and enough to drive a mature adult to, well, booze or drugs. As the '70s progressed, rock 'n' roll contributed less and less to the genre of novelty records, further evidence that the era's golden age was over.

⑦ Country Corn and Funny Folk

> "It is a private humor—a kinship humor—
> and much of it is aimed at pulling the group
> together and fending off snickers from the outside."
> —*Dorothy Horstman,* Sing Your Heart Out, Country Boy

> "It's like writing a little book. . . . It's like telling a joke.
> You can't tell it blatantly. You do that—and you can do it
> once—and then it's all over."—*Jim Stafford, on writing novelty songs*

> "Oh dear, I seem to have stumbled onto the delicate
> subject of my career."—*Loudon Wainwright III*

Humor, often earthy, sometimes raw, even childish at times, has been an important element in both country and folk music for generations. In these two genres rooted in the common experiences of ordinary people, humor has often been the glue that binds people to tradition, to a colorful past, and to one another.

For many Americans the concept of country humor was embodied in the long-running television program *Hee Haw,* with its hick jokes and cornpone comedy. But the country bumpkins that populated that show and sitcoms like *The Beverly Hillbillies* began as a Northern stereotype to describe the rural colonial Yankee. By the 1800s the now more sophisticated Yankees transferred the stereotype to the Southern hillbillies. But like the country mouse in Aesop's fable, the Southern bumpkin proved in stories and comedy sketches of the day to be innately wiser and cleverer than his city cousin.

By the same token, the country comics and novelty recording artists of this century were often surprisingly sophisticated entertainers who hid their intelligence behind a goofy grin, a silly song, and a bumpkin costume. More often than not, their audiences were in on the joke.

Minnie Pearl may have worn a hat with a price tag dangling from it and spent a lifetime on stage trying to "ketch a feller," but in real life her alter ego, Sarah Ophelia Cannon, was a cultured and sophisticated woman who lived next door to the governor's mansion in Nashville. Grandpa Jones, her male counterpart, was called "one of the premier interpreters of early country, folk and gospel music" by the Smithsonian, where his battered hat, banjo, and colored suspenders now reside. Homer and Jethro, the top duo of country comedy, were accomplished musicians who could, and often did, play jazz, pop, and Broadway material. C. W. McCall, the trucker's troubadour, was in reality the creative director of a Midwestern ad agency who dreamed up his trucker persona for a bakery account. Johnny Bond, when he wasn't singing about his "Hot Rod Lincoln," was an accomplished author, cowboy actor, and prolific songwriter, while Billy Edd Wheeler, whose only pop hit was a little ditty mourning the passing of the outhouse, was a college graduate, schoolteacher, and serious collector of folk songs. For all the earthiness of their performances, these artists put a lot of hard work and keen intelligence into their novelty songs.

The Thinking Man's Hillbillies

There is nothing in pop or rock that remotely resembles Homer and Jethro and those genres are all the poorer for it. Superb parodists, gifted musicians, and witty satirists of the country, pop, and rock music scene, they were country music's court jesters for over three decades, lampooning everyone from Patti Page to the Beatles. Beloved of their public, as only country artists are, they were equally respected and admired by their colleagues. No less a light than Hank Williams once told Homer that a song wasn't a true success until it had been butchered by Homer and Jethro.

Their real names were Henry Haynes (Homer) and Kenneth Burns (Jethro) and they knew each other from childhood, growing up in Knoxville, Tennessee. They first played and sang together (Homer on guitar and Jethro on the mandolin) on the radio when Homer was fifteen and Jethro nine. Their first group was the String Dusters, a quartet of staff musicians on Knoxville's WNOX radio station. Comedy was something they "did for kicks" according to Jethro when they were off the air. Their parodies of current song hits were so good, however, that the program director put "Homer and Jethro" on as a featured bit. When the String Dusters broke up in 1936, the two musicians went solo full time with their comedy routine.

Homer and Jethro's thirty-year reign as country's top comedy duo is unmatched in popular music. Their countless parodies run the gamut from awful to brilliant, but their superb musicianship was never in question. (Frank Driggs/Archive Photos)

Homer and Jethro graduated to nationally syndicated radio programs in 1939, but the war saw them serving in the armed forces in, respectively, the Pacific and Europe. Reunited in 1945, they worked in Cincinnati on WLW's *Midwestern Hayride,* where they met fellow musician Chet Atkins, who would become a close friend, Jethro's brother-in-law, and producer of many of their records. They first recorded for King Records in 1946 and three years later joined Spike Jones's band on tour. The same year they had their first pop hit on RCA-Victor with a countrified version of Frank Loesser's witty duet "Baby, It's Cold Outside" (#22, 1949) in which they vied for the affections of June Carter. Interestingly, the song was only part parody, with many of Loesser's lyrics remaining intact.

Their spoofs of the Hit Parade in the early '50s were often none too subtle: "Let Me Go, Lover" became "Let Me Go, Blubber" and Patti Page's "Doggie in the Window" was transformed into a hound dog in their second biggest pop hit. Although far from their best work, it featured some howlingly funny dog howls. Their last and biggest pop charter was an irresistibly silly takeoff of Johnny Horton's rousing #1 ballad, "The Battle of New Orleans." "The Battle of Kookomonga" (#14, 1959) transposed the action to a contemporary summer camp, with a troop of horny boy scouts hot on the trail of some nubile girl scouts. It won the Grammy for the Best Comedy Performance of the Year.

The sixties were the duo's peak decade with countless personal appearances from the Grand Ole Opry in Nashville to Las Vegas clubs, where, surprisingly, they were an instant hit. They produced a successful string of record albums, appeared eight times on the *Tonight Show,* and made a hit series of zany TV commercials for Kellogg's Corn Flakes.

While their arrangements and musicianship were often superb and Jethro's mandolin playing something more, their very prolificness hurt the quality of their material. But amid the dross were a number of worthy albums, such as *Any News From Nashville?* (1966), in which they skewered the country recording business from the inside out on track after track, and in a stinging parody of Buck Owens's "Act Naturally," they satirized the Vietnam War at a time when most country artists were aggressively supporting it.

"The Thinking Man's Hillbillies," as they billed themselves, ended their long run when Homer died suddenly of a heart attack in 1971 at age fifty-six. Jethro decided to continue, pairing up with a younger partner, Chicago folk singer Steve Goodman, on non-novelty albums, and gracing many other disks with his skillful mandolin playing. He died of cancer in 1989.

Country bumpkins who were as slick as any city slicker, the likes of Homer and Jethro will not likely be seen again in country music, or in pop for that matter.

Corn-Fed Comedy

The first country novelty to hit the pop charts in the rock era wasn't really a country song at all, although its creator had all the necessary credentials. Cliffie Stone was versatile in a business known for its versatility. Born in Burbank, California, he was the son of a banjo-playing country comic known as Herman the Hermit, who gave him the nickname

Cliffie Stonehead. (His real surname was Synder.) Stone began his career as a bassist in a big band and in 1935 became a deejay on a country radio station. Over the next decade and a half he oversaw many weekly country music radio shows, most prominently the *Hollywood Barn Dance* on CBS. In 1946 he joined the new label Capitol Records, and over the next two decades discovered and managed Tennessee Ernie Ford and Merle Travis, among other country stars.

Comic, singer, bandleader, composer, TV host, and behind-the-scenes kingpin of country music, Stone's pop recording career largely rests on a quirky old-time novelty called "The Popcorn Song" (#14, 1955), about a lazy kernel who was "too pooped to pop." He wrote the song and conducted the orchestra on the single, but the vocal was by Bob Roubian, who gave the jazzy lyrics a distinctly black and bluesy sound.

There was no mistaking the country roots of "Auctioneer" (#19, 1956), written and sung by fast-talking Leroy Van Dyke. Raised in Spring Fork, Missouri, Van Dyke earned a degree in agricultural science at the University of Missouri before serving in the army during the Korean War, where he began strumming the guitar and singing. After service, he worked as a livestock auctioneer, which gave him the inspiration for his first hit record, the story of a country boy who becomes a successful auctioneer. Despite a somewhat humdrum lyric, the single had an arresting opening and closing in which Van Dyke did an actual auctioneering spiel, bereft of musical accompaniment. He waited five years for his next and biggest crossover hit, "Walk on By," one of the classic country cheating songs. Ten years after "Auctioneer," the singer got a chance to play the part on screen in the film *What Am I Bid?* (1967).

Although Van Dyke had a tripping tongue, it's doubtful he could keep up with Hank Snow, whose nimble wordplay was matched by his dexterous guitar picking that gave country music a rocking beat years before the advent of rock 'n' roll. Perhaps the best example of Snow's deft way with a lyric is the novelty "I've Been Everywhere" (#68, 1962), an energized cross-country laundry list of American geography. It went #1 country and was the biggest pop hit for the "Singing Ranger."

"Traveling music" was a popular subgenre in country music; witness Snow's first big country hit "I'm Moving On" and Billy Grammer's huge crossover single of 1959, "Gotta Travel On." The same footloose yearning was a major theme of folk music (Woody Guthrie's "This Land Is Your Land" and the New Christy Minstrels' "Green, Green") and would later hold a similar appeal for rockers such as Rick Nelson ("Travelin' Man") and Dion ("The Wanderer"), although the emphasis here was less on the traveling and more on the great variety of women one could meet along the way.

The automobile provided the prime means of escape from home and responsibility to which country and pop singers aspired. Long before Dave Dudley and C. W. McCall made a mythic hero out of the long-distance trucker, the ultimate travelin' man, a classic hot rod song became one of the most recorded of country car novelties. It all started back in 1951, when Tiny Hill, a 350-pound bandleader from Illinois, recorded "Hot Rod Race" (#29), earlier that year a top five country hit for Arkie Shibley. Tiny talked while his orchestra played, describing a cross-country race between a hopped-up Ford and a Mercury, both of which are bested, in the song's climax, by a souped-up model A. The ending—like that of the Playmates' "Beep Beep" (see Chapter 10), in which a little Nash Rambler beats a Cadillac—was meant to be a joke, but nine years later country artist Charlie Ryan decided it deserved a sequel. Backed by his group, the Timberline Riders, Ryan simply took the licks from Hill's song and picked up where "Hot Rod Race" left off, boasting that he was the kid in the Model A, which had a Lincoln motor, hence the title "Hot Rod Lincoln." With its fast-moving electric guitar and a screechy harmonica doubling as a car horn and police siren, "Hot Rod Lincoln" appealed to both country and rock fans and it went to #33 pop.★ A smoother, less countrified cover by Johnny Bond peaked at #24 the same summer of 1960.

Ryan and Bond were both in their forties and a little old to be fooling around with hot rods. Bond actually seemed most at home on a horse. A radio singer in the 1930s, he joined Gene Autry's Melody Ranch in 1940 and became a singing cowboy, appearing in more than fifty films and countless television oaters. His own compositions numbered over five hundred. In the 1970s he turned to writing and pro-

---

★*Ryan's further adventures in his "Hot Rod Lincoln" were chronicled in "Side Car Cycle" (#84, 1960), in which he finds romance with a female motorcyclist, and "Hot Rod Hades," where he finally crashes and meets the Devil in hell.*

duced biographies of close pals Tex Ritter and Autry, as well as his auto-biography, *Reflections,* before succumbing to a heart attack in 1978.

Twelve years after "Hot Rod" was a hit, California country-rock band Commander Cody and His Lost Planet Airmen took the old heap out for another spin, this time into the top ten, proving the perennial appeal of rednecks in fast cars.

Nineteen-sixty-three was a year for crazes, particularly a seemingly endless configurations of teen dances. So why not a country craze? "Eefin" was a kind of hillbilly doo-wop, in which country folk sat around and made funny sounds with their mouths. The phenomenon of eefin produced a spate of zany novelty records, including "Eefeenany" by the Ardells. But the only eefin record to reach the pop charts was "Little Eeffin Annie" (#76) by Joe Perkins. The novel effect was heightened by the fact that Annie effed a chorus before getting out her words in plain English. What a speech impediment! Soon after that eefin vanished back into the hills and barely anyone noticed.

The sixties saw the disappearance of old-time country music, largely replaced by the slicker Nashville sound pioneered by producers Chet Atkins and Owen Bradley. A wave of nostalgia for the simpler country life gave Billy Edd Wheeler, songwriter and folk archivist, his only smash country hit, "Ode to the Little Brown Shack Out Back" (#50 pop, #1 country, 1965). Wheeler was inspired by an ordinance passed in a Kentucky city that prohibited outhouses. Although the subject was about as crude as you could get, the poet-troubadour's "ode" was deftly humorous and gently winning. At one point he compares himself on the outhouse seat to a "snowbird on its nest." There was a genuine cry to preserve a passing way of life and the values it represented in the plaintive chorus, "Don't let them tear that building down," that many listeners could identify with.

That same year another country institution, Grand Ole Opry stalwart Little Jimmy Dickens, surprised the recording industry with his first and only pop hit. While Little Richard, Little Anthony, and Little Willie John had heights that belied their monikers, Little Jimmy came by his nick-name honestly, standing four feet eleven inches in his stocking feet. At age seventeen he was billed on local radio as the Singing Midget and he boasted of his diminutive size in one of his biggest hits, "I'm Little But I'm Loud," which also described his dazzling cowboy suits.

Little Jimmy Dickens was already a country singing sensation for nearly two decades when "May the Bird of Paradise Fly Up Your Nose" became a major pop hit in 1965. It's clear from this publicity still that when he sang "I'm Little, But I'm Loud," he wasn't talking just about his singing. (Photo courtesy of Showtime Archives, Toronto)

For nearly two decades Little Jimmy had been delighting country audiences with such rustic reminiscences of a hardscrabble childhood as "Take an Old Cold Tater and Wait" and "Out Behind the Barn." In late 1965 he zipped up the pop and country charts with the toe-tapping pleaser "May the Bird of Paradise Fly Up Your Nose," written by composer Neal Merritt after hearing Johnny Carson coin the phrase on the *Tonight Show.* The put-down chorus was in response to such rude behavior as giving a dry cleaner a dime for his phone call after he found a $100 bill in your clothes. One of the most colorful of country performers, Little Jimmy showed he still had the stuff in a 1997 televised homage to the Grand Ole Opry when his performance of "Out Behind the Barn" proved one of the evening's highlights.

By the mid-sixties country humor was moving in a very different direction, dominated by the incredible success of Roger Miller, whose unique blend of country, jazz, and pop was the inspiration for Leroy Pullins's "I'm a Nut" (#57, 1966). Pullins, who voice-trained with Billy Edd Wheeler, was vocally a dead ringer for Miller, right down to his trademark scat singing. It was probably this striking resemblance that prevented the obviously gifted singer-songwriter from ever reaching the pop charts again.

One of the last traditional country novelties to cross over into pop was by a husband-and-wife duo from Buffalo, New York. Jack Blanchard and Misty Morgan were both performing separately when they met and fell in love in Florida in the mid-sixties and later moved to Nashville. "Tennessee Bird Walk" (#23 pop, #1 country, 1970) was a delightful nonsensical ditty with the same quirky electric guitar work that had helped make "Bird of Paradise" a hit five years earlier. Another animal novelty song, "Humphrey the Camel," gave the duo a second minor pop hit, but their funniest record may be the noncharting "Cockroach Stomp," with its doo-wop chorus of "Die, die, die, die, die, die, die."

Spiders, Snakes, Rednecks, and Truckers

It's a long way from birds that walk to spiders and snakes that slide down a pretty young thing's dress. But as the sixties turned into the seventies, subjects previously no laughing matter in country music were suddenly fair game. The artist most responsible for this changeover was Jim Stafford from Eloise, Florida. Stafford represented a new breed of singer-songwriter coming to Nashville in the sixties, more in tune with rock 'n' roll than with the traditional country music performed by the Grand Ole Opry.

Stafford came from a family of fruit pickers until his father saved up enough money to open a dry-cleaning business. In high school Jim joined his first band, the Legends, that included two future legends of country rock, Kent Lavoie of Lobo and Gram Parsons, later a founding member of the Byrds and the Flying Burrito Brothers.

Upon turning twenty-one Stafford moved to Nashville and went country, working as a sideman on guitar at the Grand Ole Opry. When his career stalled, he moved to Atlanta and began to work comedy into his musical act. He started writing novelty songs, but it was a more serious song that got the attention of record producer Phil Gernhard. "Swamp Witch" (#39, 1973) was a vivid slice of swamp rock about a bayou witch named Black Water Haddie. It was atmospheric, creepy, and mesmerizing. MGM bought the single from Stafford and Gernhard

Jim Stafford turned country novelty music on its head in the mid-seventies with novelty songs about post-adolescent sex, gay relationships, and marijuana. His star burned brightly but briefly. By 1980 he was cohosting the TV series **Those Amazing Animals.** *(Photo courtesy of Showtime Archives, Toronto)*

and released the album *Jim Stafford,* which produced three future top fifteen hits, making Stafford the hottest country novelty artist since Roger Miller burst on the scene a decade earlier.

Stafford hit his stride with "Spiders and Snakes" (#3), another prime cut of swamp rock and about as sexually suggestive as a record could get in 1974 without being banned from the airwaves. A schoolboy is seduced by a schoolmate with more experience in such matters who invites him to "do what you wanna do." The song's childish imagery only makes its theme of pubescent sexuality all the more tantalizing, along with Stafford's teasing, down-and-dirty delivery.

With "My Girl Bill" (#12, 1974) Stafford took on the forbidden topic of homosexuality, but in a way that allowed him to have it both ways. What at first appears to be a steamy sexual encounter between two males turns out to be a heart-to-heart about the girl they have both fallen for. "My Girl Bill" is actually "My Girl, Bill" with the inclusion of an all-important comma. The gender-bending joke is accentuated by Stafford's oh-so-sensitive delivery and the drippy MOR musical setting.

In his next single Stafford stretched the limits even further, daring to take the venerable country classic "Wildwood Flower" and transform it into a celebration of the joys of . . . marijuana? Stafford assumes the persona of an easy-going hick whose discovery of the mind-altering properties of the "Wildwood Weed" (#7) allow him and his brother "to take a trip and never leave the farm." The lyrics, by veteran country songwriter Don Bowman, are a hoot and Stafford's delivery makes them even funnier. Controversial though it may have been, "Wildwood Weed" was only making light of reality. By 1974 marijuana was no longer the exclusive domain of hippies. Pot-smoking had been taken up by youth all across small-town America. The plant would become a cash crop for many bankrupt farmers in the Midwest and South unable to make a living growing anything else.

Having squeezed four hits out of his first album, Stafford released a second album in 1975, *Not Just Another Pretty Foot,* and scored two more hit singles, "Your Bulldog Drinks Champagne" (#24), a shaggy dog story about a voyeur, and his second foray into the world of marijuana, "I Got Stoned and I Missed It" (#39), written by Shel Silverstein. The latter was a kind of antidote to "Wildwood Weed," that showed pot's negative effects on short-term memory. The song would be recorded by many other groups, including Dr. Hook and the Medicine Show.

Like his role model, Roger Miller, Stafford's star faded rather quickly. He reached the charts only two more times with minor hits. By then he had established himself as a major personality in television with his own summer replacement variety show. In 1978 he married country singer Bobbie Gentry, whom he met when she appeared on his TV show. Acting in television and movies replaced a sagging recording career, although Stafford wrote and performed three songs for Disney's animated film *The Fox and the Hound* in 1981.

Southern boys weren't only smoking pot, they were growing their hair long too, which got Charlie Daniels into big trouble in his first hit record, the delightful novelty "Uneasy Rider" (#9, 1973), which took its title from the 1969 Peter Fonda and Dennis Hopper movie, *Easy Rider.* Daniels, just like the two hippies in the film, is traveling through the South when his car breaks down and he finds himself at the mercy of a bunch of young rednecks. He manages to talk his way out of trouble by casting aspersions on a member of the gang and barely escapes with his skin. The intricate fiddle and guitar work behind Daniels's shaggy dog story is pure country and it's unlikely Daniels could have gotten away with his ruse if he wasn't a bit of a good ole boy himself. A session musician like Stafford for years, he quickly formed his own band and became one of the top country outlaw acts of the '70s, his popularity reaching its peak with his top three hit, the folkloric "The Devil Went Down to Georgia" in 1979.

Another figure who brought a more hip and contemporary sound to country novelty was the irrepressible Jerry Reed. An Atlanta native, Reed was recording rockabilly on Capitol Records back in 1955 when he was eighteen years old. Over the next decade he found his niche in Nashville as a songwriter ("Crazy Legs" for Gene Vincent, and "Guitar Man" and "US Male" for Elvis) and a top-notch session guitarist whose duet albums with Chet Atkins would later become classics.

By 1962 all Reed had to show for his own recording career were two minor charters, including the instrumental "Hully Gully Guitar" (#99). His breakthrough finally came in 1971, when he recorded his swamp rock classic "Amos Moses," about a rogue alligator hunter, and took it into the top ten. It was quickly followed by his signature song, the rambunctious "When You're Hot, You're Hot" (#9), which created a memorable catchphrase and established Reed as the most boisterous personality in novelty music since Ray Stevens. The song's woeful tale of a redneck gambler whose good luck runs out when he faces a judge to whom he owes money was inspired by childhood memories of watching crap games behind the Salvation Army building in his old neighborhood.

Reed's next novelty record proved he could be both funny and deadly serious at the same time. "Another Puff" is an uncompromising monologue delivered by a middle-aged Southern male whose fatal attraction to cigarettes is as much defined by a sense of fatalism as it is from his hacking cough. This unflinchingly honest portrait of a man who is doomed to lung cancer and knows it was not everyone's pipe of tobacco and only reached #65 on the charts, but it reveals Jerry Reed to be as much an artist as he is an entertainer.

Like Jim Stafford, Reed moved steadily into acting in the mid-seventies. He played a comic boon companion to Burt Reynolds in the two *Smokey and the Bandit* films and starred in two short-lived TV series, *Nashville 99* (1977) and *Concrete Cowboys* (1981). He returned to the pop charts after a long hiatus in 1982 with a song that created a new catch-phrase, "She Got the Goldmine (I Got the Shaft)" (#57).

Not all country novelty was free-spirited and liberating; some of it was mean-spirited and ugly. The folksy, down-home prejudice of "Welfare Cadillac," written and recorded by veteran country singer Guy Drake in 1970, takes a singularly dim view of the poor. The unemployed narrator uses his monthly welfare checks to meet the payments on his Cadillac. Although the song only reached #63 on the charts, it remained in the Hot One Hundred for fourteen weeks, a sign of its popularity with listeners who shared Drake's sentiments.

The last stanza darkly hints that things are going to "get even better with this new president" and his wife is already picking out *her* new Cadillac. Oddly, when the song came out, Richard Nixon was in the midst of his first term as president. In fact, "Welfare Cadillac" was a favorite of Nixon's. When Johnny Cash came to play at the White House in 1970, Nixon requested he sing it, along with "A Boy Named Sue" and Merle Haggard's "Okie From Muskogee." Cash refused. "I've only heard it ["Welfare Cadillac"] once, and there's no time to learn it, even if I wanted to," he wrote in his autobiography *Man in Black*.

If the cadillac represented the evils of the federal government and its welfare system for many country music listeners, trucks, especially

Jerry Reed paid his dues as a minor singer and songwriter for more than fifteen years before becoming a major pop recording artist in 1971 with the swamp rock classic "Amos Moses." His best work, however, may be "Another Puff," the disturbing monologue of a nicotine addict. (Photofest)

trailer trucks, symbolized everything that was good about America—free enterprise, the open road, and rugged individualism. The American trucker in popular song became a mythical figure, like the cowboy on the open range. Trucking songs had been a staple of country music since the early sixties, but in the mid-seventies C. W. McCall made them and the trucker more fashionable than ever, thanks to an ad campaign for home-baked bread that got a little out of hand.

William Fries, the alter ego of C. W., was a creative director for an Omaha, Nebraska, ad agency whose previous work experience was designing sets for a local TV station in his home state of Iowa. One of his accounts was the Mertz Bread Company, which was looking for an innovative ad campaign that would increase sales. Fries came up with a truck driver character named C. W. McCall who drove a bread truck for the Old Home Bread Company. McCall had a dog called Sloane and a waitress named Mavis he was sweet on who worked at the Old Home Filler-Up and Keep On-A-Truckin' Cafe. The television and radio ads, featuring a fast-talking Fries as McCall, were a raving success and won him a Clio award, the Oscar of television commercials.

Fries, who had loved music since his days in the University of Iowa Concert Band, saw an opportunity to break into the recording industry. With his friend Don Sears, he released a single of the jingle "The Old Home Filler-Up and Keep On-A-Truckin' Cafe," and sold 30,000 copies on his own label in just three weeks. MGM Records took notice and picked up the single for national distribution. It peaked at #54 on the *Billboard* pop charts. Fries, aka C. W. McCall, was signed to a recording contract. An album of engaging trucker songs, *Wolf Creek Pass,* was released. Fries's dry sense of humor and his shrewd way with a story infused the title song, a hilarious, terror-filled ride down a notorious pass in a truck with no brakes loaded with live chickens. "Wolf Creek Pass" squeaked into the top forty at #40 for one week. This modest chart success prepared no one for the phenomenal success of his next single.

Citizens' Band (CB) Radio had been a necessary part of the trucker's equipment for years, but it took on a new importance with the fuel shortage of the mid-seventies and the new federally regulated 55-miles-per-hour speed limit. Both of these developments spelled trouble for truckers, who now used their CBs to check out where the cheapest gas could be bought and to keep tags on the whereabouts of the highway patrol (read "Smokey"). These funny little two-way radios and the colorful lingo of CB made the trucker a glamorous figure in pop culture. Before long CBs were appearing in cars and station wagons and it seemed that every suburban mom and commuter dad was signing on as "Red Hot Mama" and "The Road Warrior."

McCall's "Convoy," the tale of a group of truckers who ban together to fend off Smokey and make up for lost time, roared to #1 and became a million seller. McCall's earlier records were noted for their good-natured humor and lack of pretense, two qualities sorely missing from "Convoy." Action director Sam Peckinpah made one of his worst movies, *Convoy,* inspired by the song, in 1978. Soon after, the CB bubble burst and sales plummeted. Fries had one more minor hit, quit the road, and went back to advertising. In 1982 he moved to California and was elected mayor of the town of Ouray.

He may look like a truck-driving man, but C. W. McCall (aka William Fries) was actually an advertising man turned recording artist. He created the McCall character for an ad campaign for a Midwest bread company, Old Home Bread. (Photofest)

The migration of ordinary folk from the country to the city and eventually out to the suburbs was completed in the seventies and no songwriter explored the phenomenon more whimsically than Nashville's Bobby Russell. His biggest pop hit, "Saturday Morning Confusion" (#28, 1971), was about Daddy dealing with a houseful of kids on his day off. There was no hot rod Lincoln for Russell to make his getaway in, only the family station wagon. He couldn't tear out for six days on the road in his semi or pickup truck because he was employed in a low-level white-collar job in a local high-tech company. There was no outhouse out back for relief, no wildwood weed growing in the cabbage patch. Country corn had been transmuted into microwave popcorn. All the rich flavor of country life was about gone. And so was the novelty. It had been replaced by the uniform sameness of suburbia. And that's not much to laugh about.

Childish Nonsense and Sophisticated Satire

In "The Folk Singer," their satirical attack on the sixties' folk phenomenon set to the strains of "La Habanera" from Bizet's *Carmen,* Homer and Jethro summed up the situation tersely with the line "There's more folk singers now than there are folk." This might well have seemed the case when the Kingston Trio and Peter, Paul & Mary were turning out hit after hit and *Hootenanny,* TV's first folk music series, was broadcast weekly from a different college campus.

Folk music came in for a lot of kidding in those days of Kennedy sophistication, culminating in Allan Sherman's million-selling album, *My Son, the Folk Singer.* As comic Shelly Berman put it, the folk song "is an art form in which a considerable number of geese die." But while there was plenty of gloom and doom in many of the traditional folk songs these artists sang, there was another, more life-affirming side to folk music that could be funny, silly, and sometimes sublimely nonsensical.

Both the serious and the childish worlds of folk have been well captured by the dean of American folk singers, Pete Seeger, whose albums of children's songs have been perennial favorites. The composer of "We Shall Overcome" and "Where Have All the Flowers Gone?" had his only solo charting pop single with a sly satire on American middle-class conformity, Malvina Reynolds's "Little Boxes" (#70, 1964), recorded live at his historic Carnegie Hall concert in June 1963. "Little Boxes" follows the children of the middle class from their Levittown box homes, to the university, to boxed-in professional careers, and ultimately to the coffins in which they are deposited. (A cover version by an early feminist folk group called the Womenfolk has the distinction of being the shortest record to make the charts in the rock era, clocking in at 1:00.)

Years earlier, Seeger was a member of the first folk group to crack the pop charts, the Weavers, who had a #2 hit with their version of the Southern Highlands folk song "On Top of Old Smoky." The song was neatly parodied in 1963 by folk singer Tom Glazer, backed by the Do-Re-Mi Children's Choir. "On Top of Spaghetti" (#14) was a nonsensical sing-a-long that tells the tragic path of a slippery meatball. As serious a folk archivist as Seeger, Glazer continued to record popular children's albums into the late sixties, while pursuing a second career as a pop songwriter ("Melody of Love," "More," "Skokiaan").

Among the most successful of the new wave of contemporary folk groups were the Kingston Trio, who zoomed to fame in 1958 with the starkly tragic tale of "Tom Dooley," highlighted by Dave Guard's rough-hewn baritone and twangy banjo. Two years later the group gave the tale of another murderer a comic twist in "Bad Man Blunder" (#37, 1960). The dimwitted outlaw-narrator, a master of understatement, casually shoots a deputy down, is captured, put on trial, and sentenced to ninety-nine years. He ends his tale with the aside, "I sure have learned my lesson."

But the Kingston Trio's most celebrated novelty song was a more contemporary folk ballad about poor Charley, a citizen of Boston who is trapped on the "M.T.A. (Metropolitan Transit Authority of Boston)" (#15, 1959), because he refused to pay the fare increase. Written in 1948, the comical protest song was adapted from "The Wreck of the Old 97," country music's first million-selling record in 1924.

Better known for their sense of humor were the Limeliters, another folk trio who balanced the lilting lyric tenor of Glenn Yarborough with the sophisticated wit of bass Lou Gottlieb. The bespectacled Gottlieb, who played bass fiddle, titled himself the group's "comic-arranger-musicologist." A graduate of UCLA and the U.S. Army Band, he was a student of Arnold Schoenberg, creator of the twelve-tone row. Gottlieb's doctoral thesis in musicology was "Liturgical Polyphony of the 15th Century" and his unique choral arrangements for the trio were surpassed only by his witty, deadpan commentary on such popular numbers as "The Monks of St. Bernard" and "Madeira, M'Dear," written by the English novelty duo Flanders and Swan. Both these songs appeared on their million-selling album *Tonight: In Person*. While their albums sold phenomenally well, the Limeliters had only one minor hit single, "A Dollar Down" (#60, 1961), a satire on the American obsession for buying on the installment plan. Gottlieb left the group in late 1962 after surviving a plane crash and in 1966 he established an "alternative community" on a ranch in Sonoma County, California. He died in July 1996.

Peter, Paul & Mary's sense of humor rarely surfaced on the songs for which they are best known, although they had as good a resident comic as Gottlieb in former stand-up man Paul Stookey. Their "Big Blue Frog" was a concert favorite, but a more sophisticated novelty was "Frogg" (#32, 1961), a contemporary take on the sixteenth-century English folk song "Frog Went A-Courting" by the Brothers Four, none of whom, by the way, were related. In their version, Froggie picks up a hat-check girl at the Coconut Grove who eventually rejects him because he's a "horny toad."

Another fresh take on a childhood favorite was "Don't Let the Rain Come Down (Crooked Little Man)," freely adapted by rockabilly singer Ersel Hickey and sung with infectious charm by the Serendipity Singers, who at nine members were one of the biggest folk ensembles this side of the New Christy Minstrels. The sparse instrumentation, which included bongo drums set to a calypso beat, propelled "Crooked Little Man" all the way to #6 on the charts in early 1964. The follow-up, "Beans in My Ears" (#30), was a similarly winning piece of folk nonsense that poked gentle fun at the generation gap. That gap was growing larger by the minute and would soon make the folk revival, with its family-style sing-a-longs, a quaint relic of the past.

The new folk music that was changing all this was championed by Bob Dylan and Joan Baez, who, like Pete Seeger and Woody Guthrie before them, sang about social and political change. If they had an immediate precursor it was the Chad Mitchell Trio, who were able to find humor in everything from contemporary politics to historic ax murders. Their "Lizzie Borden" (#44, 1962) is an impish and witty romp, filled with ghoulish puns ("Her father said, 'Lizzie, cut it out!' and that's exactly what she did"). Interestingly, the folk-like ballad was written by tunesmith Michael Brown for the hit Broadway revue *New Faces of 1952*.

The Mitchell Trio, so named because the lead tenor's name was felt to be the most marketable, was one of the few folk groups whose members didn't play instruments. They were backed on guitar and banjo on "Lizzie" and other sides by one Jim McGuinn, who had earlier worked with the Limeliters. McGuinn would later change his name to Roger, turn in his banjo for a twelve-string guitar, and help found the proto-folk rock group the Byrds. Joe Frazier, who replaced original baritone Mike Pugh, brought a social consciousness and political bent

More political in their humor than most '60s folk groups, the Chad Mitchell Trio was also one of the few folk groups that played no instruments. Stringman Jim McGuinn (far left) backed them on many of their early recordings. He later changed his name to Roger and formed the first folk rock super group, the Byrds. (Photofest)

to the Chad Mitchell Trio, with such biting political satires as "The John Birch Society" (#99, 1962) and "Barry's Boys," a vaudeville soft-shoe number that put Republican presidential candidate Barry Goldwater in historical perspective.

Another folk group whose albums far outsold their singles, the Chad Mitchell Trio's last charter was the childlike "The Marvelous Toy" (#43, 1964). Mitchell left the group the following year for a solo career but allowed the group to retain his last name as the Mitchell Trio. Frazier

In performance Tommy (left) was the dumb half of the Smothers Brothers and Dickie was the smart one. But in real life Tommy was the brains and the driving force behind the duo, especially when they invaded television with their controversial **Smothers Brothers Comedy Hour,** *which was eventually cancelled for its outspokenness about the Vietnam War and other social issues of the day. (From the collection of Ronald L. Smith)*

left two years later and eventually became an Episcopal priest. The two were replaced by John Denver and Rod Boise. When Kobluk left, Mitchell withdrew rights to his name and the group floundered as Denver, Boise and Johnson. Denver went on to a successful solo career devoid of humor, except for the hillbilly romp "I'm a Country Boy." Mitchell became entertainment director for a river boat franchise in Louisiana before being arrested on drug charges.

Far more political than even the Mitchell Trio were the Smothers Brothers, although there is little evidence of it on their early albums. Their one charting single was the teen death song parody "Jenny Brown" (#84, 1963). As much a comedy act as a folk singing duo, Tom and Dick Smothers largely based their humor on sibling rivalry. Their *Smothers Brothers Comedy Hour* (1967-69) on CBS was the most radical television show of its time, openly criticizing the Johnson administration and its handling of the Vietnam War. One program featured Pete Seeger singing the antiwar "Waist Deep in the Big Muddy," which the network deleted before air time. Seeger, who hadn't been on network television since he was blacklisted in the fifties, came back at a later time to perform the song. When the *Smothers Brothers Comedy Hour* was cancelled in June 1969, CBS filled its Sunday night slot with *Hee Haw.*

By the time the Irish Rovers took Shel Silverstein's gentle fable "The Unicorn" into the top ten in 1968, the folk revival was long gone, replaced by the folk rock made popular by the Byrds, the Mamas and the Papas, and the Lovin' Spoonful. While authentically Irish to a man, the Irish Rovers had actually formed in Alberta, Canada. A perennial St. Patrick's day act, the folk quintet reemerged on the charts thirteen years later as the Rovers with the rowdy "Wasn't That a Party" (#37).

But the folk party wasn't over, it had simply reinvented itself. In the seventies fresh sensibilities would bring new meaning and resonance to the whimsical, populist idiom of folk humor.

Getting Personal

As the socially conscious sixties gave way to the "me" generation of the seventies, mainstream folk music underwent similar changes. While this may have been bad for social causes, it was very good for novelty.

If Bob Dylan was the prototypical folk singer of the sixties, Loudon Wainwright III might well have filled that role for the seventies and eighties. There is a rich irony here, for when Wainwright first signed with Atlantic Records in 1970, they heralded him as "the new Dylan."★ Instead, they got a very different kind of folk singer. Wainwright's two Atlantic albums proved far too bitter to attract a large audience, although the critics loved them. *Album III,* his first on Columbia, provided a catchy ode to road kill, "Dead Skunk," that became his first, and to date only, pop hit (#16, 1973). Wainwright claimed to have dashed the song off in fifteen minutes to satisfy people who found his material too intellectual. Of course, he underestimated the critics, who saw the dead skunk "in the middle of the road" as a symbol for unpleasant reality rearing its ugly head (stink?) in suburbia. Some even saw it as a metaphor for the Vietnam War, which was finally winding down after eight years of fighting.

While Wainwright may not have been your typical war protester, he was well acquainted with suburbia and its pleasures. Born in North Carolina in 1946, he is a direct descendant of New Amsterdam's first governor, Peter Stuyvesant. His grandfather, the first Loudon Wainwright, was a captain of industry in the insurance business and his father was a well-respected journalist, author, and columnist for *Life* magazine. Loudon grew up in upper-class Bedford, New York, and attended a private school in Delaware that years later served as the setting for the movie *Dead Poets' Society.*

Although he made his debut as a folk singer in a San Francisco coffeehouse at sixteen, his main ambition was to be an actor. He studied acting at the Carnegie Mellon Institute in Pittsburgh, but dropped out in 1967 and hitchhiked to San Francisco during the "Summer of Love." Returning to New York, he started to write songs.

After the success of "Dead Skunk," Wainwright turned increasingly inward for his inspiration. Called by some "the Woody Allen of folk," many of his songs are about the ups and downs of his personal life—his relationships with women, his children, and his two failed marriages (to Kate McGarrigle and to Suzy Roche of the Roches). All this might be heavy going if the singer were not blessed with a most eccentric and disarming sense of humor. A master of self-mockery, he illuminates such

---

★Unable to get tickets to a Bob Dylan–Van Morrison concert at Madison Square Garden in early 1998, Wainwright wrote ruefully in an op-ed piece for the New York Times, *"The new Bob Dylan can't get in to see the old Bob Dylan."*

ordinary experiences as a first date to a trip for take-out food with his razor-sharp wit and keen intelligence.

While he largely steers clear of traditional social causes, Wainwright does vent his anger on the dark side of the entertainment business in such perceptive songs as "Career Moves," "The Grammy Song" (he's never won one), and "How Old Are You?" which takes on talk show interviews and clinging fans. When he does sing from the heart, the results can be surprisingly poignant, as in two songs to his children,

Loudon Wainwright III represented a new breed of folk singers in the seventies, more interested in expressing the vagaries of his own life than in exploring social issues. After twenty-five years on the circuit, his songs are still funny, fresh, and pertinent. (Platt Collection/Archive Photos)

"Your Mother and I" and "Five Years Old." One of his children, Rufus, has followed in his footsteps and is a successful singer.

Firmly rooted musically in the traditional folk-blues idiom, Wainwright's songs are deceptively simple, their craft hidden beneath a spontaneous style, as if he were composing as he sings. Loudon Wainwright, in the words of *New York Times* music critic Stephen Holden, remains, after a quarter century, "the most candid diarist among the singer-songwriters [of] confessional poetry in popular song."

Other folkies used the confessional mode to poke fun at the pretensions of the "back to nature" movement that grew out of the sixties. None found more success than Larry Groce, whose "Junk Food Junkie" (#9, 1976) turned the tables on the macrobiotic set. Wittily written, if sloppily played before a live audience at a Santa Monica coffeehouse (at one point Groce blows his entrance on the chorus and has another go at it), "Junk Food Junkie" was about a natural food cook and expert who after dark gives in to his cravings for Big Macs and Hostess Twinkles.

Groce's excursion into satire may have been in reaction to a career that included recording innocuous children's songs such as "Winnie the Pooh for President" for Disney's Vista label. But further attempts by his label, Warner Bros., to turn him into a novelty singer failed and soon he was back doing kiddie material on tape and video for Disney as well as a folk concert series for PBS.

Sex was another favorite subject for the new folkies of the seventies and eighties. Jud Strunk, an eccentric performer who toured the world at one point with a "one-man show" for the U.S. Armed Services, made his mark on the charts with the sentimental ballad "Daisy a Day" (#14, 1973). He followed it two years later with the bawdy novelty "The Biggest Parakeets in Town" (#50), a euphemism for women's breasts. The impressive boobs, the lady's husband learns to his chagrin after their wedding night, are, alas, detachable. A regular on TV's *Laugh-In,* Strunk died in a plane crash in 1981.

Sexual innuendo was taken to greater heights by cabaret singer Meri Wilson in "Telephone Man," a surprise top twenty hit in 1977. Wilson's girlish, giggly delivery of her double entendres in a homey seduction was both a turn-off and a turn-on. Even more raunchy was a follow-up single, "Peter the Meter Reader," who orders her to "take me to your box." Peter petered out however, and Meri never came within striking distance of the charts again, although she remains a favorite on the Dr. Demento show. When last heard from, the Georgia native was a high school choir director in Atlanta.

A more prominent member of the eighties' folk revival was Christine Lavin, whose main concession to traditional folk is playing an acoustical guitar. One of her signature numbers, "Sensitive New Age Guys," mocks the men who, weaned on the values of the folk movement, carry infants on their backs and weep at movies like *Three Men and a Baby*. A male chorus of every sensitive guy in New York City make this a memorably zany sing-a-long.

There is nothing sensitive about the male groups at the other end of the folkie revival who have sprouted in the Midwest and who prefer a cold can of beer in a cabin to a cup of latte in a Greenwich Village coffeehouse. Groups like Michigan's Da Yoopers and Wisconsin's the Happy Schnapps Combo revel in their gauche male camaraderie. Their attitude is neatly summed up in the Combo's "new age polka" romp, "No, I Don't Wanna Do Dat," which celebrates the overthrow of middle-class responsibility, replacing it with a zany anarchy that the Marx Brothers might have appreciated.

Giddy, gutsy, and at times sublimely foolish, the "new folk" reflects the yearnings of common people as well as the alienated individual, with more candidness and humor than their colleagues from an earlier era. The long tradition of humor in folk music continues unhampered and often uninhibited into the twenty-first century—a refreshing antidote to all that is serious and solemn in our self-obsessed society.

⑧ Rock Laughs at Itself

> **"Silhouettes made a big hit with 'Get a Job,' which consists largely of sounds like Sha-Da-Da-Da, Yip-Yip-Yip and no discernible melody."**—Life *magazine, 1958*

> **"The only thing I regret is that when we got on the cover we were a bunch of assholes and we had nothing to say."**
> —*Dennis Locorriere of Dr. Hook in 1987* Rolling Stone
> *interview on their hit "The Cover of Rolling Stone"*

It may well be said that rock 'n' roll has a sense of humor, but rarely has that humor been unleashed on itself. In the fifties Stan Freberg blasted rock for what he perceived as unintelligible lyrics and a monotonous beat, but few rock artists since have made fun of themselves so directly. Fortunately, those few who have done so have provided us with plenty of laughter and some memorable music.

Elvismania!

Elvis Presley was the first and most famous rock star, and the peculiar mannerisms of his performing style made him the target of humor from all sides. In 1956, the year Presley burst onto the national scene, there was a plethora of Elvis novelty records, each hoping to cash in on his popularity as much as to have some fun with it. "Dear Elvis (Pages 1 & 2)" by Audrey, was a "break-in" record, using the technique pioneered by Buchanan and Goodman only a few months earlier. Despite being an awful record, it was one of the few Elvis novelties to chart at #87. Rockabilly singer Janis Martin, who was known as the female Elvis, weighed in with "My Boy Elvis." November saw Lou Monte promote "Elvis Presley for President" and Christmas brought "I Want Elvis for Christmas," an early effort from the songwriting team of Bobby Darin and Don Kirshner. There were two released versions of this holiday novelty, an excruciating one by Debbie Dabner and a more palatable one by the Holly Twins, Glenell and Janell, which had the added fillip of a young Eddie Cochran impersonating the King.

When Elvis was drafted into the army in 1956 there were mournful farewells like Genee Harris's "Bye Bye Elvis," as well as martial hymns like "Marching Elvis" by the Greats and "Alright, Private" by Mo Klein and the Sergeants ("Who's the joker with the blue suede combat boots?").

Interestingly, the best Elvis novelty never mentioned his name once. "The All American Boy" (#2, 1959) remains both a classic novelty and classic fifties' rocker, enhanced by singer-songwriter Bobby Bare's delicious "talking blues," a rambling guitar, and sly lyrics that charted the rise of an Elvis-style rock star and his inevitable rendezvous with Uncle Sam. ("Gimme that guitar, boy. Here, take this rifle.")

Born in Ironton, Ohio, Bare formed his first band while still in his teens. The group relocated to Long Beach, California, where they eked out a precarious existence playing clubs and road houses. A recording contract with Capitol led to a couple of forgettable releases and then came Bare's draft notice, about seven months after Elvis got his. He

Since the success of his "The All American Boy," about the rise of an Elvis-like teen idol, Bobby Bare has had an up-and-down career in rock and country, but he has never lost his sense of humor. (Photofest)

returned to Ohio for induction, where he ran into old friend and fellow musician Bill Parsons, who had just finished his tour of duty in the service. And that's where the story takes a strange twist.

Parsons was putting together a demo tape in hopes of landing a recording contract and Bare, with a few days left before his hitch, agreed to help him. They paid for a three-hour session in the studio of Cincinnati's King Records. Parsons recorded his composition "Rubber Dolly" and Bare did his "The All American Boy." It was supposed to be a demo tape to help Parsons learn the song and later record it himself. But that never happened. Instead, the studio sent the tape, with Parsons's name on it, to a studio owned by Fraternity Records, where they could duplicate the acetates. Fraternity owner Harry Carlson heard "The All American Boy" and smelled a hit. He bought the tape for $500 (Bare and Parsons were paid $50 each) and released it. Imagine the shock Bare received a few months later while in basic training at Fort Knox, when he heard his song on the radio, with Bill Parsons named as the artist!

Meanwhile, Parsons was lip-synching Bare's vocal on *American Bandstand* and enjoying the hit of his life.★ Bare bore his pal no rancor and when he returned from the service, he recorded for Fraternity under his own name, including a sequel to "Boy," "I'm Hanging Up My Rifle," which didn't sell. In 1962 producer Chet Atkins signed Bare to RCA in Nashville and he had a string of memorable pop-country ballads. In 1965 Bare abandoned the pop market for straight country and continued to make vital recordings in the genre for two decades, earning him the title "the Springsteen of country" (see Chapter 10). As for Bill Parsons, he made a few recordings of his own in the early 1960s and then disappeared without a trace.

When Elvis returned to civilian life in 1960 and resumed his career there were plenty of teen idols competing with him for record sales and Elvismania cooled considerably. One of the last Elvis novelties of the period was Mike Sarne's "My Baby's Just Crazy 'Bout Elvis" which came out in 1963. A few months later, Sarne's baby—and everybody else's—would be crazy for someone else: a quartet of long-haired musicians from England. The British had landed.

★*Although Bare was revealed to be the singer and songwriter of "The All American Boy" in 1960, for many years after that books and articles continued to cite Parsons as the vocalist.*

Beatlemania!

Unlike Elvis, the Beatles showed a strong affinity for novelty from the very beginning of their career. The Coasters were one of their favorite American groups and of the fifteen songs they taped for their Decca audition on New Year's Day in 1962, two were Coasters' hits, "Searchin'" and "Three Cool Cats." When Decca turned the Beatles down, their audition tape for George Martin at EMI included another Coasters' song, "Besame Mucho," a regular favorite of their stage repertoire in Hamburg, Germany. All three of these rare recordings are included on *The Beatles Anthology 1*.

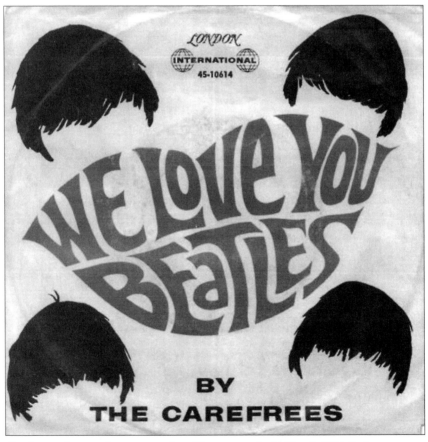

Beatles novelty records were ground out like sausages in 1964 and 1965. Only a very few ever made the charts, including this cheerful anthem from a trio of British song-birds. Note the prominence given to the Fab Four's mop haircuts on the picture sleeve. (From the collection of Don McLaughlin)

As the Beatles' music evolved, many of their own compositions flirted with novelty, exuding a wry, eccentric sense of humor that was distinctly British. John Lennon's love of word play and his childlike imagination ran riot on such "novel" songs as "Penny Lane," "Yellow Submarine," "An Octopus's Garden," and "I Am The Walrus."

It seems fitting, therefore, that no sooner had the Beatles hit American shores than they inspired literally hundreds of novelty songs. While few of these novelties bear a second (first?) hearing, they reveal much about America's various responses to the Beatles.

The sheer exuberance of Beatlemania is best captured in "We Love You Beatles" (#39, 1964) by three British girls who called themselves the Carefrees. The melody was lifted from a chant to the fictitious teen idol Conrad Birdie in the 1960 Broadway musical *Bye Bye Birdie*. The song got valuable exposure when American Beatlemaniacs serenaded the Fab Four with it outside the Plaza Hotel, where they stayed during their first celebrated visit to the States. Similar adulation was expressed by "We Love The Beatles" by the Vernon Girls and "Yeh, Yeh, We Love 'Em All" by Little Cheryl. The Beatles' first American hit, "I Wanna Hold Your Hand," found ready responses in "I'll Let You Hold My Hand" by the Bootles and "Yes, You Can Hold My Hand" by the Beatlettes, not to be confused with the Beatle-Ettes, who responded to the flip side, "I Saw Her Standing There," with their answer record, "Only Seventeen."

The end of the Beatles' first American tour brought forth "Beatles, Please Come Back," a decent girl group number from Gigi Parker and the Lonelies, while veteran British actress Dora Bryan ended the year with the Yuletide wish "All I Want for Christmas Is a Beatle."

Among the individual group members, none garnered more song tributes than the sad-faced drummer Ringo, whose very homeliness seemed to bring out all the maternal instinct in teenage girls. There was "Ringo" by the Starlettes and "Ringo Did It" by Veronica Lee and the Moniques, while the Young World Singers demanded "Ringo for President." Actor Lorne Greene went all the way to #1 on the *Billboard* charts with the Western ballad "Ringo," which probably wouldn't have done half so well if it didn't have a Beatle for a namesake. One-hit wonder Larry Finnegan ("Dear One") rushed out "A Tribute to Ringo Starr (The Other Ringo)" using Greene's "Ringo" melody, but to little avail. More convoluted a tribute was "You Can't Go Far Without a Guitar (Unless You're Ringo Starr)" by Neil Sheppard. Phil Spector, under the prodding of Sonny Bono, produced "Ringo, I Love You," sung by Sonny's girlfriend Cherilyn Sarkasian LaPier, who recorded it under the name Bonnie Jo Mason. The record stiffed and Spector lost interest in Cherilyn, although Sonny didn't. They were married in Tijuana, Mexico, a short time later and within a year were the hottest married couple on disk—Sonny and Cher.

Ringo's marriage to Maureen Cox on February 11, 1965, caused Penny Valentine to lament "I Want to Kiss Ringo Goodbye" and Angie and the Chicklettes to warble the more selfless "Treat Him Tender, Maureen (Now That Ringo Belongs To You)."

Paul, the cute one, was the recipient of "A Letter to Paul" by Tracy Steel. The rumors of his death after the appearance of a barefooted Paul on the *Abbey Road* album inspired "Brother Paul" by Billy Shears and the All-Americans and "Ballad of Paul" by Mystery Tour.

John, the controversial one, incurred the wrath of millions of Americans when he declared that the Beatles were more popular than Jesus Christ, which caused Rainbo to express her divided loyalties in "John You Went Too Far This Time." Nearly a decade later Rainbo would reemerge as film star Sissy Spacek.

The distinctive Beatle mop haircuts inspired nearly as many novelties as the boys themselves. "My Boyfriend Got a Beatle Haircut" by Donna Lynn (#83) was one of the most appealing Beatle novelties, thanks to a catchy melody and bouncy arrangement. It probably didn't hurt that it was released on Capitol, the Beatles' label in America. Almost as successful was "The Boy With the Beatle Haircut" by the Swans (#85). Then there was the more descriptive "The Guy With the Long Liverpool Haircut" by the Outsiders (not to be confused with the group that sang "Time Won't Let Me" two years later) and "I Want to Hold Your Hair" by the Bagels. "My Beatle Haircut" by the Twiliters was a rare example of a Beatle novelty by a black R&B group. Scott Douglas revealed the Beatles' tonsorial secrets in "The Beatles' Barber."

Beatle envy was a common emotion among American rockers in 1964 and found full expression in "I Dreamed I Was A Beatle" by Murray Kellum, "A Beatle I Want to Be" by former Cricket Sonny Curtis, "I Want to Be a Beatle" by Bobby Wilding, and "I Wanna Be a

Beatle" by Gene Cornish and the Unbeatables. Shortly after, Cornish and Felix Cavaliere formed what would become one of the best post-Beatle American rock bands, the Young Rascals.

Those American bands who weren't ready to leap on the Beatle bandwagon wanted to bust it up. A backlash to Beatlemania was expressed in the braggadocio of "I'm Better Than the Beatles" by Brad Berwick and the Bugs (they, of course, weren't), "I Ain't No Beatle" by Jack White, "Gonna Send 'Em Home" by Homer and Jethro, and "The Beatle-Bomb," an instrumental by the Exterminators, who attempted to end their careers with bug spray. Allan Sherman voiced his disdain in "Pop Hates the Beatles," one of his lesser parodies, sung to the tune of "Pop Goes the Weasel." Far wittier was "Beatle Crazy" by folkie Bill Clifton ("These guys between them sure got some hair/I'm losing mine, Don't seem fair.") Bill Buchanan, of Buchanan and Goodman fame, with his new partner Howard Greenfield, gave the Beatles the break-in treatment in "The Invasion," which recast his classic "The Flying Saucer" by replacing the invading Martians with the Beatles, referred to as "The Four Mops." It ends with a manic Buchanan warning "America, this is the end!"

Buchanan was not the only established recording artist to be seduced into releasing a Beatle novelty. The Angels forgot all about their boyfriend being back and sang the virtues of "Little Beatle Boy." Johnny and the Hurricanes, who played with the Beatles in German clubs in their early days, sang the "Saga of the Beatles" to the tune of "The Ballad of Davy Crockett," and the revered Ella Fitzgerald abandoned jazz momentarily for the "Beatle Beat."

By 1965 the tide of Beatlemania had receded and with it, so did Beatles novelty songs. They reappeared in 1970 when the group announced that they were disbanding. A rash of novelties urged them to "Get Back Beatles" (Gerard Kenny and the New York Band), "Come Back Beatles" (The People), and "John, Paul, Ringo and George (Please Get Together Again)" by Tina Allen. Unlike the Beatles themselves, few listeners were sorry to see the novelty songs about them go, but listening to even the most crass and poorly produced of them today is a nostalgia trip to a more innocent time when a four-man band captured the hearts of a continent.

Name Dropping

Novelties about a particular singer or group were largely restricted to phenomena like Elvis and the Beatles. However, recording artists looking for a hit record quickly discovered that just mentioning a hit song title or recording artist in a lyric could help sell a record. And the more titles and names you could cram in, the better.

One of the first and most successful of these name droppers was Larry Williams, whose novelty "Short Fat Fannie" (#5, 1957) was a parody of Little Richard's "Long Tall Sally." More important, the song contained no fewer than a dozen popular song titles, including four hits by Little Richard and three by Elvis Presley. But Williams was more than a one-shot novelty artist. His follow-up, "Boney Maronie" was a solid rocker in its own right, and "Slow Down," the flip of his last fifties' hit, "Dizzy, Miss Lizzy," was rediscovered years later by the Beatles, who recorded it along with two other Williams' songs. However, this renewed interest in his work came too late to revive Larry Williams's career, which had been derailed by an arrest for drug dealing in 1960. He committed suicide in 1980.

In "Everyone Was There" (#96, 1958), Bob Kayli got all the characters together from current hits (Peggy Sue, the Purple People Eater, and so on) for a party. Kayli was the nom de disque of Robert Gordy, brother of Berry Gordy, Jr., owner of Motown Records. According to Berry, no black singer in Detroit wanted to record his brother's "white-sounding song," so with Berry's encouragement, he recorded it himself. In his autobiography, *To Be Loved,* Berry reports what happened when Robert sang his record on Dick Clark's *American Bandstand.* "People were shocked. This white-sounding record did not go with his black face. Bob Kayli was history. When that happened I realized this was not just about good or bad records, this was about race."

The Three Friends clearly sounded black on their song-title-crammed "Dedicated (To the Songs I Love)" (#89, 1961), a clever takeoff on the Shirelles' "Dedicated (To the One I Love)." The group sounded a lot like the Coasters and most of the songs they referred to were hits by black artists.

Mark Dinning, whose weepy death-rock ballad "Teen Angel" went #1 in early 1960, did a clever twist on the name dropping format in

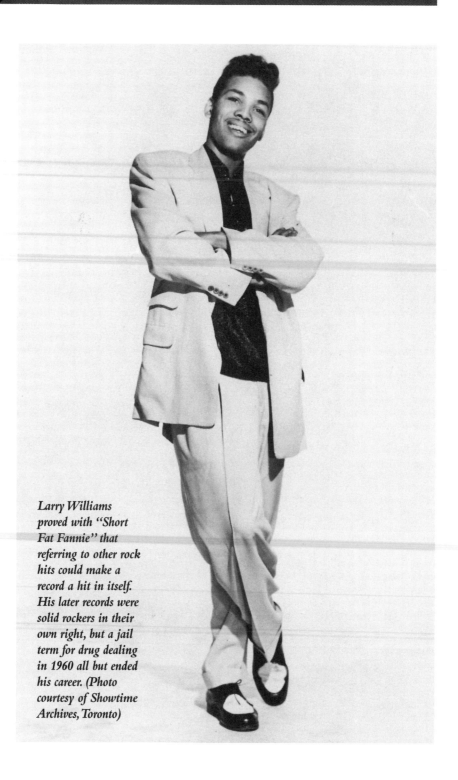

Larry Williams proved with "Short Fat Fannie" that referring to other rock hits could make a record a hit in itself. His later records were solid rockers in their own right, but a jail term for drug dealing in 1960 all but ended his career. (Photo courtesy of Showtime Archives, Toronto)

"Top Forty, News, Weather and Sports" (#81, 1961), his last charting single. He portrays a kid who dozes off while listening to the radio as he works on his current events homework assignment. When he reads it aloud in class, newsworthy figures like President Eisenhower and Fidel Castro are scrambled in a surreal mix with pop song titles, ball scores, and weather forecasts.

Another unlikely novelty artist who took a stab at this subgenre was Jimmie Beaumont, lead singer of the white doo-wop group the Skyliners. His "Everybody's Crying" name-drops not only the titles of heartbreaking hits, but also the artists who recorded them, from Dion to Gene McDaniels. The lyrics were clever, the melody rousing, and Beaumont sang his heart out. So why did this record stall at #100?

Another response to the rash of death rock and crying records at the decade's start, but much more successful, was "Let's Think About Living" (#7, 1960) written by Boudleaux and Felice Bryant and performed by rockabilly singer Bob Luman. Interestingly, the lyrics don't refer to any actual death-rock songs but to recent hits by Marty Robbins and the Everly Brothers, for whom the Bryants were something of house song-writers. Luman, who never repeated his pop success, went on to fame as a country artist.

Despite this record's message, there was definitely money to be made thinking about and singing about death, particularly dead rock stars. Buddy Holly, Ritchie Valens, and J. P. Richardson (aka the Big Bopper) were still warm in their graves after the crash of their small plane in February 1959 when record companies began rushing out tributes for their fans. The most successful was "Three Stars" (#11, 1959), a turgid ballad narrated by California deejay Tommy Dee with vocal backing by Carol Kay and the Teen-Aires. Dee pictured the dead rock stars sitting up in heaven like members of the Holy Trinity. ("Buddy's singing for God now," goes the lyric.)

Almost as lachrymose was "Teenage Heaven" (#58, 1963) by Johnny Cymbal, who three years earlier had come out with one of the most gruesome of death disks, "The Water Is Red," in which his girl gets eaten by a shark! After Cymbal pays his respects at the shrine of Holly and company, an angel shows him the rock stars who would be there "one hundred years from today," conveniently allowing him to name a slew of current teen singers, a few of whom have since gone on to their heavenly reward (Elvis, Rick Nelson, and Cymbal himself).

Western singer and cowboy star Tex Ritter did the same for country music's departed stars in "I Dreamed of a Hill-Billy Heaven" (#20, 1961), but had the good humor to include his own name in the golden book, which caused him to do a double take midsong.

Then there was "Soul Heaven" (#99, 1965) narrated by the Dixie Drifter (aka Enoch Gregory, a New York City disk jockey). Interestingly, Gregory's heaven is not ruled by God but by three black singers, two of whom, Nat King Cole and Dinah Washington, were better known as pop than soul singers.

While many recording artists drew on the names of other artists—both living and dead—to sell their records, a few had the chutzpa to sing about themselves. One artist who regularly sang his own exaggerated praises was Bo Diddley. Born Elias McDaniel, his well-known pseudonym means "funny storyteller" in African. Tales of his daring exploits as told in "Bo Diddley," "Hey Bo Diddley," and "Who Do You Love" had little actual autobiographical detail in them, but the fascinating "The Story of Bo Diddley" mixed fact and fiction to chart Bo's rise to stardom.

In the sixties autobiography became more common in pop songs, as artists drew more and more on their personal experiences for material. In 1969 the Beatles produced "The Ballad of John and Yoko" (#8), which told in colorful detail the surprise marriage and celebrated honeymoon of John Lennon and Yoko Oko, which took them from Gilbraltar to Amsterdam, where they stayed in bed for a week growing their hair for peace, and then on to Vienna. Although the song went to #1 in England, it only peaked at #8 stateside, partially due to the fact that radio stations and some listeners were offended by the "blasphemous lyrics" that compared John and Yoko to Christ (something Lennon had gotten into trouble for years earlier). For all its good humor and frankness, the record did little to patch up the differences between the other band members and John's new bride. In less than a year the Beatles, although still officially a group, had ceased recording together.

The best autobiodisc, however, was produced by the Mamas and the Papas. Written by group leader John Phillips and his then wife Michelle, "Creeque Alley" (#5) was a good-natured shaggy dog of a song about the group's evolution as their various paths crossed and they formed the group that would make them all famous. Along the way, jokes are made about Mama Cass's weight and the group's drug-taking. This summing up of their history, unfortunately, was their last top ten hit. Within a year and a half, differences among members would cause one of the best American bands of the sixties to break up.

Perhaps the most intriguing entry in this mini-genre was "Moulty" (#90, 1966) by the Massachusetts garage band the Barbarians, whose first hit was the Beatle-bashing "Are You a Boy Or Are You a Girl." "Moulty" was the inspirational saga, complete with wailing harmonica, of band leader and drummer Victor "Moulty" Moulton, who lost his left hand when the homemade lead-pipe-and-gasoline bomb he had been making exploded. What he had intended to do with the bomb was never alluded to in his self-penned song. But, hey, it was the sixties.

Bomp-a-Bomp-a-Rama-Lama-Ding-Dong (Get Down Get Down)

The various styles of rock each have their own idiosyncratic characteristics as distinct in their way as the historical periods of classical music. There's the joyful nonsense syllables of doo-wop, the driving, mechanized beat of disco, and the reverberating fuzz-tone guitars and shrieking vocals of heavy metal, punk, and shock rock. Plenty here to parody and satirize, although the attempts to do so have been, alas, few and far between.

Early rock often came the closest to self parody, but maybe that was the point. When the Silhouettes sang about the frustrations of trying to "Get a Job," the message may have been downbeat, but who could feel down with all those sha-na-nas and dip-dip-dip-dips in the chorus? Little Richard was pure exuberance when he sang "Whomp-bomp-a-loo-bomp-a-whomp-bam-boone" in "Tutti Frutti," regardless of what it all meant.

The year 1961 saw a renaissance of doo-wop, which had all but disappeared from the musical scene a few years earlier. But now it was filtered through an even greater comic sensibility. The Marcels, an integrated vocal group from Pittsburgh, produced a doo-wop version of Rodgers and Hart's 1935 standard "Blue Moon" that had more "bomp-da-a-bomps" than the Silhouettes' "Get a Job" had "sha-na-nas." Bass man Fred Johnson battled lead singer Cornelius "Nini" Harp's falsetto for attention and took the song to #1. The Marcels had fun playing around with a few more golden oldies, most notably "Heartaches" (#7), which began exuberantly "It's us! We're back again!" But there were no more returns to the charts for the group after their version of "My Melancholy Baby" in early 1962.

The success of "Blue Moon" caused a New York deejay to recall another funny doo-wop song, one first recorded three years earlier. The disk, "Rama Lama Ding Dong" by the Edsels, had been a local hit in Baltimore on Dub Records. (The label had erroneously given it as "Lama Lama Ding Dong.") The deejay spun the record and an immediate demand got it released on the Twin label. It shot to #21 on the charts.

"Rama Lama Ding Dong" is a joyous two minutes of doo-wop, with a great bass opening of the title phrase and as wild a sax break as has ever been put on wax. How can you not fall in love with a record that contains the line "I've got a girl named Rama Lama Lama Lama Ding Dong?" The sheer exuberance of the over-the-top delivery and lyrics both parody the form and pay it a loving tribute.

As for the Edsels, they quickly re-formed after having broken up three years earlier, and released three singles for Capitol, including two dance numbers—"Do You Love Me" and "Shake Sherry Shake"—that Motown's the Contours would later turn into hits. But the Edsels, like the ill-fated car they were named after, quickly disappeared once more into obscurity.

But leave it to a songwriter to have the last word on the subject. Barry Mann's "Who Put the Bomp" (#7, 1961) is a comic ode to the man who created all these crazy catchphrases "and made my baby fall in love with me." Mann, one half of the songwriting team of Weill-Mann with his wife, Cynthia Weill, were perhaps the most thoughtful and socially conscious of the songwriting teams to come out of the Brill Building in the late '50s and early '60s. They were well qualified to mock the banality of nonsense rock lyrics, since they employed them in their songs far less often than their competitors Carole King and Gerry Goffin and Jeff Barry★ and Ellie Greenwich. Interestingly, "Bomp," which was Mann's debut as a solo artist, was cowritten not by Weill, but by Gerry Goffin.

Among the answer songs that sprang up after "Bomp" hit was "I Put the Bomp" by an aging and increasingly desperate Frankie Lymon, who

---

★*Barry, who sang with Greenwich in the girl group the Raindrops, also spoofed his own music in such novelties as "It's Called Rock and Roll" and "Teen Quartet."*

did put the bomp in rock but would soon end up as another on rock music's long list of casualties. Another answer song was "We're the Guys" by Bob (Feldman) and Jerry (Goldstein), who several years later as the Strangeloves put a Bo Diddley beat into their big hit "I Want Candy."

"Bomp" was actually Barry Mann's second foray into satire, having written the delicious "She Say (Oom Dooby Doom)" (#18) for the Diamonds in 1959, his first hit song. The Diamonds, a white cover group from Canada, are best remembered for "Little Darlin'" (#2, 1957) perhaps the first rock record that delved deeply into self-parody.

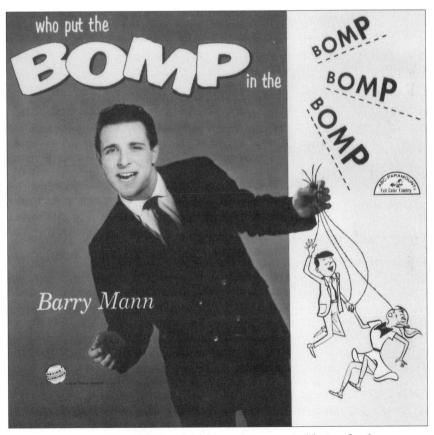

Barry Mann was well qualified to poke fun at the nonsensical lyrics of rock songs, having written a few of them himself. With his wife and partner Cynthia Weill, Mann went on to write some of the grittiest socially conscious songs of the mid-sixties, including "On Broadway," "Kicks," and "We Gotta Get Out of This Place." Bomp Bomp Bomp indeed. (Photo courtesy of Showtime Archives, Toronto)

Their offbeat version of the Gladiolas' original, with its flighty falsetto and justly famous comic bass recitation, supposedly developed after long hours of rehearsing the song before the recording session made them giddy.

Mann was backed on "Who Put the Bomp" by the Halos, who had their own novelty hit that year, "Nag," and Ronnie Bright of the Cadillacs, who did the song's bass voice, a part he repeated on Johnny Cymbal's "Mr. Bass Man" (#16, 1963). Catchy and charming, "Mr. Bass Man" was a loving tribute to the backbone and anchor of rock doo-wop, released a year or so before the bass man almost disappeared from pop music. It was Canadian Cymbal's first and biggest hit after several years of floundering in several genres, including death rock and teen idoldom. He would reemerge as Derek, one of several pseudonyms, with the hit "Cinnamon" in 1968. A talented performer, writer, and producer, Johnny Cymbal died of a heart attack at age forty-eight in 1993.

Few musical trends in rock have been as detested as disco. The style was so pervasive by 1976 that Rick Dees, one of a long line of deejays who became novelty artists, had little trouble taking his kooky "Disco Duck" to the top of the charts. With a catchy "quack quack" beat that made it a good disco number in spite of itself, "Disco Duck" is about the inexplicable transformation on the dance floor of a disco don into a duck.

Dees got the idea from "The Duck," a dance hit of 1965 by Jackie Lee, and took it to Estelle Axton for her Memphis label, Fretone. It first became a regional hit, but Dees's station, WMPS, fearful of a conflict-of-interest suit, wouldn't let Dees play the song and actually fired him when he merely talked about the record. Dees, of course, got the last laugh with his million-seller, and went on to become morning deejay at a top L.A. station and host of TV's *Solid Gold* and later his own short-lived late-night talk show. Along the way he produced more novelties, the best of which is "Eat My Shorts" (#75, 1984), a merciless satire of the Barry Manilow school of soft-rock ballads.

A far more biting disco parody was Frank Zappa's "Dancin' Fool" (#45, 1977), about a man who commits "social suicide" every time he steps onto the disco floor. No ordinary novelty song, it had offbeat instrumentation and weird echo effects, the kind of experimentation that was Zappa's hallmark. Also typical of this social satirist, it is as much a putdown of the culture that surrounds disco as well as the music itself.

Zappa, who died of prostate cancer in 1996, was a restless innovator whose musical styles ranged from doo-wop, his first love, to electronic music, and just about everything in between. His trio of chart records in a long and productive career (the other two were "Don't Eat the Yellow Snow" and "Valley Girl," featuring his daughter Moon Unit) barely scratch the surface of Zappa's talent. Novel though much of his music is, it rarely qualifies as novelty music in the strict sense, and thus largely falls outside the scope of this book.

Green Jellÿ, a twelve-man rock band from Kenmore, New York, put their main focus not on recordings but music videos, which they made in a Hollywood studio that Frank Zappa once owned. Their "Three Little Pigs" (#17, 1993) is a delicious send-up of the angst-filled death-rock divas of glam rock from Alice Cooper to Marilyn Manson. The Big Bad Wolf's cry of "Little pig, little pig, let me come in!" shows to advantage all the hot air expelled by these self-dramatizing rock stars. Like Zappa's rare-charting singles, "Three Little Pigs" was an anomaly in 1993 and Green Jellÿ (aka Green Jellö) has largely returned to the TV studio.

Julie Brown, another charter member of the video MTV scene, has been called the "Lucille Ball of the '90s." Her "The Homecoming Queen Has a Gun" is a hilarious send-up of the '60s girl groups, both the Shelley Fabres "Johnny Angel" variety and the angst-ridden Shangri-Las "Leader of the Pack" school. There's also, for good measure, a few sharp pokes at the valley girls of the '90s.

Taking Care of Business

Behind the music, rock 'n' roll has always been a business, and often a cutthroat one. Even in its wild and innocent days, money talked and artists learned that they let others take care of their business at their peril. Record executives, A&R men, promoters, agents, and deejays preyed on the talent with a ruthless voracity. When in more recent years recording artists have come to have more control over their careers and finances, they often have exhibited a self-indulgence that would do a Roman emperor proud. It comes as no surprise that the seamy business of rock has rarely been depicted in the music. What sane recording artists would dare expose the industry and themselves?

One of the first records to cast a slightly jaded eye at the record industry was a snappy novelty by Brook Benton, that underrated soul singer whose class act kept him on the charts for seven years in the sixties. "Hit Record" (#45, 1962) was hardly a biting satire, but beneath the fun it made a serious point about the assembly line mentality of the recording industry in the early '60s, where all too often the songs and the artists seemed interchangeable.

One element Benton left out of the equation in "Hit Record" was payola—illegal payoffs to deejays to play a new disk. The payola scandal broke in 1960 and ended the career of Alan Freed among others, although younger, smoother operators like Dick Clark got off with a wrist slap.

That same year Stan Freberg came out with "The Old Payola Roll Blues (Sides 1 & 2)," his last charting single. Part 1 is a reasonably funny satire on the teen idol syndrome, then at its height. In Part 2, an unscrupulous record promoter, played by Jesse White, goes to a radio station and tries to persuade the deejay to spin the new single by his latest discovery by offering him payola. Freberg's righteous, big-band-loving deejay turns down the money as much because he hates rock 'n' roll as for any ethical reasons, making this one of Freberg's most earnest and least funny records.

By the mid-sixties large record companies were eating up the independents and the pressure for groups to produce hits was greater than ever. The pressure was well captured in the Beatles' "Paperback Writer" (#1, 1966), where the publishing of pulp fiction is only a stand-in for the record industry. The song was so rhythmically appealing that the message of the lyrics was probably lost on most listeners. More anguished was the Byrds' "So You Want to Be a Rock 'N' Roll Star" (#28, 1967), which, with its screaming fans (actually taped at a real Byrds' concert) and its keening trumpet solo by Hugh Masakela, had a cold and rather exotic feel that was disorienting. Chris Hillman and Roger McGuinn, who wrote the song, were supposedly inspired by the overnight success of the Monkees, a group created and prepackaged for a television series.

The trouble with "Rock 'N' Roll Star," Rick Nelson's maudlin if pretty "Teen Age Idol" (#5, 1962), and other odes to the empty lives of rock stars was their complete lack of humor. More lighthearted and appealing was "Nashville Cats" (#8, 1967) by the Lovin' Spoonful, which was actually recorded in Nashville. The song celebrated the "1,352 guitar-pickers" who were eking out a living in Music City's recording studios, replacing celebrity with a solid, if anonymous, professionalism.

By the early seventies the rock groups who did "make it" were often bloated by their excesses and possessed egos that could sink ships. This image of the coddled, self-obsessed rock star was depicted masterfully by songwriter Shel Silverstein in "The Cover of Rolling Stone" and performed to a fare-thee-well by Dr. Hook and the Medicine Show. This good-time country rock band was formed in New Jersey in 1968 by Alabama native Roy Sawyer and Dennis Locorriere. Sawyer got his nom de disque from the eyepatch he wore after losing his right eye in an auto accident. Through their manager the group met Silverstein, who was impressed enough to ask them to record his score

Dr. Hook and the Medicine Show explored the excesses of '70s rock groups as no one has before or since in "The Cover of Rolling Stone," which made them a super group themselves. While their music got slicker and more commercial with time, Dr. Hook retained a refreshing sense of humor about their work. Among their favorite hijinks was appearing as their own opening act in concert. (Photo courtesy of Showtime Archives, Toronto)

for the film *Who Is Harry Kellerman And Why Is He Saying These Terrible Things About Me?* starring Dustin Hoffman. The black comedy, released in 1972, lasted about as long as it took to say the title, but the exposure got the band a contract with Columbia Records and a lasting collaborator in Silverstein, who wrote a number of songs for their debut album. Among them was their first hit single, the intentionally overwrought ballad "Sylvia's Mother" (#5, 1972), and its follow-up, "Carry Me, Carrie" (#71).

But it was their next hit, "The Cover of Rolling Stone" (#6, 1973), that made their careers and showed rock stars to be at once self-indulgent and hopelessly star struck (ready to buy "five copies for my mother"), complete with compliant groupies and mystic gurus "showing us a better way." One of the funniest and most biting novelty songs of the decade, its success did indeed get the group on the cover of *Rolling Stone* magazine, only a month after the song hit the charts. Both song and magazine benefited from the exposure. Before the song came out, *Rolling Stone* was still a struggling little journal. After, it was a national phenomenon.

Unfortunately, Dr. Hook (the Medicine Show was dropped from the name soon after) delivered only two more novelties. "Roland the Roadie and Gertrude the Groupie" (#83), looked at the other end of the rock hierarchy with an unflinching honesty and ribald humor that may have kept the song from becoming a bigger hit. "The Millionaire" (#95, 1975) was another offbeat look at success, this time from the perspective of a guy who, with disarming candor, admits he fell accidentally into his fortune, while he uses it to get whatever he wants.

After switching labels to Capitol, the group's music became safer and less adventurous. In a few short years they had become the thing they had satirized in "Cover"—a self-satisfied super group. "I became a product with a patch and a hat," says Sawyer, who left the band in 1983. The band split up in 1985 after twenty-one chart entries and a clutch of gold and platinum records. Such is the price of fame in the business of rock.

9 A Zany Little Christmas

Our modern-day Christmas is a holiday for merriment, merchandising, and music. And the music is as well merchandised as anything else. While traditional carols remain popular, Yuletide pop songs have rivaled them for air space on radio, in music stores, and on department store PA systems. Novelty songs have established a special niche in holiday music that has been extremely lucrative ever since Spike Jones's unleashed "All I Want for Christmas Is My Two Front Teeth" on the world and Gene Autry warbled "Rudolph the Red-Nosed Reindeer." Every singer offered "Rudolph" before Autry turned it down, and so might have the singing cowboy if his wife hadn't persuaded him to record it.

But few of the recording artists considered in this chapter had to be coaxed into singing a Christmas novelty song. They knew from Autry's experience that there was gold in them there silly seasonal songs. Autry's version of "Rudolph" went to #1 on the Billboard charts in 1949 and has sold millions of copies since.

Like the children noted in Santa's big book, Christmas novelty songs have generally fallen into two categories—good and bad. The "good" songs, like "Rudolph," are often aimed at the children in us and celebrate the holiday with heart-warming humor and fantasy. The "bad" songs, by their very irreverence, undermine modern Christmas's emotional and materialistic excesses. While the latter has often had the more satisfying and lasting impact, it is the former that has usually sold more records.

Naughty but Nice

Christmas, we are constantly being told, is for children. And what could be more appealing than having a child sing a Christmas song? Spike Jones made fun of such holiday sentimentality in his "All I Want for Christmas" (#1, 1948), which featured singer George Rock imitating a tot missing his front teeth. But the Baby Boomer fifties seemed the perfect time for real prepubescent cherubs to wail holiday tunes. One of the first was Jimmy Boyd. The twelve-year-old kid from McComb, Mississippi, had a #1 hit in 1952 with the sentimental "I Saw Mommy Kissing Santa Claus," whom, everyone except little Jimmy knew, was actually Daddy in disguise.★

Then in December 1955, with rock just starting to shake up the airwaves, came "Nuttin' for Christmas," which made recording stars, however briefly, of three tuneful tykes. The song was a semi-clever catalogue of the pranks pulled by a mischievous child who is "gettin' nuttin' for Christmas, 'cause I ain't been nothin' but bad." Seven-year-old Barry Gordon, already a four-year pro of television and stage, had the original top ten version on MGM, although one truly wonders why. The slow tempo and arch orchestration by Art Mooney (who took top billing on the label with his orchestra) detract from what little charm the lyric and melody have, and Gordon is too young to have been much of a Dennis the Menace anyway. Joe Ward, who recorded a cover for King Records, had a year up on Gordon and gave the lyric a little more grit. A third version for Capitol by Ricky Zahnd, who, at age nine was the old man of the trio, trailed Ward on the charts, #21 to #20.

None of these jolly juveniles had much more of a recording career, although Gordon managed to return a few months later with "Rock Around Mother Goose" (#52). A successful child actor for years, he was

---

★*Comic Kip Addotta gave the song a contemporary twist in the 1980s with "I Saw Daddy Kissing Santa Claus." The physical lovemaking went far beyond kissing, but the song was saved from the censors when it was revealed just in time that it was Mommy wearing the Santa suit.*

Seven-year-old Barry Gordon demonstrates some of the swagger that helped sell over two million copies of "Nuttin' for Christmas," the novelty hit of 1955. While the song's chorus was brash Tin Pan Alley, the verse melody was adapted from the traditional old French song "Vive la Companie." (Photofest)

most memorable as Jason Robards's son in *A Thousand Clowns* on Broadway and in the movie version, but rock fans may best remember him as the paper boy who had eyes for Jayne Mansfield in the film *The Girl Can't Help It.* Joe Ward grew up to become a successful songwriter and producer, while Zahnd became a lawyer and was vice president of the New York Knicks and Rangers in the 1980s.

"Nuttin'" was covered by adult artists too, everyone from the Fontaine Sisters (#36) to Homer and Jethro, who called their version "Hurtin' for Christmas." But the best of them all was Stan Freberg's zany version with a member of his comic repertory company portraying a

Little Brenda Lee, as she was first billed, was all of eleven when she recorded this Christmas novelty on a hot July day in 1956 in Owen Bradley's Nashville studio. Two years later she had a far bigger seasonal hit with "Rockin' Around the Christmas Tree." (From the collection of Don McLaughlin)

bizarrely hyperactive child. Freberg himself makes a guest appearance in the closing moments as a larcenous Santa Claus who shows just how "bad" this widdle kid is. Freberg was already a veteran producer of Christmas novelties, having scored in 1953 with his "Christmas Dragnet" (#13), a somewhat schmaltzy sequel to his million-selling "St. George and the Dragonet."

Three years after "Nuttin'" little Augie Rios, another Broadway child actor, had a hit with the bilingual "¿Dònde Està Santa Claus?" (Where Is Santa Claus?). But the best child Christmas singer in the pack was twelve-year-old "Little Brenda Lee" (as she was billed on her first releases for Decca's Children's Series). Two years before she recorded the classic "Rockin' Around the Christmas Tree" she belted out the delightful countrified novelty "I'm Gonna Lasso Santa Claus." The *Billboard* review of the record praised little Brenda's "loud, piercing voice," comparing it to Barry Gordon's! Among the record's finer points are an irresistible steel guitar hook by Grady Martin and a lyric that says Brenda wants to catch Santa so she can make him give toys to all the "boys and girls who don't have none." A most refreshing note of altruism in a season all too often overstuffed with greed.

Christmas Critters

Animals run a close second to children as icons of Christmas cuteness. While sheep and cows were prominent at the manger, it is Santa's reindeer that have garnered the most pop songs. "Rudolph," which remains the quintessential Christmas novelty song, began life as a lyric in a 1939 ad campaign for Montgomery Ward department stores. The shiny-nosed reindeer was the hero of an illustrated poem, given as a free handout for store shoppers. In 1947 songwriter Johnny Marks, a friend of the ad copywriter who wrote the poem, set it to music. "Rudolph" has been interpreted and reinterpreted by dozens of recording artists since Autry first brought him out of Santa's stable. Spike Jones played fast and free with him in 1950 with Santa and the Four Reindeer on backup vocal (#7). The Cadillacs turned Rudolph R&B in 1956, while the white trio the Melodeers from Brooklyn gave him the full doo-wop treatment in 1960 (#71). The same year saw the Chipmunks, who had the biggest Christmas novelty of the era with the seasonal "The Chipmunk Song," sing their version of "Rudolph" (#21), which ended with long-suffering Dave seeking shelter from the arctic cold. More saccharine still was "The Happy Reindeer" (#34, 1959) sung by Dancer, Prancer, and Nervous (The Singing Reindeer), a studio concoction that sounded suspiciously like the Chipmunks.

Pioneer country rocker Hank Snow gave Rudolph and company a rockabilly beat in "Reindeer Boogie" (1953, 1966), while Johnny Horton's charming "They Shined Up Rudolph's Nose" kept the beat with Christmas chimes. But perhaps the best permutation on the original was Chuck Berry's "Run Rudolph Run" (#69, 1958), which was

The Singing Dogs version of "Jingle Bells" was released on this EP (extended play) single in 1955 and became a hit all over again in 1971. When the single was first released, Life magazine challenged dog meister Weismann (aka Don Charles) to record a new song from random dog barks. He obliged, using the talents of two German shepherds, a poodle, a terrier, and a pinscher and splicing the taped barks together in his studio. (From the collection of Don McLaughlin)

basically his own "Carol," with new lyrics. (Berry was a master at recycling his own songs.) Nonetheless, it glowed with that inimitable Berry wit and driving guitar.

More in the juvenile category was Lou Monte's "Dominick the Donkey (The Italian Christmas Donkey)" (#114, 1960). Monte would find much greater success a few years later with Italian mice and pussycats. Then there was Don Charles (aka Carl Weismann), an enterprising Dane who trained five dogs to bark in sequence to the music of "Jingle Bells."* The holiday tune was one of four dog barkers on an EP (extended-play) disc Charles made in Copenhagen and which sold half a million copies in America in 1955 (see Chapter 1). Fifteen years later, New York deejay Howard Smith unearthed the original 45 and began playing the Singing Dogs' version of "Jingle Bells" as a holiday gag. Listener response was phenomenal. Smith received calls from dog owners who claimed their pooches sang along with the record. RCA dug up the original at its Indianapolis plant and rushed it into release. In December 1971 the record sold 420,000 copies in just three weeks. This time, unlike the time of its first release, few listeners questioned whether the dog barks were electronically enhanced, a charge Charles vehemently denied, doggone it!

Santa, Is That You?

No symbol of the holiday season has been more pervasive in our society than jolly old Saint Nick himself. From bona fide saint to the secular embodiment of Christmas as a roaring good time, Santa has been the central character in many a seasonal novelty.

With the birth of the rock era, it was inevitable that Santa would get with the times and try some of the new dance steps, perhaps in an effort to slim down that waistline. The Moonglows got him rocking with their jump tune "Hey Santa Claus" (1953) while the Enchanters urged him to "Mambo Santa Mambo" (1956). The Martells marveled at a "Rockin' Santa Claus" (1959) while the Marcels, in a typically lively performance, taught him the latest dance craze in "Merry Twist-mas" (1961), one of the better twist records despite its novelty status. Country artist George

---

A feline version by the Jingle Cats appeared in the early 1990s. Other recent versions of "Jingle Bells" have featured various farm animals and one, human babies.

Jones, perhaps taking a cue from Jimmy Boyd, caught "My Mom and Santa Claus" (1965) twisting all over the house on Christmas Eve.

Outer space became a dangerous place for St. Nick in the late '50s with the dawning of the space race. In "Santa and the Satellite" (#32, 1957) Buchanan and Goodman took Santa into the stratosphere, where his sleigh was hijacked by those nasty little Martians. Although not among the best of the duo's break-in singles, the two-part record had some nice surreal touches, like when the Martians, who are pulling Santa's sleigh through space, break into the opening chorus of Thurston Harrison's "Little Bitty Pretty One."

In "Santa and the Purple People Eater" (1958), one of several sequels to his #1 novelty that same year, Sheb Wooley describes how Santa's sleigh nearly collides with Sputnik when the jolly fellow is saved in the nick (no pun intended) of time by the Purple People Eater.

In "Monster's Holiday," (#30, 1962), Bobby "Boris" Pickett's worthy follow-up to "Monster Mash," poor Santa is kidnapped with sleigh by Frankenstein, Dracula, and friends. In the end they see the error of their ways and are rewarded with presents from Santa, including an electric shaver for the Wolf Man. The original Wolf Man, Lon Chaney, Jr., covered the song, but even he couldn't top Pickett's exit line in the original, delivered in his best Karloffian accent: "Where is that reindeer with the *red* nose?"

Rudolph is also absent from Ray Stevens's equally delightful "Santa Claus Is Watching You" (#45, 1963), replaced by Clyde the Camel, who appeared in Stevens's previous hit, "Ahab the Arab." The song has some of the rollicking zaniness of the Coasters and even features a King Curtis-like yakety sax break.

The Beach Boys were less frantic but as harmonically melodic as ever on "Little Santa Nick," paying as much attention to Santa's cool airborne bobsled and its accessories as the little guy himself. The following year they returned with "The Man With All the Toys," concentrating on the goodies in the sack.

Gift taking, as opposed to gift giving, has been a major theme of Santa novelty songs in these acquisitive times. One of the first and best examples is "Santa Baby" (#4, 1953), in which the seductive Eartha Kitt plays gold digger to Santa's sugar daddy and ticks off with lascivious delight the luxuries she wants under her tree. Equally self-aggrandizing but more down-to-earth was Pearl Bailey, who only wanted Santa to bring her "A Five Pound Box of Money" (1960). Interestingly, the song was inspired by the payola scandal that broke that year.

The Surfaris' "A Surfin' Christmas List" (1963) was topped, no surprise, by a new surfboard. The Trashmen asked Santa to bring them a "Real Live Doll" (1966), revealing a softer side to the wild men who gave the world "Surfin' Bird" two years earlier. Then there was "Surfin' Santa" (1964) by one Lord Douglas Byron, which sounded like "Alley Oop" gone to the beach, which is not surprising since it was produced by former head Hollywood Argyle Gary Paxton.

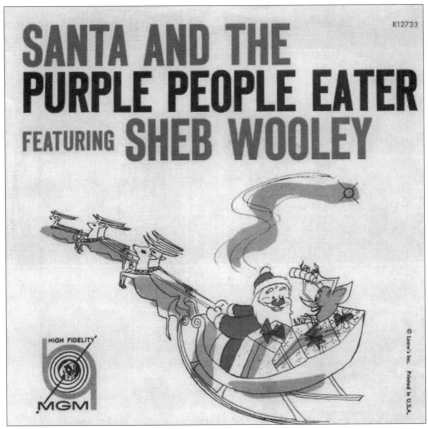

"Santa and the Purple People Eater" attempted to cash in on the popularity of Sheb Wooley's first novelty hit earlier the same year. Note the Purple People Eater playing the horn on his head and Sputnik orbiting in the background. (From the collection of Don McLaughlin)

One of the best of the Santa request songs is Johnny Preston's charming "I Want a Rock 'n' Roll Guitar" (1960), delivered by a hip little kid who tells Santa he can keep his bag of toys if he'll just deliver a six string. The same year saw the release of what must surely be one of the most bizarre of the subgenre, "Who Says There Ain't No Santa Claus" by Ron Holden and the Thunderbirds. This Coaster-like novelty has the hero collecting double indemnity when his nagging wife dies accidentally. He is later accused of murdering her, goes to jail, and ends up in the electric chair, finally realizing his Santa benefactor was indeed only a fantasy.

Elmo and Patsy hardly look like your typical novelty song duo, but their recording of "Grandma Got Run Over by a Reindeer" remains a Yuletide classic. They later divorced and Elmo pursued a second career as a veterinarian. (From the collection of Don McLaughlin)

By the early 1970s Santa Claus had largely fallen into disrepute in novelty records, skeptically viewed as a representative of the well-fed Establishment. In the Kinks' "Father Christmas" a department-store Santa is mugged by a group of slum kids, who tell him to give his toys "to the little rich boys," a stinging indictment of the inequity of our social system—on both sides of the Atlantic. Santa's fondness for strong stimulants became an issue in Clyde Lasley's blues-based "Santa Came Home Drunk" and "Santa Got a DWI" by Sherwin Linton, which logically led to "Grandma Got Run Over by a Reindeer." In this, one of the last and best Christmas novelties to reach the pop charts, Santa stands accused of vehicular manslaughter.

Songwriter Randy Brooks's choice comic premise manages to triumph over the less-than-dynamic performance of Elmo and Patsy and a jingly, campy arrangement. Besides sending up Santa, "Grandma" is a merciless satire of American family holiday togetherness, as Grandma's untimely demise on Christmas Eve barely dampens the family's capacity for beer, card playing, and football games.

The song's rise to novelty stardom was a torturous one. The husband-and-wife duo of Elmo Shropshire and Patsy Trigg first recorded it on a tiny label in Fayetteville, Tennessee, in 1979. It barely made a ripple in the recording industry and the team recorded it again three years later on the country Oink label, which was picked up by novelty song king-maker Dr. Demento on his nationally syndicated radio program. From there it took off, rising to #1 in 1982 on *Billboard*'s special Christmas chart. It was recorded yet again on the Epic label in 1984.

Elmo and Patsy, who originally called themselves the Homestead Act, seemed bewildered by their newfound fame and had little more to offer in the way of novelties. They divorced in 1985 and continued to record separately for a time. Today Elmo is a part-time veterinarian. One wonders if he's ever treated a wounded reindeer.

Cracked Carols

If Santa has been up for grabs, Christmas carols have also been popular targets of novelty artists. They have had great fun in setting these age-old melodies of Christmas past to contemporary lyrics that skewer the rampant materialism and commercialism of Christmas present.

Tom Lehrer perhaps did it best in his "A Christmas Carol," which contains short parodies of several religious carols. Since then most novelty artists have preferred to play with the more secular carols, perhaps to avoid the disapproval of the faithful.

A favorite target has been "The Twelve Days of Christmas" with its absurd laundry list of gifts. Allan Sherman had a go at it with his "Twelve Gifts of Christmas," in which the traditional presents were replaced by modern kitsch, including a calendar with the name of his insurance man, a simulated alligator wallet, and most notably a Japanese transistor radio. ("It has holes in it you can listen right through.")

Then there was the distinctively Canadian version from Bob and Doug McKenzie (aka Rick Moranis and Dave Thomas) whose litany included three French toast, two turtlenecks and . . . a beer. Unable to keep up with the sprightly music track behind them, one of them grumbles, "This should just be the two days of Christmas."

The song takes a sinister turn in "A Terrorist Christmas" by James and Kling, who receive a knife with a very sharp blade, M-16s, hand grenades, and ultimately twelve nuclear Holocausts. (The point is made, boys.) Considerably funnier is "The Twelve Pains of Christmas" by the Bob Rivers Comedy Corporation which neatly captures all the little miseries of contemporary Christmas, from putting up Christmas lights to sitting through stale TV specials.

Clement Moore's "The Night Before Christmas" was rendered in "Scandahoovian" by Yogi Yorgesson (aka Harry Stewart) and interpolated in his corny but quaint "I Yust Go Nuts at Christmas," a top five hit of Christmas 1949. Stewart was an equal opportunity ethnic novelty singer and also recorded funny songs in German, Mexican, and Japanese accents, the last as Harry Kari and His Six Saki Sippers. The Davis Sisters (Skeeter and Betty Jack, no relation) gave the song a rockabilly bounce in their endearing "Christmas Boogie" (1953). Betty Jack died in a car accident soon after, and Skeeter Davis went on to a successful solo career.

"Jingle Bells," the one Christmas song that has nothing to do with Christmas, has been parodied mercilessly. The Singing Dogs barked it, the Jingle Cats meowed it, St. Nick guffawed his way through it, José Jimenez gave us "Hingle Bells," and Yogi Yorgesson waxed the definitive Nordic version, "Yingle Bells." But our personal favorite is "Rusty

Chevrolet" by Da Yoopers, who demonstrated that sliding on ice in a four-door heap is about as much fun as cruising around in that one-horse open sleigh.

Perhaps the most ambitious carol send-up, if you can call it that, is Stan Freberg's nearly seven-minute-long musical extravaganza, "Green Chritma" (#44, 1958), a parody of Dickens's "A Christmas Carol," with Scrooge as the head of a Madison Avenue advertising agency. Although the satire of the merchandising of Christmas now seems tame and obvious, at the time it was highly controversial.

Stan Freberg looks perplexed by Capitol's failure to promote his nearly seven-minute reworking of Dickens's "A Christmas Carol" that transformed Scrooge into an advertising executive. The label found the recording too controversial and tried to get Freberg to drop a reference to Christ's birth. Considering the little air play it received because of its length and subject matter, it's surprising that it reached #44 on the **Billboard** *charts. (From the collection of Don McLaughlin)*

In his autobiography, Freberg claimed that Capitol Records president Lloyd Dunn warned him he would "never work again in the advertising business" if the record was released. Instead two of the companies satirized in the record—Marlboro cigarettes and Coca-Cola—asked Freberg to create ad campaigns for them six months after the record came out. Yes, Stan, there really *is* a Santa Claus.

Although it doesn't parody a Christmas carol, we'd like to mention "Somebody Stole My Santa Suit" (1987) by Dan Hicks and the Christmas Jug Band, which is actually set loosely to the tune of "Somebody Stole My Gal." It's a great song that begins in justified anger and ends on a note of Christian forgiveness—recapturing some of the true Christmas spirit that we thought was gone with all that discarded wrapping paper.

Christmas Present

"Grandma Got Run Over by a Reindeer" was effectively the last Christmas novelty to create a major stir on the pop charts. With changing musical tastes, novelty records in general were an endangered species by the late 1970s. Retaining an interest in the holiday, many artists sang its praises, or more often its flaws, on album tracks that were rarely released as singles. The Waitresses, one of the hottest bands (albeit briefly) of the New York new wave in the early '80s, put out the infectious "Christmas Wrapping" (read Rapping) on their first album, *I Can Rule the World If I Could Only Get the Parts* (1982). The late Patty Donahue's insouciant girl group vocal and the clever lyrics provide a stressed-out perspective of the overworked holiday that has a surprising happy ending when romance enters the picture.

But "Christmas Wrapping" was an anomaly. Most recording artists who took on Christmas in the '80s and '90s saw it through the jaded eye of the satirist, as in Mona Abboud's precious version of Jim Rusk's "The Pretty Little Dolly," which catalogs the lifelike attributes of the ultimate Christmas present, which will turn blue and die if you put a plastic bag over its head. Originally written for a sixties' musical revue, the song has been sung on television by Carol Burnett, Lily Tomlin, and Abboud herself on the *Tonight Show,* a performance which in 1980 was released as a single to little acclaim.

The Christmas office party with its flowing alcohol and loss of inhibitions was tackled by Indianapolis morning deejays Bob Kevion and Tom Greisall, aka the Bob and Tom Band, on "It's Christmas and I Wonder Where I Am." The same theme got a more serious, if sentimental, treatment in Commodore Cody's "Daddy's Drinkin' Up Our Christmas" (1973), one of the few country Christmas novelties to pack the kind of stark honesty that infuses the best of country music.

For trenchant comment, however, few Christmas novelties can top "Christmas Is Coming Twice This Year" by the Hollytones, three high school buddies from Costa Mesa, California, who have made Christmas novelties their specialty. Their first was "How's Santa Gonna Find Us (In a Fallout Shelter)." "Christmas Is Coming Twice This Year," from the CD *Gridlock Christmas* (1992), has a feel-good sing-songy chorus that is countered by the conversations of two manipulative '90s kids who play their divorced parents against each other to increase the goodies under the tree.

This brings us to the ultimate Christmas send-up, "Weird Al" Yankovic's "Christmas at Ground Zero," which cheerily contemplates a Yuletide after the bomb falls. With all this angst and enmity directed at it, what's a poor holiday to do? Say "Humbug!" and crawl back under the covers until New Year's Eve.

⑩ They All Sang Novelty

"In my own mind, I didn't see myself continuing to make novelty songs all my life."—*Brian Hyland*

"There's this song 'Short People.' It's really a joke. I like other ones on the album better but the audiences go for that one."—*Randy Newman*

"My name is Sue! How do you do?"
—*Johnny Cash, "A Boy Named Sue"*

Red Ingle had a problem. Having played sax with Spike Jones and his City Slickers for nearly five years on some of the finest novelty records of the 1940s, he was about to strike out on his own with his new group, the Natural Seven. While Jones's satirical style was eccentrically eclectic, Ingle thought he could parody pop songs using a decidedly hillbilly beat.

He was all set to record his first single for Capitol, a rustic spoof of the old evergreen "Temptation," lately a big hit for pop crooner Perry Como. The problem was that the girl he had hired as vocalist for the session was nowhere to be found. Then at the last moment a young singer who was already one of Capitol's biggest recording artists volunteered to fill in. Jo Stafford was known for singing ballads, but underneath the serious facade beat the heart of a natural cut-up. For Ingle's record, Stafford adopted a backwoods drawl that would have made Daisy Mae green with envy.

Capitol executives agreed reluctantly to release "Temptation (Tim-Tayhsun)" but refused to allow Stafford's name to appear on the label. The singer was identified as Cinderella G. Stump, and the record, to everyone's surprise, climbed to #1 on the pop charts in June 1947. Stafford made one more country novelty that year, "Feudin' and Fightin'" (#6), this time under her real name, before returning to the ballads and upbeat pop tunes that would make her a legend in the fifties. Red Ingle and the Natural Seven had a few more novelty hits before fading into obscurity. Their last *Billboard* charter in late 1948 was "Serutan Yob (A Song for Backward Boys and Girls Under 40)," a parody of the Nat King Cole hit "Nature Boy."

Jo Stafford is just one of a long line of "serious" recording artists who have relished the opportunity to kick up their heels and have some fun recording a novelty song or two. Some artists have even had their greatest success with a silly song. And many performers who later went on to bigger and better things found novelty a way to get their foot in the industry's door. Some are grateful for the opportunity that novelty provided them; others would rather forget those misspent hours in the recording studio. But we won't let them do that, will we?

Dizzy Debuts

Fifteen-year-old Brian Hyland's dreams of teen stardom surely didn't include a #1 novelty record, but then let's remember his cousin was Larry Fine of the Three Stooges, so it might have been hereditary. The budding youngster from Queens, New York, was grateful to land a contract with Kapp Records in 1960 and readily agreed to record the Paul Vance-Lee Pockriss ditty with the preposterous title "Itsy Bitsy Teenie Weenie Yellow Polkadot Bikini."

Executive Dave Kapp planned to put Hyland on his Leader subsidiary, not wanting Kapp, the label of pianist Roger Williams, to be tainted by anything resembling rock 'n' roll. He also had his doubts about "Bikini," whose lyrics he found slightly risqué, until writer Vance convinced him that the girl in the bikini was modeled on his two-year-old daughter. There was, however, no reference in the song to the wearer's age, unlike the little girl in the Ames Brothers' 1954 hit "The Naughty Lady of Shady Lane."

With Hyland's boyish vocal, the more worldly girl who teasingly introduced the chorus ("One-two-three-four, Tell the people what she wore"), and the cutesy arrangement, "Bikini" shot to the top of the charts, remaining in the top forty for thirteen weeks, well past bikini weather. The follow-up was another too-cute novelty in motion, "Four Little Heels (The Clickity-Clack Song)" (#73). By the time Kapp issued an album of novelties, *The Bashful Blonde,* Hyland wondered if he would ever get to record anything else.

Fortunately, around this time he met another talented songwriting duo, Gary Geld and Peter Udell, whose forte was ballads. They helped get him signed to ABC-Paramount, where his first release, "Make Me Belong to You," included such suggestive lyrics as "Make me behave, make me your slave." From girl watching at the beach to heavy-duty masochism was a big jump, but Hyland made the transition without missing a beat. By the time he recorded his biggest ballad the following year, Geld and Udell's melancholy "Sealed with a Kiss," all thoughts of little girls in bikinis had faded and Hyland's position as a teen idol was secure.

High school heartthrob Brian Hyland seemed destined to remain a novelty artist after the phenomenal success of "Itsy Bitsy Teenie Weenie Yellow Polkadot Bikini," but he managed the difficult transition to teen idoldom within a year. Novelty, however, may well be in Hyland's genes—Larry Fine of the Three Stooges was his cousin.

Joe South made less of a splash with his first hit single, 1958's "The Purple People Eater Meets the Witch Doctor" (#47). This blatant ripoff of two of the biggest novelty records of the year was written and first recorded by the Big Bopper (aka J. P. Richardson) as the B side of his classic "Chantilly Lace." The Bopper's version had more gusto, but South had the hit with the same Chipmunk-like voices that David Seville used in "Witch Doctor."

"It was one of those embarrassing songs you couldn't perform unless you had a puppet show going on behind you," South said in a 1991 *Goldmine* interview. Ten years later, after a long stint as a session musician and a songwriter, he reemerged with his top twenty hit "Games People Play." And you can bet that when he received his two Grammys for the song, he made no mention of his first appearance on the charts.

Chubby Checker is the King of the Twist, but few fans will recall that his first hit wasn't a dance record but a novelty song. Born Ernest Evans, he entertained customers in a Philadelphia poultry shop with jokes and funny songs while he plucked the chickens. Evans's talent for impersonating well-known singers brought him to the attention of Kal Mann, president of Parkway Records and Dick Clark of *American Bandstand*. At Clark's request, Ernest made a singing Christmas card for him that included impressions of different singers crooning "Jingle Bells." Among the vocalists Evans spoofed was Fats Domino, leading Clark's wife to dub the fledgling singer Chubby Checker.

Mann thought the idea of the recording was clever and had Checker do a similar treatment of the nursery rhyme "Mary Had a Little Lamb" for his first Parkway release. The premise of "The Class" was teacher Chubby asking his students, all well-known rock stars, to recite "Mary." The impersonations, which included Fats, Elvis, the Coasters, and, curiously, drummer Cozy Cole ("Mary—Part 2") are clever if not particularly memorable. The record's highlight is when Chubby goes down the hall to the kindergarten to hear little teen idols Frankie, Ricky, and Fabian, who sing like the Chipmunks.

"The Class" was a sizable hit, peaking at #38 on the charts and was followed by a handful of novelties that went nowhere. One of these, "The Jet," is an attempt to make a novelty dance hit, complete with jetlike sound effects and a beat not very different from the twist. After suffering through such drivel as "Dancing Dinosaur," Checker was given "The Twist" to record, a dance that was certainly a novelty, and the rest is history.

Like Chubby Checker, Jan Berry and Dean Torrence were known for having a wild sense of humor. They formed a trio with Arnie Ginsberg and had a top ten hit in 1958 with "Jennie Lee," a rocking number about a famous L.A. burlesque dancer that they recorded in Jan's parents' garage. The record label read "Jan and Arnie," because Dean, who sang

Before he was crowned king of the twist, Chubby Checker cut a handful of novelty songs, the first of which capitalized on his gift for mimicking other singers. (Archive Photos).

lead vocal, had gone into the service before the record was released. When Dean returned from his hitch, he and Jan signed with Herb Alpert and Lou Adler's Dore label in 1959 and had their second hit. "Baby Talk" (#10) was a silly doo-wop tune with the two singers imitating infants in love, which *Billboard*'s reviewer, for some strange reason, found "rather distasteful." On further releases, Jan and Dean retained their California doo-wop sound but moved away from novelty material. A few years later they joined the Beach Boys in the surfing craze with Brian Wilson's "Surf City," but never quite abandoned novelty—remember "The Little Old Lady (from Pasadena)"? Then in 1966, just before their careers came to a jarring halt when Dean had a near-fatal car accident, they returned to the novelty form with "Batman"(#66), a tribute to the hit TV series based on the caped crusader.

Another fan of doo-wop was Queens native Paul Simon, who in 1957 teamed up with his friend and neighbor Art Garfunkel and recorded "Hey Schoolgirl" as Tom (Graph) and Jerry (Landis). The record became a modest hit (#49) and got them a spot on *American Bandstand*. Several follow-ups flopped and Simon enrolled in Queens College. While studying music theory, he continued to record solo under the pseudonym Jerry Landis and in early 1963 released the catchy novelty "The Lone Teen Ranger," a mild spoof on the popular *Lone Ranger* TV series. Simon's neo-doo-wop-heavy vocal hook and a busy arrangement that included a bit of the *William Tell Overture* propelled the single into the Hot One Hundred for three weeks, peaking at #97.

Over the next few years Simon would continue to put out records under a half-dozen names including Paul Kane, Harrison Gregory, True Taylor, and Tic and the Triumphs, who would scrape the charts with their prototypic car tune, "Motorcycle." After trying his hand at nearly every genre of rock, Simon was finally drawn to the folk revival and regrouped with his old pal Garfunkel in late 1965 to record "The Sounds of Silence." And there was nothing funny about that.

One of Simon's classmates at Queens College was Carole Klein, who would soon leave college for an apprenticeship in singing and songwriting at New York's legendary Brill Building. Here, with Simon, she recorded demos of new songs for other artists. Under the name Carole King she recorded a handful of singles including "Short Mort," a parody of Annette's "Tall Paul," and "Oh! Neil," an answer song to

Neil Sedaka's hit "Oh! Carol," which was written for her. These and other novelties brought her to the attention of Don Kirshner, who signed her and her new husband, David Goffin, to his Aldon Music company, and the career of one of the top songwriting teams of the early sixties was launched.

Bobby Darin, another Kirshner protégé, began his recording career with a cover of Lonnie Donegan's "Rock Island Line." His next single was "Silly Willie," which *Billboard* called a "fast and furious bit of non-sense." But it would be another two years before Darin hit pay dirt with a kooky novelty rocker he wrote in twelve minutes called "Splish Splash."

Another talented singer-songwriter who, like Simon and King, hailed from Queens was Paul Evans. He played a sexually frustrated teen squiring a bevy of beauties and his Casanova friend Fred around town in his first hit, "Seven Little Girls Sitting in the Back Seat" (#9, 1959). The teasing girl chorus was sung by "the Curls," two singers moonlighting from Perry Como's chorale group.

Less unhappy in the novelty category than some, Evans wrote his own semi-novelty, "Happy-Go-Lucky-Me" (#10, 1960) and in 1962 sang the giddy, drunken "Feeling No Pain," which failed to chart. After that he thrived for many years as a successful songwriter ("Roses Are Red" for Bobby Vinton) and jingle writer. Today he continues to market his songs on one of the most ambitious web sites put out by a vintage recording artist.

Girl problems were also at the heart of the first recording efforts of two teen idols of the early '60s. Former Mouseketeer Paul Petersen was already an established star on the popular sitcom *The Donna Reed Show* when he recorded "She Can't Find Her Keys" (#19, 1962). This rather clever specialty number found Paul waiting impatiently on the doorstep for a goodnight kiss while his date rummages through her pocketbook. The lyric was a laundry list of everything she had in her purse, from Presley records to a kitchen sink. In a 1998 *Goldmine* interview with writer Sandy Steward Benjamin, Petersen confessed that to this day he has "to keep the lyrics in my hand in order to get through it."

Eddie Hodges was only fourteen when he recorded another doorstep novelty, "I'm Gonna Knock On Your Door" (#12, 1961), but he was already a seasoned veteran of television, movies (he sang "High Hopes" with Frank Sinatra in *A Hole in the Head*), and Broadway (the musical *The Music Man*). "I'm Gonna Knock" was notable for its clever use of sound effects (doors knocking, bells buzzing, windows rapping). The next year little Eddie graduated to light, upbeat ballads like Phil Everly's now sexually incorrect "Girls, Girls, Girls (Were Made to Love)."

Midlife Crisis

So much for ambitious beginnings. But what would possess an already established recording artist to record a novelty record? Ask Bo Diddley that question and he might just laugh in your face. After all, novelty gave him the biggest pop hit of his long and illustrious career. Born Ellas McDaniel, Bo had been making some of the most innovative and exciting rock 'n' roll in America for nearly half a decade. Yet his grand anthem "Bo Diddley," while a #1 R&B hit in 1955, didn't even register on the pop charts. Unlike his great contemporary Chuck Berry, Bo's music, even with that infectious beat, was considered "too black" for the white teen market.

The story goes that Bo was jokingly trading insults with his maracas player, the legendary Jerome Green, during a coffee break in the studio when engineer Ron Maylow happened to listen in on them. Maylow found something worth hearing as they dissed each other and turned on a tape recorder. When Bo learned what Maylow had been up to, he was mystified. After much editing and cleaning up, Bo's label Chess released the spoken novelty as "Say Man." It eventually rose to #20 on the pop charts, Bo Diddley's first and only top forty record.

While some of the exchanges in "Say Man" are downright corny, others have the classic hyperbolic humor of Southern folklore ("That chick was so ugly that she had to sneak up on a glass just to get a drink of water!") The background musical jamming punctuates the punch lines with a powerful percussive beat. The late Robert Palmer called "Say Man" the first rap track, and though this may be stretching the point, the earthy humor and comic braggadocio of Bo's music has surely influenced today's rap and gangsta music.

Macho posturing was also responsible for the only hit novelty record that Buddy Holly and the Crickets made. The group was on tour in Australia in 1958 when Holly's drummer, Jerry Allison, was taken by the

Bo Diddley and his right-hand man, maracas player Jerome Green, mix it up in matching jackets. The pair's off-the-wall verbal sparring led to Bo's only top forty pop hit, "Say Man," in 1959. (Photo courtesy of Showtime Archives, Toronto)

original rocker "Wild One" by Aussie rockabilly artist Johnny O'Keefe, who opened the show for the Crickets. Allison liked it so much that he began singing it as part of their set. But while O'Keefe sang it straight, Allison mumbled the lyrics, "trying," he said, "to sound like Jimmy Cagney 'you dirty rat.'"

Holly didn't much like the song or Allison's interpretation, but went along with recording it. Allison wasn't particularly proud of the side, either. "I said I didn't want anyone to know who it was, because I thought it was really atrocious," he said in an interview with Holly biographer John Goldrosen, and recorded it under his middle name Ivan.

The public found the song, now retitled "Real Wild Child," goofily appealing and it rose to #68 on the charts. Holly, for all his disdain, must have gotten into the spirit, because in the instrumental break his lead guitar does a neat parody of the celesta break on his own "Everyday."*

The Playmates, three college students from the University of Connecticut, began in the early fifties primarily as a comedy act called the Nitwits. But when they signed with Roulette Records in 1957 they transformed themselves into a male harmony group whose specialty was romantic ballads like their first hit, "Jo-Ann" (#19, 1958). Later that year they reverted to their comic roots when handed a novelty song about an impromptu road race between a Cadillac and a little Nash Rambler. What made "Beep Beep" (#4) so memorable was not only its tortoise-and-hare story line, but the clever way in which the Playmates slowly accelerated their delivery as the cars went faster and faster. The final punchline, with the driver of the little Rambler calling out as he leaves the Caddy in the dust, "Buddy, how can I get this car out of second gear?" is a winner. The group came back the next year with the delight-ful semi-novelty "What Is Love?" before returning to more traditional ballad material. They ended their run on the charts in 1962 with another novelty, "Keep Your Hands in Your Pockets" (#88).

---

*Holly wasn't above delving into novelty on his own. According to his old friend Waylon Jennings, Buddy attempted to release a cover of Little Richard's "Slippin' and Slidin'" in a speeded-up Chipmunks' version. However, the record company released it at the wrong speed and the effect was lost. "Buddy thought those high, squeaky voices were the coolest thing," Jennings wrote in his autobiography.

There are those who think the entire career of teen idol Frankie Avalon was a novelty. After all, he turned the flimsy "Dede Dinah" into his first hit by holding his nose while he sang it. After seventeen charting singles in three years, Avalon came out with "The Puppet Song" (#56, 1960), the B side of the ballad "A Perfect Love." It was about a little puppet maker whose prayers bring his wooden creations to life (sound familiar?). The puppets sounded like the Chipmunks with colds

The Playmates live up to their original name, the Nitwits. They moved effortlessly from comedy to straight ballads like "Jo-Ann," then back to comedy with the classic car novelty song "Beep Beep." (Photo courtesy of Showtime Archives, Toronto)

and the song was as treacly sentimental as anything Avalon recorded in his five-year run on the charts.

Fellow teen idol James Darren also had a novel recording career, but one far more interesting than Avalon's. An actor with little singing ability, his specialty was masochistic songs like his biggest hit, "Goodbye Cruel World" (#3, 1961), which his label Colpix promoted to radio stations with a modeled figure of a man about to flush himself down a toilet. The song's sideshow motif was accentuated by a shrieking circus calliope that was actually the voice of composer Gloria Shayne speeded up. Darren's only full-out novelty was "Conscience" (#11, 1962), in which he played both a teen Lothario and his conscience, which admonishes him not to break the girl's heart on an impending date. The clever lyrics by Barry Mann and Cynthia Weill were supported by an imaginative arrangement: sweet woodwinds accompanying the voice of conscience and blaring horns backing the teen wolf.

Perry Como was hardly a teen idol, but in the fifties he had incorporated some of the beat of rock into such hits as "Papa Loves Mambo," "KoKo Mo," and "Juke Box Baby." He had tried his hand at novelties, too, with "A—You're Adorable," and "Bibbidi-Bobbidi-Boo" from Walt Disney's animated film *Cinderella*. Then in 1960 he came out with "Delaware" (#22), an ingenious bit of geographic punning ("What did Delaware, boys? She wore a brand New Jersey"). Set to a martial beat, it sounded like an authentic army marching song, but it had actually been written by tunesmith Irving Gordon, whose love of verbal gymnastics went back to the days when he wrote "Who's on First?" for Abbott and Costello. "Delaware" went all the way to #3 in Great Britain, where such witty wordplay was more appreciated.

By the seventies, novelty songs were few and far between. But three singer-songwriters, all free and independent spirits, brought humor and imagination to their forays into the genre.

Harry Edward Nelson III (aka Nilsson) was a hard act to categorize, although it was just this versatility that led John Lennon to name him as his favorite American singer. Best known for "Everybody's Talking," the theme song from *Midnight Cowboy*, and the monster ballad "Without You," he also produced the wistfully whimsical "Me and My Arrow" (#34, 1971) from his ninety-minute animated TV special, *The Point*, and the infectiously quirky "Coconut" (#8, 1972), about a witch doctor's love remedy. Nilsson, who never took himself too seriously, retired from the recording industry in the 1980s to devote himself to film production. He died of a heart attack at age fifty-two in 1994.

One of Nilsson's closest colleagues was Randy Newman, whose rich character studies and offbeat songs never came near the pop charts until the darkly comic "Short People" (#2, 1977) struck the public's funny bone. Like many of Newman's best songs, "Short People" was filtered through an adopted persona and was meant to be a tongue-in-cheek putdown of bigotry. Many listeners missed the point and accused Newman of making fun of people who are, well . . . vertically challenged.

"It was the worst kind of hit anyone could have," Newman told writer Joe Smith. "It was like having 'Purple People Eater.' I'd try to watch a ball game and the band would play the song and the announcer would make jokes about it. It was too noisy. I prefer quiet money."

Jimmy Buffet, like Nilsson, is a man of many talents. A correspondent for *Billboard* back in the late sixties, he moved to Key West in 1971, where he eventually opened a store named after his biggest hit, "Margaritaville" and put out his own line of tropical clothing. "Cheeseburger in Paradise" (#32, 1978), his only novelty hit, bears a similarity to Larry Groce's "Junk Food Junkie," although Buffet's take on his passion for fast food has a far more philosophical bent than Groce's. A true thinking man's novelty song.

Strange Swan Songs

Few singers were as popular in the 1940s as Vaughn Monroe, whose rich baritone permeated the airwaves through the mid-fifties. A band leader and trumpeter (he'd won his first championship in Wisconsin at age fourteen), Monroe enjoyed singing all kinds of music and had a special fondness for cowboy songs, like "Riders in the Sky," which he took to #1 in 1949. By the mid-fifties, with his brand of singing in sharp decline, Monroe made a surprise cover of the rock novelty "Black Denim Trousers" (#38) and the following year had his last top forty hit with the offbeat folkish "In the Middle of the House" (#11),* which is

---

*Rusty Draper, another Hit Parader with a penchant for Western themes, also had a top twenty version of the song.

a cheery tale of a homeowner who uses the train tracks going through his house to dispense of annoying bill collectors and boorish relatives. In the end he makes the mistake of sitting down in the middle of the house himself and is cut off in midline by the roar of the 109. The childlike melody and homey lyrics work nicely with the bizarre doings, but the production is rather antiseptic. It would have taken the twisted mind of a Nervous Norvus to make the most of the song's black humor.

Pat Boone, the Vaughn Monroe of the rock era, ended his long run in the top forty with a wild novelty that he has called one of his two favorite songs. (The other is "Love Letters in the Sand." Go figure.) Boone was sitting in a club in the Philippines when he heard David Dante's version of "Speedy Gonzales," then the #1 record in that country. Boone instantly fell in love with the catchy novelty and wanted to record it. Randy Wood, head of Dot Records, Boone's label, was less enthusiastic and told his star to stick with the blander ballad material with which he had become associated. But Boone persisted and Wood finally relented and released his version of the novelty song in 1962.

Although filled with denigrating stereotypes of Hispanics, "Speedy" was a lively record, bolstered by two "guest" artists: an unbilled Robin Ward, whose caterwauling senorita gets to my eleven-year-old daughter every time, and the original voice of Speedy, Mel Blanc, whose comic interjections did nothing for U.S.-Mexican relations. ("Hey, Rosita, come quick! Down at the cantina they are giving green stamps with tequila.") Interestingly, despite the negative response by Hispanic groups in this country, "Speedy Gonzales" went to #1 in several South American countries.

It was Blanc's participation, and not the Hispanic stereotypes, that got Boone and Dot in trouble. Warner Bros. filed an $850,000 damage suit against both parties in U.S. District Court for unfair competition and the unrequested use of their copyrighted cartoon character and voice. Although the cartoon mouse was never portrayed in the song, the complaint declared that Blanc's voice was "a vital part of his personality and hence of his public appeal." The suit was settled amicably. "Speedy" was such a big hit (#6) that there was plenty of money to go around and Warner Bros. got its share.

Robin Ward's screeching serenade was later lifted almost note for note by Elton John in his 1973 hit "Crocodile Rock," perhaps the

America's cleanest teen idol, Pat Boone, ended his incredible run of top forty hits with "Speedy Gonzales," a novelty based on the Warner Bros.' cartoon character. The film studio sued both Boone and Mel Blanc, who provided Speedy's voice. Surprisingly, Boone has recently returned to the novelty field with an album of heavy metal songs.

only time that the King of Covers himself was ripped off. Wisely, Boone didn't press it.

Another teen idol fallen on hard times in 1962 was Joe Dowell, who reached #1 a year earlier with "Wooden Heart," the German folk-like ballad that Elvis crooned in *G.I. Blues* (1960). His last charting single was a watery version of the tortoise and the hare, "Little Red Rented Rowboat" (#23). After that, he was up the creek without a paddle.

Unlike Pat Boone, Johnny Cash was well known for his quirky sense of humor. Somehow a funny song from the dry, deep-voiced man in black was very funny indeed. Cash capitalized on this in his 1968 album, *Everybody Loves a Nut,* which consisted only of novelties and had cover art by MAD magazine artist Jack Davis.

Possessing an independent spirit, Cash often swam against the conservative current of country music. In 1966 he skewered the political posturing of all musicians in "One on the Right Is on the Left" (#46, 1966), although the song focused on radical folkies.

A few years later he was preparing for a second live album to be recorded during a concert at San Quentin Penitentiary when a Nashville producer sent him "A Boy Named Sue," by the unsung king of novelty songwriters, Shel Silverstein, who died in May 1999. The singer got the song so late that he didn't have time to learn the lyrics, as he reported in his autobiography, *Man in Black,* and had to lay the sheet music down in front of him on the concert stage. "I have a new song," he explained to the inmates. "I don't know it yet, but I'll sing it to you as best I can."

Cash's slightly out of kilter rendition, seasoned with the authentic robust laughter of the inmates, helped to make "Sue" a stand-out on the album, *Folsom Prison Blues.* This shaggy dog song about a showdown between a son and his wayward father who gave him "that awful name" was a natural for Cash and zoomed to #2 for three weeks, giving him the biggest pop hit of his long career. The album eventually sold six million copies and the single three million, making Johnny Cash Columbia's best-selling artist of 1969. Cash's last charting pop single in 1976 was also a novelty song, "One Piece at a Time" (#29), about an auto plant worker who smuggles out car parts and builds himself a Cadillac in his garage.

Another country music renegade who rediscovered novelty in the 1970s was Bobby Bare. After the auspicious beginning of "The All American Boy," Bare settled into a saner country groove producing some of the best of the Nashville country songs in the early sixties. He later plumbed the themes of loneliness and infidelity with greater artistry and honesty than most country singers in a string of country hits.

In 1973 Bare teamed up with the ubiquitous Shel Silverstein to produce the landmark album *Bobby Bare Sings Lullabys, Legends and Lies*, which brought him back into a comic mode. The album produced the

Comedy has long been a part of Johnny Cash's act. His grim image and rough, dry vocals are the perfect foil for a novelty song. Shel Silverstein's "A Boy Named Sue" gave him the biggest hit of his pop career and inspired Jane Morgan to record "A Girl Named Johnny Cash." (Photofest)

#1 country hit "Marie Laveau," a poignant duo with his five-year-old son; "What If . . .," his last pop hit at #41; and "The Winner," a hilarious character study of male machismo gone loony. There was even a tongue-in-cheek religious number, "Dropkick Me Jesus (Through the Goalpost of Life)," written by Paul Craft and reported to be Bill Clinton's favorite song.

The biggest benefactor of a late-date novelty is rock pioneer Chuck Berry. Berry's sharp sense of humor has infused his classic rockers from the music-crazy heroine of "Sweet Little Sixteen" to that unbudgable seatbelt in "No Particular Place to Go." It seems ironic that Berry should finally find his way to #1 with a silly, throwaway novelty that had been around for decades and was a staple of his concert act for years. "My Ding-A-Ling" (1972) had been written and recorded by New Orleans legend Dave Bartholomew way back in 1952. It had been recorded under different titles by several R&B groups through the fifties, most prominently as "Toy Bell" by the Bees in 1954.

Berry's version of this ode to the male organ was one of the raunchiest and most inventive. The live recording (made, Berry claims, without his knowledge) was performed in England, a nation where the disk would probably have been banned a few years earlier. The 35,000 students at the Lanchester Ballroom in Coventry joined in the saucy sing-a-long, with some memorable adlibs from Berry. Silly or not, the record sales were a well-deserved bonanza for the often underpaid and now aging rocker. "A two-hundred-fifty-thousand dollar check, the largest I'd ever received, was handed to me while crossing Fifth Avenue," Berry wrote in his autobiography. "I stubbed my toe on the curb as I was counting the zeros."

The lowly novelty has bolstered the careers of many of our biggest rock stars—young, old, and in mid-career—who found themselves laughing all the way to the bank.

As we enter the new millennium, novelty songs appear to be a dead genre. This is not news. With the exception of "Weird Al" Yankovic, novelty songs have been an endangered species since the early '80s. Very few have made the charts since then and only a handful of those have broken into the top forty.

Chuck Berry gave the world more than a dozen rock classics, but it took seventeen years and an old song about penis preoccupation to put him on top of the charts. "My Ding-A-Ling" was written and first produced by Dave Bartholomew in 1952. Later versions included "The Real Thing," "Toy Bell," and Berry's own "My Tambourine." (Photofest)

But the spirit of novelty is far from dead. Weird Al's popularity among teens and preteens who flock to his concerts and buy his CDs shows that a generation that never heard Spike Jones, Stan Freberg, or Allan Sherman is receptive to humor in music. Meanwhile, new groups explore the strange and the novel. Witness the wild eclecticism of the Squirrel Nut Zippers and the creative sampling of Beck. The Dr. Demento show continues to promote the golden age of novelty as well as serving as a showcase for newer talent that, if not busting up the charts, is at least producing high-quality novelty music that has attracted a devoted following—groups like Da Yoopers and the Christmas-obsessed Hollytones. Anthologies from the golden age continue to sell well to baby boomers and their offspring.

The possibility of a novelty renaissance looks unlikely at present, but who can say? If the future brings the same kinds of stresses and fears that we experienced in the Cold War years of the 1950s and the social upheaval of the 1960s, we may need music that makes us laugh more than ever. And if things really go awry, what better song to sing on the eve of destruction than Tom Lehrer's "We'll All Go Together When We Go"? Sweet dreams.

Bibliography

Books

Berry, Chuck. *The Autobiography*. New York: Harmony Books, 1987.

Breithaupt, Don, and Jeff Breithaupt. *Precious and Few: Pop Music in the Early Seventies*. New York: St. Martin's Press, 1996.

Bronson, Fred. *The Billboard Book of Number One Hits*. New York: Billboard Books, 1988.

————. *Billboard's Hottest Hot 100 Hits*. New York: Billboard Books, 1995.

Brown, Ashley, ed. *The Marshall Cavendish Illustrated History of Popular Music*. 6 vols. New York: Marshall Cavendish, 1989.

Cash, Johnny. *Man in Black*. Grand Rapids, Mich.: Zondervan Publishing House, 1975.

Clifford, Mike, consultant. *The Harmony Illustrated Encyclopedia of Rock*. New York: Harmony Books, 1988.

Current Biography. New York: H.H. Wilson, 1954, 1958, 1966, 1978.

Dellar, Fred. *The Harmony Illustrated Encyclopedia of Country Music*. London: Salamander Books, 1986.

Evans, Hillary. *From Other Worlds: Aliens, Abductions and UFOs*. Pleasantville, N.Y.: Readers Digest, 1998.

Fox, Ted. *In the Groove: The People Behind the Music*. New York: St. Martin's Press, 1986.

Freberg, Stan. *It Only Hurts When I Laugh*. New York: Times Books, 1988.

Glubok, Shirley. *The Art of the Comic Strip*. New York: Macmillan, 1979.

Goldrosen, John, and John Beecher. *Remembering Buddy: The Definitive Biography of Buddy Holly*. New York: Viking Penguin, 1986.

Gordy, Berry. *To Be Loved: The Music, the Magic, the Memories of Motown*. New York: Warner Books, 1994.

Gottfried, Martin. *Broadway Musicals*. New York: Harry Abrams, 1980.

Gregory, Hugh. *Who's Who in Country Music*. London: Weidenfield and Nicolson, 1993.

Hardy, Phil, and Dave Laing. *Encyclopedia of Rock*. New York: Schirmer Books, 1988.

Heslam, David, ed. *The Rock 'n' Roll Years*. New York: Crescent Books, 1990.

Horstman, Dorothy. *Sing Your Heart Out, Country Boy*. Nashville: Country Music Foundation Press, 1996.

Humphries, Patrick. *Paul Simon: Still Crazy After All These Years*. New York: Doubleday, 1988.

Jancik, Wayne. *The Billboard Book of One-Hit Wonders*. New York: Billboard Books, 1998.

Jancik, Wayne, and Tad Lathrop. *Cult Rockers.* New York: Simon and Schuster, 1995.

Jennings, Waylon, with Lenny Kaye. *Waylon: An Autobiography.* New York: Warner Books, 1996.

Kingsbury, Paul. *The Grand Ole Opry History of Country Music.* New York: Villard Books, 1995.

Larkin, Colin, ed. *The Guinness Encyclopedia of Popular Music.* 6 vols. Middlesex, England: Guinness Publishing, 1995.

McAleer, Dave. *Encyclopedia of Hits: The 1960s.* London: Blonford, 1996.

McNeil, Alex. *Total Television.* New York: Viking Penguin, 1984.

Marsh, Dave, and James Bernard. *The New Book of Rock Lists.* New York: Simon and Schuster, 1994.

Marsh, Dave, and Steve Propes. *Merry Christmas, Baby: Holiday Music from Bing to Sting.* Boston: Little, Brown, 1993.

Miller, Jim, ed. *The Rolling Stone Illustrated History of Rock and Roll.* New York: Random House, 1980.

Moses, Robert, and Beth Rowen, eds. *1996 Information Please Almanac.* Boston: Houghton Mifflin, 1995.

Murrells, Joseph. *Million Selling Records from the 1900s to the 1980s.* New York: Avco Publishing, 1985.

Nite, Norm N. *Rock On: The Illustrated Encyclopedia of Rock 'n' Roll: The Solid Gold Years.* New York: Thomas Crowell, 1974.

————. *Rock On: The Illustrated Encyclopedia of Rock 'n' Roll: The Modern Years, 1964-Present.* New York: Thomas Crowell, 1978.

O'Neil, Thomas. *The Grammys: For the Record.* New York: Penguin Books, 1993.

Palmer, Robert. *Rock and Roll: An Unruly History.* New York: Harmony Books, 1995.

Panati, Charles. *Extraordinary Origins of Everyday Things.* New York: Harper, 1987.

Phillips, John with Jim Jerome. *Papa John: An Autobiography.* Garden City, N.Y.: Doubleday, 1986.

Pollock, Bruce. *In Their Own Words.* New York: Macmillan, 1975.

Schaffner, Nicholas. *The Boys from Liverpool: John, Paul, George, Ringo.* New York: Methuen, 1980.

Schipper, Henry. *Broken Record: The Inside Story of the Grammy Awards.* New York: Birch Lane Press, 1992.

Shaw, Arnold. *Black Popular Music in America.* New York: Schirmer Books, 1986.

————. *The Rockin' '50s: The Decade That Transformed the Pop Music Scene.* New York: Hawthorn Books, 1974.

Smith, Joe. *Off the Record: An Oral History of Popular Music.* New York: Warner Books, 1988.

Stambler, Irwin. *Encyclopedia of Pop, Rock and Soul.* New York: St. Martin's Press, 1989.

Stambler, Irwin, and Grelun London. *The Encyclopedia of Folk, Country and Western Music.* New York: St. Martin's Press, 1984.

Tichi, Cecelia, ed. *Reading Country Music: Steel Guitars, Opry Stars, and Honky-Tonk Bars.* Durham, N.C.: Duke University Press, 1998.

Tosches, Nick. *Unsung Heroes of Rock 'n' Roll.* New York: Charles Scribner's Sons, 1984.

Warner, Jay. *Billboard's American Rock 'n' Roll in Review.* New York: Schirmer Books, 1997.

———. *The Billboard Book of American Singing Groups: A History, 1940–1990.* New York: Billboard Books, 1992.

Weiner, Ed. *The TV Guide TV Book.* New York: Harper Perennial, 1992.

Whitburn, Joel. *The Billboard Book of Top 40 Hits.* New York: Billboard Books, 1992.

———. *Pop Hits 1940–1954.* Menomonee Falls, Wis.: Record Research, 1994.

———. *Top Pop Singles 1955–1996.* Menomonee Falls, Wis.: Record Research, 1997.

Periodicals

"Allan Sherman Dips into Disk, Movie Production." *Billboard,* October 19, 1963, p. 2.

"Alvin Gets Prexy Call." *Billboard,* August 1960, p. 8.

"Alvin Plunges into Side Lines." *Billboard,* April 6, 1963, p. 16.

"'Baby Talk' Clicks for Jan and Dean." *Billboard,* August 31, 1959, p. 20.

Baker, Glenn A. "Pop Schlock: A Guide to Tasteless Records." *Goldmine,* October 24, 1986, pp. 32, 64.

Benjamin, Sandy Street. "Joe South: Games People Play." *Goldmine,* March 8, 1991, pp. 54, 140, 185.

———. "Paul Petersen." *Goldmine,* January 30, 1998, pp. 14, 15.

———. "The Rivingtons: The Papas of Oom-Mow-Mow." *Goldmine,* September 22, 1989, pp. 115, 118.

"Bob McFadden Hits Charts with Mummy." *Billboard,* September 7, 1959, p. 18.

"Boone Sued for Using Cartoon Figure Voice." *Billboard,* March 2, 1963, p. 3.

Brown, Tony. "Conceited? They always say that when you're successful, says Lonnie Donegan." *Melody Maker,* May 4, 1957, p. 3.

Browne, David. "Where Are They Now? Dr. Hook and the Medicine Show." *Rolling Stone,* September 10. 1987.

Cafarelli, Carl. "One Hit Wonder: Barry Mann." *Goldmine,* December 30, 1988.

"The Caroling Dogs of Copenhagen." *Life,* December 19, 1955, pp. 93, 94.

"Charlie Ryan Hip with 'Hot Rod Lincoln.'" *Billboard,* May 4, 1960, p. 26.

"Cheech Marin Working on Multi-projects." *Connecticut Post,* August 25, 1997, p. A5.

"Chipmunks' Daddy Says No Renewal at Liberty." *Billboard,* April 20, 1963, p. 3.

"'Chipmunks' Sue 'The Doctor.'" *Billboard,* February 2, 1959.

Cole, Gloria. "One Nutty Show." *Connecticut Post,* February 28, 1997, pp. E1, E6.

Cooney, Christine M. "Weird Al Just Wants to Have Fun." *Connecticut Post,* May 24, 1996, pp. E1, E3.

Cooper, B. Lee. "Bear Cats, Chipmunks, and Slip-In Mules: The 'Answer Song' in Contemporary American Recordings, 1950-1985." *Popular Music & Society,* Fall 1988, pp. 57-77.

———. "Sultry Songs as High Humor." *Popular Music & Society,* Spring 1993, pp. 71–85.

"Country Comic Minnie Pearl" [obituary]. *Connecticut Post,* March 5, 1996.

Dawborn, Bob. "The Scots-Born Irish Hill-Billy from London." *Melody Maker,* May 10, 1956, p. 11.

Dawson, Jim. "The Cadets and the Jacks: Meanwhile Back in the Jungle." *Goldmine,* April 26, 1996, pp. 54ff.

Domingues, Robert. "Cheech Rides High with 'Chum' Roles," *Connecticut Post,* April 20, 1998, p. D4.

Dowd, Maureen. "Sinners and Spinners on the Equator." *New York Times,* March 25, 1998, p. A23.

Eden, Dawn. "Brian Hyland: Bikinis, Gypsies, Jokers and Stooges." *Goldmine,* April 15, 1994, pp. 63-66, 195.

Fink, Stu. "One Hit Wonders: Napoleon XIV." *Goldmine,* December 30, 1988, p. 15.

———. "Rolf Harris." *Goldmine,* December 30, 1988, p. 20

———. "The Pipkins." *Goldmine,* December 30, 1988, p. 74.

"Frankie Yankovic, 83; Accordion-Playing Polka King" [obituary]. *Connecticut Post,* October 15, 1998, p. B5.

"Grandpa Jones, 84; 'Hee Haw' Character" [obituary]. *Connecticut Post,* February 20, 1998, p. C5.

Grendysa, Peter. "The Coasters: Hall of Fame Profiles." *Goldmine,* February 26, 1988, p. 10.

———. "One Hit Wonders: The Fendermen." *Goldmine,* December 30, 1988, p. 12.

Grimes, William. "Tiny Tim, Singer, Dies at 64; Flirted, Chastely, with Fame" [obituary]. *New York Times,* December 2, 1996, p. B10.

———. "Lou Gottlieb, 72, the Bass Player for 1960's Folk Trio Limeliters" [obituary]. *New York Times,* July 14, 1996.

Heatley, Michael. "Rolf Harris: Kangaroo Court Jester." *Goldmine,* October 13, 1995, pp. 189, 190.

Hill, Randal C. "The Big Bopper: The Short, Happy Life of Jiles Perry Richardson." *Goldmine,* March 13, 1987, p. 22.

———. "One Hit Wonders: The Hollywood Argyles." *Goldmine,* December 30, 1988, p. 20.

———. "Bobby 'Boris' Pickett." *Goldmine,* December 30, 1988, p. 25.

Holden, Stephen. "Roger Miller, Quirky Country Singer and Songwriter Is Dead at 56" [obituary]. *New York Times,* October 27, 1992, p. B4.

———. "Minnie Pearl Is Dead at 83; Star of 'The Grand Ole Opry'" [obituary]. *New York Times,* March 6, 1996.

"Irving Gordon, 81; Wrote 'Unforgettable'" [obituary]. *Connecticut Post,* December 3, 1996.

Kidd, Tom. "Tiny Tim Tiptoes Again." *Goldmine,* September 21, 1990, pp. 40, 60.

Knight, Tim. "Big Bopper: From Head Waiter to Rock 'N' Roll Hero." *Goldmine,* February 10, 1989, pp. 12, 13, 29.

"Liberty Preps Chipmunk Push for TV Show Tie-In." *Billboard,* September 25, 1961, p. 4.

Miller, Billy. "The Papa Oom Mow Mow Whoa Dad Bird Dance Beat of the Trashmen." *Kicks,* no. 7, 1992, pp. 6–16.

Miller, Chuck. "Alien Nation: The Story of Dickie Goodman." *Goldmine,* September 12, 1997, pp. 144ff.

———. "Ray Stevens and His Streaks of Success." *Goldmine,* April 9, 1999, pp. 40ff.

Montgomery, Scott. "The Invisible Randy Newman: The Metric Music to Reprise Years (1960–95)." *Goldmine,* September 1, 1995, pp. 17–24, 26ff.

Myers, Gary. "Dante and the Evergreens." *Goldmine,* October 13, 1995, pp. 196, 198.

"Night Harbingers of Horror." *Life,* May 26, 1958, pp. 63–65.

"Novelty LP a Riot in Atlanta." *Billboard,* October 27, 1962, p. 1.

Pareles, Jon. "With Dues Long Paid, Musicians Reap Awards." *New York Times,* February 28, 1998, pp. B9, B18.

———. "Carl Perkins, Dies at 65; Rockabilly Pioneer Wrote 'Blue Suede Shoes'" [obituary]. *New York Times,* January 20, 1998, p. B12.

Pike, Jon R. "The Trashmen: The Bird Is the Word." *Goldmine,* September 22, 1989, p. 115.

"The Popular People Eater." *Life,* June 30, 1958, p. 89.

Saxon, Wolfgang. "Louis Jones, 84, Country Music's Grandpa" [obitutary]. *New York Times,* February 21, 1998, p. B20.

Scharnott, Jim. "Salutes to Stevens, Sherman, and Nervous Norvus." *Goldmine,* November 21, 1986, p. 73.

Scherman, Tony. "Country." *American Heritage,* November 1994, pp. 38–40, 42ff.

Scutt, Roger. "Roger Miller C & W King." *Billboard,* April 24, 1965, p. 4.

"Sherman Says No to TV Till After Moore Show." *Billboard,* December 15, 1962, p. 5.

Slim, Almost. "Bobby Marchan: Larry Darnell Was His Idol." *Goldmine,* September 25, 1987, pp. 88, 92.

———. "Clarence 'Frogman' Henry: New Orleans Is His Home." *Goldmine,* May 22, 1987, pp. 16, 73.

"'Space Girl' Contest Hot." *Billboard,* February 2, 1959, p. 2.

"Squirrels Everywhere at Once" *Billboard,* October 1959, p. 8.

"Squirrels Score with Solid Smash: Uh! Oh!" *Billboard,* November 30, 1959, p. 21.

Tamarkin, Jeff. "Allan Sherman: Folk Singer, Celebrity, Nut." *Goldmine,* September 11, 1987, pp. 22, 75.

———. "Flying Saucer Rock 'N' Roll: A Space Odyssey." *Goldmine,* February 12, 1988, pp. 22, 30, 129.

———. "One Hit Wonders: The New Vaudeville Band." *Goldmine,* December 30, 1988, p. 12.

———. "Roger Miller: King of the Country-Pop Road." *Goldmine,* May 22, 1987, pp. 16, 68.

———. "Roger Miller, 'King of the Road,' Dead at 56" [obituary]. *Goldmine,* November 27, 1992, p. 7.

———. "Vanilla Nice: Boone in the U.S.A." *Goldmine,* February 22, 1991, pp. 8–14, 18, 127.

———. "White House Funnies: Presidential Satire Records." *Goldmine,* November 18, 1988, pp. 27, 83–85.

Tauber, Peter. "The Cynic Who Never Soured." *New York Times Magazine,* November 2, 1997, pp. 50, 51.

"Teen Tunes out of Time." *Life,* March 5, 1956, pp. 127, 128.

Thompson, Dave. "The Footnote Archives [Lonnie Donegan]." *Goldmine,* September 12, 1997, p. 36.

"Tiny Tim Buried with Tulips, Ukulele." *Connecticut Post,* December 5, 1996, p. A8.

"T-R-A-N-S-F-U-S-I-O-N . . ." *Life,* June 11, 1956, p. 137.

Wainwright, Loudon, III. "Stones and Spice. And Bob." *New York Times,* January 16, 1998, p. A25.

Web sites to check out for novelty songs

http://www.drdemento.com
This is the official Dr. Demento web site.

http://www.execpc.com/~brikrn
Novelty record collector Brian Korn lists his collection in alphabetical order.

http://3rdSE.com
Picture sleeve collector Don McLaughlin displays a portion of his extensive collection, including many novelty records.

http://www.oldiesmusic.com/links.htm
Web site features biographical information on many rock recording artists, including some of the better-known novelty artists.

Discography

Recommended Listening

All titles are on CD, unless otherwise noted.

Introduction

The Best of Louis Jordan. MCA Records MCAD-4079.

Musical Depreciation Revue: The Spike Jones Anthology. Rhino Records R2 71574 DRC21112 (double CD).

Songs and More Songs by Tom Lehrer. Rhino Records R2 72776.

Chapter 1: Flying Saucers and Singing Chipmunks

Dickie Goodman and Friends: Greatest Fables. Hot Productions HTCD 33205-2.

Buchanan and Goodman: Politically Correct? Lunartick Records LT000 (double CD).

The Very Best of the Chipmunks with David Seville. EMI CDP 7 91684 2.

The Very Best of Lou Monte. Taragon Records TARCD-1030.

Sheb Wooley: The Purple People Eater. Bear Family Records BCD 16149-AH.

Sheb Wooley: Wild and Wooley, Big Unruly Me. Bear Family Records BCD 16150-AH.

Hellooo Baby! The Best of the Big Bopper 1954–1959. Rhino Records R2 70164.

Chapter 2: Soul Humor

Voodoo Jive: The Best of Screamin' Jay Hawkins. Rhino Records R2 70947.

The Coasters: 50 Coastin' Classics. Rhino Records R2 71090 (double CD).

The Best of the Cadillacs. Rhino Records R2 70955.

The Olympics' All-Time Greatest Hits. Sandstone D233078-2.

The Minit Records Story. EMI, Legends Series E2 30879 (double CD, contains all charting singles of Ernie K-Doe).

Lee Dorsey Wheelin' and Dealin': The Definitive Collection. Arista Records 18980.

The Best of Rufus Thomas. Rhino Records R2 72490.

The Very Best of Shirley Ellis. Taragon Records TARCD-1005.

Chapter 3: Parody, the Sincerest Form of Flattery

Stan Freberg. Collectors Series Capitol Records CDP7916272.

My Son, the Greatest: The Best of Allan Sherman. Rhino Records R2 75771.

The Four Preps. Collectors Series Capitol Records CDP7916262.

"Weird Al" Yankovic's Greatest Hits. Way Moby 32008-2.

Chapter 4: Monsters, Madmen and Other One-Hit Weirdos

Halloween Hits. Rhino Records R2 70535

Napoleon XIV: The Second Coming. Rhino Records R2 72402.

The Royal Guardsmen Anthology. One Way Records S21-18147.

Batmania: Songs Inspired by the Batman TV Series. Varese Sarabande VSD-5821.

The Best of Peter and Gordon. Rhino Records R2 70748-2.

Chapter 5: Ray Stevens and Roger Miller: Kings of Sixties Novelty

Ray Stevens: Ahab the Arab. Special Music Company 838 169-2.

Ray Stevens Greatest Hits. MCA Records MCAD-5918.

Roger Miller: King of the Road. Bear Family Records BCD15477.

Chapter 6: Bring on the Comics!

The Jazzy Old Philosopher. Red Dragon JK 57756.

Jerry Lewis. Collectors Series Capitol Records CDD7931962.

Cheech and Chong: Greatest Hit. Warner Bros. 3614.

Chapter 7: Country Corn and Funny Folk

America's Song Butchers: The Weird World of Homer and Jethro. Razor & Tie RE 2130-2.

Dr. Demento's Country Corn. Rhino Records R2 72125.

Jim Stafford. Polydor 833 073-2.

The Very Best of the Chad Mitchell Trio. Vanguard 79494-2.

One Man Guy: The Best of Loudon Wainwright 1982–1986. Music Club MCCD 166.

Chapter 8: Rock Laughs at Itself

The Essential Bobby Bare. RCA 67405-2.

Flabby Road: 26 Of The All Time Greatest Beatle Novelty Songs. (Vols. I & II). Orange Records OR4444 and OR4445.

The Best of Larry Williams. Ace Specialty CDCH 917.

The Best of the Marcels. Rhino Records R2 70953.

Chapter 9: A Zany Little Christmas

Bah! Humbug! Laserlight 12 777.

Bummed Out Christmas! Rhino Records R2 70912.

Dr. Demento Presents The Greatest Christmas Novelty CD of All Time. Rhino Records R2 75755.

Hillbilly Holiday. Rhino Records R2 70195.

Legends of Christmas Past: A Rock 'n' R&B Holiday Collection. EMI 7-99987-2.

Rockin' Little Christmas. MCA Records MCAD-25084.

Collections and Anthologies

Dr. Demento 20th Anniversary Collection: The Greatest Novelty Records of All Time. R2 70743 (double CD).

Dr. Demento 25th Anniversary Collection: More of the Greatest Novelty Records of All Time. Rhino R2 72124 (double CD).

Silly Songs. K-Tel 30362.

Wacky Weirdos. K-Tel 30372.

Your Hit Parade: Golden Goofers. Time-Life HPD-40.

Your Hit Parade: The Fun-Time '50s and '60s. Time-Life HPD-35.

Appendix

Sixty-five of the Best Novelty Songs of the Rock Era

(listed in alphabetical order according to artist)

"The All American Boy" ....Bobby Bare

"Shaving Cream" ....Benny Bell

"Hit Record" ....Brook Benton

"Chantilly Lace" ....The Big Bopper

"The Flying Saucer (Pts. 1 & 2)" ....Buchanan and Goodman

"Cheeseburger in Paradise" ....Jimmy Buffet

"A Boy Named Sue" ....Johnny Cash

"Black Denim Trousers and Motorcycle Boots" ....The Cheers

"Rubber Biscuit" ....The Chips

"Yakety Yak," "Charlie Brown,"
　　　　　"Shoppin' for Clothes," "D.W. Washburn" ....The Coasters

"Don't Go Near the Eskimos" ....Ben Colder

"I Want My Baby Back" ....Jimmy Cross

"Rusty Chevrolet" ....Da Yoopers

"The Leader of the Laundromat" ....The Detergents

"The Cover of Rolling Stone" ....Dr. Hook and the Medicine Show

"Does Your Chewing Gum Lose Its Flavor" ....Lonnie Donegan

"My Boomerang Won't Come Back" ....Charlie Drake

"The Clapping Song" ....Shirley Ellis

"Grandma Got Run Over by a Reindeer" ....Elmo and Patsy

"The Big Draft" ....The Four Preps

"Wun'erful, Wun'erful (Side-uh One and Side-uh Two)" ....Stan Freberg

"The Ballad of Irving" ....Frank Gallop

"The Last Blast of the Blasted Bugler" ....Sonny Gianotta

"Junk Food Junkie" ....Larry Groce

"No, I Don't Wanna Do Dat" ....The Happy Schnapps Combo

"I Put a Spell on You" ....Screamin' Jay Hawkins

"Psycho" ....Bobby Hendricks

"Hide and Go Seek, Pt. 2" ....Bunker Hill

"Alley Oop" ....The Hollywood Argyles

"The Battle of Kookamonga" ....Homer and Jethro

"Stranded in the Jungle"..The Jayhawks/The Cadets

"Mother-in-Law"..Ernie K-Doe

"The Old Philosopher" ....Eddie Lawrence

"Creeque Alley"...The Mamas and the Papas

"Who Put the Bomp" ....Barry Mann

"There's Something on Your Mind, Part 2" ....Bobby Marchan

"Wolf Creek Pass" ....C. W. McCall

"Lizzie Borden" ....The Chad Mitchell Trio

"Queen of the House" ....Jody Miller

"Dang Me," "King of the Road"...Roger Miller

"They're Coming to Take Me Away, Ha, Haaa" ....Napoleon XIV

"Deteriorata"..The National Lampoon

"Transfusion" ....Nervous Norvus

"Short People" ....Randy Newman

"Monster Mash"..Bobby "Boris" Pickett

"Beep Beep" ....The Playmates

"Another Puff"...Jerry Reed

"Papa-Oom-Mow-Mow"..The Rivingtons

"Smokey Joe's Cafe" ....The Robins

"Cinderella" ....Jack Ross

"Hello Muddah, Hello Fadduh!" ....Allan Sherman

"Wildwood Weed" ....Jim Stafford

"Pink Shoelaces" ....Dodie Stevens

"Ahab the Arab," "Gitarzan" ....Ray Stevens

"Tip-Toe Through the Tulips" ....Tiny Tim

"Surfin' Bird"..The Trashmen

"The Little Space Girl" ....Jesse Lee Turner

"Dead Skunk"..Loudon Wainwright III

"Christmas Wrapping"..The Waitresses

"Smells Like Nirvana" ...."Weird Al" Yankovic

Index

Abboud, Mona, 210
ABC-Paramount, 214
Adderley, Cannonball, 19
Addotta, Kip, 198
Adler, Lou, 103, 146, 217
"Ahab the Arab," 121, 122, 123, 125–126, 204
"Ain't Got No Home," 37
"Ain't Nobody Here But Us Chickens," 4, 38
"(Ain't That) Just Like Me," 50
Aldon Music, 82, 218
Alfi and Harry, 14
Allen, Steve, 19, 137
Allen, Sue, 23
"The All American Boy," 25, 179, 180, 228
The Alley Cats, 64
"Alley Oop," 101, 102–103, 105, 120
"Alligator Wine," 42
Allison, Jerry, 219, 221
"All I Want for Christmas Is My Two Front Teeth," 197, 198
"Along Came Jones," 49, 52, 123
Alpert, Herb, 103, 217
"Alvin for President," 17
The Alvin Show, 16, 17–18
"Ambrose (Part Five)," 137
"Amos Moses," 163, 165
Ancell, Bob, 12
"Another Puff," 164, 165
Any News From Nashville?, 155
"Ape Call," 28–29
Appel, Dave, 90
The Applejacks, 90
Argo, 54
Arvee, 53, 54
Asher, Peter, 112
Atco, 47
Atkins, Chet, 127, 154, 158, 163, 180
Atlantic Records, 47
"At Smokey Joe's Cafe," 46–47
"The Auctioneer," 156
Autry, Gene, 197, 201
Avalon, Frankie, 222–223
Axton, Estelle, 192
Aykroyd, Dan, 149–150

"Baby Sittin' Boogie," 21
Bacharach, Burt, 88
The Bachelors, 80
Backus, Jim, 136–137
"Bad Man Blunder," 169

"Bad News," 97
Bagdasarian, Adam, 17
Bagdasarian, Ross, Sr.
    See Seville, David
Bagdasarian, Ross, Jr., 15, 18
Baker, Mickey, 41
"The Ballad of Irving," 100
"The Banana Boat Story," 12
Banashak, Joe, 56
The Barbarians, 189
Barber, Chris, 107
Bare, Bobby, 7, 25, 179–180, 228–229
Barnaby, 123
Barnes and Barnes, 8
Barnum, H.B., 100
The Barron Knights, 80
Bartholomew, Dave, 229, 230
"Basketball Jones," 146
"The Battle of Kookomonga," 155
The Beach Boys, 204
"Beans and Cornbread," 4, 38
"Bear Cat," 61
The Beatles, 49, 181–182, 185, 188, 194
Beaumont, Jimmie, 187
Beck, 231
Beck, Jackson, 83
"Beep Beep," 157, 221, 222
The Bees, 229
Bell, Benny, 117
Bellard, Bruce, 78, 81
The Belmonts, 35–36
Belushi, John, 149–150
Belvin, Jesse, 52
Bendix, Ralf, 21
Bennett, Joe, 24, 25
Benton, Brook, 193–194
Berman, Shelly, 134
Bernal, Gil, 46–47
Berry, Chuck, 6, 44, 229, 230
Berry, Jan, 216–217
Berry, Richard, 45–46, 104
"Besame Mucho," 49, 181
Big Ben, 29
The Big Bopper, 32–36, 60, 215
"The Big Bopper Show," 33
"Big Bopper's Wedding," 35
"Big Boy Pete," 54, 104
"The Big Draft," 79, 80
"Big Name Button," 24
"Bird Bath," 97
"The Bird's the Word," 55, 96

Bizet, Georges, 168
"Black Denim Trousers," 23, 24, 224
"Black Slacks," 24
Blanc, Mel, 101, 225, 226
"The Blob," 88
"Blue Moon" (The Marcels), 189, 190
The Blues Brothers, 149–150, 151
"Blue Suede Shoes," 25
Bob B. Soxx and the Blue Jeans, 64
Bobby Bare Sings Lullabys, Legends and Lies, 228–229
The Bob Rivers Comedy Corporation, 208
Boise, Rod, 173
Bond, Johnny, 153, 157–158
Bono, Sonny, 183
Boogaloo and His Gallant Crew, 50
Boone, Pat, 225, 226
"Born in East L.A.," 148
Bowman, Don, 162
Boyd, Jimmy, 198
"A Boy Named Sue," 212, 227, 228
Bradley, Owen, 158, 200
Brennan, Walter, 143
Brent Records, 102
Bright, Ronnie, 192
"Brontosaurus Stomp," 78
Brooks, Randy, 207
The Brothers Four, 170
Brown, Julie, 193
Brownsville Station, 89
Bryant, Boudleaux, 187
Bryant, Felice, 187
Buchanan, Bill, 9–12, 13, 15, 27, 178, 184, 204
"Buchanan and Goodman on Trial," 11–12
The Buena Vistas, 60
Buffet, Jimmy, 224
Bullet, 31
Burland, Alexander "Sascha," 19
Burns, George, 143
Burns, Horace J. "Happy," 126–127
Burns, Kenneth, 127, 153.
    See also Homer and Jethro
Burrows, Tony, 118
Butler, Artie, 50
Butler, Daws, 69
The Button Down Mind, 134
The Byrds, 194
Byrnes, Edd, 26, 27

The Cadets, 38–39, 40
The Cadillacs, 50, 51, 55, 201
Cameo Records, 90, 91
Canned Heat, 18
Cannon, Sarah Ophelia.
    See Pearl, Minnie
Capitol Records, 66, 68, 73, 78, 80,
    81, 84, 116, 120, 136, 139–140,
    156, 163, 179, 183, 190, 196,
    198, 209, 210, 212
Capizzi, Lenny, 91
Caprice Records, 25
The Carefrees, 181, 182
Carlin, George, 145
Carlson, Harry, 180
Carney, Art, 139
Carroll, Earl, 50
Cash, Johnny, 7, 164, 212, 227, 228
Cavaliere, Felix, 54, 184
"A Certain Girl," 56, 57
The Chad Mitchell Trio, 170–173
The Challengers, 52
Champion, Harry, 112
Chaney, Lon, 204
"Chantilly Lace," 34, 35, 36, 215
Charles, Don, 202, 203
"Charlie Brown," 44–45, 49
"The Chase," 32
Chase, Lincoln, 62, 63
Checker, 54
Checker, Chubby, 7, 215–216
Cheech and Chong, 145–148, 149
The Cheers, 23–24
"Cheeseburger in Paradise," 224
Cher, 183
Chess, 219
"Chinese Rock and Egg Roll," 137
Chipmunk Punk, 18
The Chipmunks, 5, 14, 15–18, 32, 143,
    201–202, 215, 221, 222–223
"The Chipmunk Song," 17, 18,
    19, 201
The Chips, 37, 43, 149
Chong, Thomas, 145–148, 149
Christie, Susan, 116
"Christmas at Ground Zero," 211
"Christmas Is Coming Twice
    This Year," 211
The Christmas Jug Band, 210
"Christmas Wrapping," 210
"Christy Christmas," 200
"Chug A Lug," 128
"Church Key," 97
"Cinderella," 138–139
The City Slickers, 4–5, 212
"The Clapping Song," 62, 64
Clark, Dick, 103, 185, 194, 215
"The Class," 215

Claudra, 28
Clifford, Buzz, 21
Clooney, Rosemary, 14
"Close the Door," 88
"Clothes Line," 50
The Clovers, 51, 52
The Clowns, 55, 57, 58
The Coasters, 4, 24, 32, 39, 43–45,
    46, 47–51, 52, 53, 54, 55,
    59, 120, 121, 123, 181, 185,
    204, 206
Cobb, Ed, 78, 81
Cochran, Eddie, 6, 179
Colder, Ben, 32, 65, 76–77.
    See also Wooley, Sheb
Collins, Aaron, 38, 39
Colpix, 223
Columbia, 14, 19, 40, 174, 196, 227
"Come On-a My House, 14
Como, Perry, 223
"Conscience," 223
"Convoy," 167
Convy, Bert, 23
Cooper, B. Lee, 9
Cooper, Marty, 100
Cornish, Gene, 184
Cosby, Bill, 141–143
"The Cover of Rolling Stone,"
    178, 195, 196
"Cowboy Boots," 101
The Cowboy Church Sunday
    School, 9, 15
Cox, Wally, 139
Craft, Paul, 229
Creedence Clearwater Revival, 42
"Creeque Alley," 188–189
The Crickets, 219, 221
Crier, Arthur, 55
Criner, John, 52
Cropper, Steve, 149, 150
Cross, Jimmy, 82–83
"The Crusher," 97
The Crypt-Kickers, 92
Crystal, Billy, 145
"The Curley Shuffle," 145
The Curls, 218
Curtis, King, 47, 48–49, 50, 204
Cymbal, Johnny, 187, 192

Dabner, Debbie, 179
Daily, Pappy, 35
Daly, Tyne, 70
Dana, Bill, 137–138
"Dancin' Fool," 192
"Dang Me," 121, 128, 131
Daniels, Charlie, 163
Dante, David, 225
Dante, Ron, 82

Dante and the Evergreens, 102,
    103–104
Darian, Fred, 99
Darin, Bobby, 50, 109, 178–179, 218
Darnell, Larry, 58
Darren, James, 223
Davis, Jack, 227
Davis, Skeeter, 208
Davis, Willie, 39
The Davis Sisters, 208
Da Yoopers, 177, 209, 231
"Dead Skunk," 174
"Dear Elvis," 178
Decca, 107, 127, 140, 181, 200, 201
Dee, Tommy, 187
Dees, Rick, 192
"Delaware," 223
"Delicious!," 137
DeLong, Al, 99
Demon Records, 52
Denver, John, 173
Denver, Boise and Johnson, 173
Derek. See Cymbal, Johnny
"Der Fuehrer's Face," 4
The Detergents, 82
"Deteriorata," 83
"Detroit City No. 2," 77
"The Devil Went Down to
    Georgia," 153
Diamond, 28
The Diamonds, 191–192
Dickens, Little Jimmy, 158–160
Dicky Doo and the Don'ts, 24–25
Diddley, Bo, 7, 36, 188, 191, 219, 220
"Dinner with Drac," 90–91
Dinning, Mark, 185, 187
Dion, 35–36
"Disco Duck," 192
The Dixie Drifter, 188
"Does Your Chewing Gum Lose
    Its Flavor on the Bedpost
    Overnight?," 107, 109, 121
Domino, Fats, 12
Donegan, Lonnie, 107–109, 218
Donohue, Patty, 210
"Don't Go Near the Eskimos,"
    76–77
"Don't Let the Rain Come Down
    (Crooked Little Man)," 170
"Don't You Just Know It," 57
Dootone, 11
Dor, 91
Do-Re-Mi Children's Choir, 169
Dore Records, 148, 217
Dorsey, Lee, 56, 60–61
Dot Records, 28, 29, 109, 225
The Dovells, 60
Dowell, Joe, 227

"Down Home Girl," 50
"Down in Mexico," 47
Downs, Hugh, 21
Drake, Charlie, 109
Drake, Guy, 164
Drake, Jimmy, 28–29
Draper, Rusty, 224
Dr. Demento, 2, 7–8, 83, 84, 85, 93, 117, 177, 207, 231
Dr. Hook and the Medicine Show, 178, 195–196
The Drifters, 42, 51, 59
Dr. Jive, 59
Drowty, Don, 103
Dub Records, 190
Dudley, 100
Dudley, Dave, 101, 157
Dunn, Donald, 149, 150
Dunn, Lloyd, 210
Durante, Jimmy, 143
Durgom, Bullets, 73
D.W. Washburne," 50–51
The Dyna-Sores, 102, 103

"Eat It," 84, 85
Ebb, Fred, 21
Eddy, Duane, 54
The Edsels, 190
Eisler, Ed. See Lawrence, Eddie, 135
El Clod, 100
Elliott, Don, 19
Ellis, Shirley, 25, 59, 62–64
Elmo and Patsy, 206, 207
Ely, Jack, 104
Embee, 29
EMI, 181
Epic, 207
Era Records, 99
Ernie (Sesame Street), 106
Evans, Ernest. See Checker, Chubby
Evans, Paul, 218
The Everly Brothers, 6
Everybody Loves a Nut, 227
"Everybody's Crying," 187
"Everyone Was There," 185

Feature Records, 33
The Fendermen, 100
Ferrera, Peter, 93
The Fireflies, 24
Fire Records, 57
The First Family, 75, 134
The Five Blobs, 88
"The Flying Saucer," 10–11, 15, 27, 31, 184
"The Flying Saucer Goes West," 12
"Flying Saucer the Second," 12
"The Folk Singer," 168

The Fontaine Sisters, 200
Foray, June, 69
The Four Jokers, 28
The Four Preps, 78–81
Fowley, Kim, 101–102
Foxx, Charlie, 62
Foxx, Inez, 62
"Framed," 46
Fraternity Records, 180
Frazier, Dallas, 101, 102–103
Frazier, Joe, 171–173
Freberg, Stan, 5, 7, 65–70, 83, 178, 194, 197, 200–201, 209–210, 231
Freed, Alan, 11, 42, 194
Freeman, Ernie, 103
Frees, Paul, 5
Fretone, 192
Fries, William. See McCall, C.W.
"Frogg," 170
The Funk Brothers, 62

Gallop, Frank, 100
Gardner, Carl, 46, 47, 48, 49, 51, 52
Garfield, Gil, 23
Garfunkel, Art, 217
Garpax, 92, 93
Gas, Sir Frederick, 5
Gaudio, Bob, 24
Geld, Gary, 214
Gernhard, Phil, 161
"Get a Job," 178, 189
Gilbert and Sullivan, 74
"Gimme Dat Ding," 118
Ginsberg, Arnie, 216
Gioanotta, Sonny, 99–100
"Gitarzan," 122, 123, 126
Glazer, Tom, 169
Goffin, Gerry, 190
Go, Johnny, Go, 51
Goldner, George, 11
"Goodbye Cruel World," 223
"Good Lovin'," 54
Goodman, Richard "Dickie," 6, 9–13, 15, 27, 178, 204
Gordon, Barry, 198–200, 201
Gordon, Irving, 223
Gordy, Berry, Jr., 185
Gordy, Robert. See Kayli, Bob
Gottlieb, Lou, 169–170
Gourdine, Anthony, 40
Granahan, Gerry, 24–25
Grand, 40
"Grandma Got Run Over by a Reindeer," 206, 207, 210
Graph, Tom, 217
Green, Jerome, 219, 220
Greenaway, Roger, 118
"Green Chritma," 197, 209–210

"The Green Door," 88
Greenfield, Howard "Hal," 12, 103–104, 184
Green Jellÿ, 193
Gregory, Enoch, 188
Griffith, Andy, 9, 136
Groce, Larry, 176, 224
Guard, Dave, 169
Gunter, Cornell, 49, 51
Guy, Billy, 45, 47, 48, 50, 51, 52

Hackett, Buddy, 137
Hall, Rene, 103
The Halos, 55, 192
Hamblen, Stuart, 15
Hamilton, Ralph "Waldo," 47
Hanover-Signature Records, 19
Hansen, Barry. See Dr. Demento
The Happy Schnapps Combo, 177
Harp, Cornelius "Nini," 189
Harris, Kent, 50
Harris, Phil, 87–88
Harris, Rolf, 87, 109–111
Harrison, George, 146
Harrison, Thurston, 54
"Harry the Hairy Ape," 121, 122, 123
Hart, Lorenz, 189
Hawkins, Screamin' Jay, 40–43
Haynes, Henry, 153.
See also Homer and Jethro
"Hello Muddah, Hello Fadduh," 74–75
Hendricks, Bobby, 58–59
Henry, Clarence "Frogman," 37
Henson, Jim, 106
"Here Comes the Judge," 59–60
Herman's Hermits, 111–112
"Hey Schoolgirl," 217
Hickey, Ersel, 170
Hicks, Dan, 210
"Hide and Go Seek," 61
Hill, Bunker, 61
Hill, Tiny, 157
Hillman, Chris, 194
Hinckley, Don, 137
"Hit Record," 194
Hodges, Eddie, 218–219
Holden, Ron, 206
Holly, Buddy, 32, 35, 35–36, 219, 221
Holly, Glenell, 179
Holly, Janell, 179
The Hollytones, 211, 231
The Holly Twins, 179
The Hollywood Argyles, 102, 103, 104
Homer and Jethro, 65, 77, 153–155, 168, 184, 200
The Homestead Act, 207

"Hoppy, Gene and Me," 101
Horrible Records, 116
Horstman, Dorothy, 152
"Hot Rod Lincoln," 32, 153, 157, 158
"Hot Rod Race," 157
Hudson, Bob, 148
Hudson and Landry, 148
Hughes, Leon, 47, 49
Humphrey, Phil, 100
Hyland, Brian, 212, 213–214

"Idol with the Golden Head," 48
"I Dreamed of a Hill-Billy
      Heaven," 188
"I Got Stoned and I Missed It," 162
"I Lost on Jeopardy," 85
"I Love Onions," 116
"I'm Gonna Knock on Your Door,"
      218–219
"I'm Gonna Lasso Santa Claus,"
      200, 201
"I'm Henry VIII, I Am," 112
"I'm Little, But I'm Loud," 158, 159
The Imperials, 40
"Impossible," 137
"I Must Be Dreaming," 46
Ingle, Red, 212–213
Ingraham, Marvin, 78
Inside Shelly Berman, 134
"In the Middle of the House,"
      224–225
"The Invasion," 12, 184
"I Put a Spell on You," 40–43
The Irish Rovers, 173
"I Saw Mommy Kissing Santa
      Claus," 198
"Itsy Bitsy Teenie Weenie Yellow
      Polkadot Bikini," 7, 82, 213, 214
"I've Got You Under My Skin"
      (Freberg), 68
The Ivy Three, 104
"(I Wanna) Dance With the
      Teacher," 53
"I Want Elvis for Christmas," 178–179
"I Want My Baby Back," 82–83
"I Went to Your Wedding," 5, 137

Jack, Betty, 208
James and Kling, 208
Jan and Dean, 216–217
The Jayhawks, 38, 39, 40, 54
The Jaynetts, 62
Jennings, Waylon, 36
"Jeremiah Peabody's Poly
      Unsaturated Quick Dissolving
      Fast Action Pleasant Tasting
      Green and Purple Pills, 120–121
Jim Stafford, 162

"Jingle Bells (Laughing All the
      Way)" (St. Nick), 137
"Jingle Bells" (The Singing Dogs),
      202, 203
John, Robert, 25
"John and Marsha," 65, 66–67, 68
The Johnny Mann Singers, 143
Johnson, (Chad Mitchell Trio), 173
Johnson, Betty, 20–21
Johnson, Fred, 189
Johnson, James, 38, 39
Johnson, Plas, 31–32, 103
"The Jolly Green Giant," 54, 104
Jones, George, 36
Jones, Grandpa, 153
Jones, Spike, 3, 4–5, 65, 66, 137, 197,
      198, 201, 212, 231
Jones, Will "Dub," 39, 49, 50, 51
Jordan, Louis, 3–4, 5, 38
José Jimenez The Astronaut, 137–138
Jubilee, 137
Jump 'N The Saddle, 145
"Junk Food Junkie," 176, 224
Justis, Bill, 123

Kador, Ernest, Jr. See K-Doe, Ernie
Kapp, Dave, 213
Kapp Records, 213
Karloff, Boris, 92–93
Kay, Carol, 187
Kayli, Bob, 185
K-Doe, Ernie, 3, 8, 55, 56, 57, 60
Kermit the Frog, 106
Khaury, Herbert. See Tiny Tim
King, Carole, 146, 217–218
"King of the Road," 128, 130
King Records, 154, 180, 198
The Kingsmen, 54, 104–105
The Kingston Trio, 169
"King Tut," 143, 144, 145
Kirshner, Don, 178–179, 218
Klein, Alan, 113
Klein, Carole. See King, Carole
The Knack, 84
Kobluk, 173
"Kookie, Kookie (Lend Me Your
      Comb)," 27, 91
Koppelman, Charles, 104
Kosher Comedy, 117

"Lady Godiva," 112
Landesman, Rocco, 131–132
Landis, Jerry, 217
Landry, Ron, 148
LaPier, Cherilyn Sarkasian. See Cher
Larson, Glen, 78, 81
"The Last Blast of the Blasted
      Bugler," 99–100

Laurie, Linda, 137
Lavin, Christine, 177
Lawrence, Eddie, 135–136
Leader, 213
"Leader of the Laundromat," 82
Leander, Mike, 112
Lee, Brenda, 18, 200
Lee, Curtis, 55
Lee, Gary, 151
Lehrer, Tom, 5–6, 83, 95, 208, 231
Leiber, Jerry, 4, 7, 23–24, 39, 42,
      43–51, 52, 53, 59
Lennon, John, 182, 188
"Let's Think About Living," 187
"A Letter to the Beatles," 81
Levy, Jack, 54
Lewis, Jerry, 139–140
Lewis, Smiley "Laughing," 12
Liberty Records, 14, 17, 55
"Like a Surgeon," 85
The Limeliters, 169–170, 171
Little Anthony, 40
"The Little Blue Man," 21
"Little Boxes," 168–169
"Little Darlin'," 191–192
"Little Effin Annie," 158
"Little Ole Man (Uptight–
      Everything's Alright)," 141, 143
"Little Red Riding Hood," 35
Little Richard, 189
"The Little Space Girl," 19, 20, 21
"Lizzie Borden," 170, 171
Locorriere, Dennis, 178, 195
London Records, 28, 92, 181
"The Lone Teen Ranger," 217
Long, Shorty, 60
"Louie, Louie," 104
Love, Darlene, 146
"Love Potion Number Nine," 51, 52
"Loving You Has Made Me
      Bananas," 116
Lowe, Bernie, 90
Lowe, Jim, 88
Luft, Sid, 139
Luman, Bob, 187
Luniverse, 11
Lute Records, 101–102

Mabley, Moms, 143
MacNeille, Tress, 85
The Magistrates, 60
Maitland, Mike, 73
Mama Cass, 189
The Mamas and the Papas, 188–189
Manchester, Melissa, 83
Mann, Barry, 103–104, 190–192, 223
Mann, Kal, 215
The Marathons, 39, 54, 100

The Marcels, 189
Marchan, Bobby, 57–58
Marin, Richard "Cheech," 134, 145–148, 149
Markham, Pigmeat, 59, 60
Marks, Guy, 116
Marks, Johnny, 201–202
"Martian Boogie," 89
"Martian Hop," 88
Martin, George, 109, 181
Martin, Grady, 201
Martin, Steve, 134, 143–145
Masakela, Hugh, 194
Maxim, Arnold, 40–41
"May the Bird of Paradise Fly Up Your Nose," 159, 160
Maylow, Ron, 219
Mayorga, Lincoln, 78
MCA Records, 125, 148
McCall, C.W., 153, 157, 166–168
McCrae, John, 92
McFadden, Bob, 91
McGuinn, Jim/Roger, 171, 194
The McKenzie Brothers, 151, 208
McKuen, Rod, 91
McLean, Phil, 81
McPhatter, Clyde, 59
Meader, Vaughn, 75, 134
The Melodeers, 201
The Memphis Horns, 62
Menken, Shepard, 18
Mercury Records, 33, 35, 36, 120–121, 122, 128
Merrick, David, 70
Merritt, Neal, 160
MGM Records, 19, 31, 76–77, 161–162, 166, 198, 205
Miller, Elva, 116
Miller, Jody, 130
Miller, Mitch, 14
Miller, Roger, 7, 119, 121, 123, 126–133, 160, 162, 163
Minit Records, 55–56, 61
Minkin, Bill, 82
Mitchell, Chad, 171, 172, 173
"Mockingbird," 62
Modern, 38–39, 45
The Monkees, 51
Monroe, Vaughn, 224–225
"Monster Mash," 91, 103, 149, 204
"Monster's Holiday," 204
Monte, Lou, 21–23, 203
Monument, 122–123
Mooney, Art, 198
Moranis, Rick, 151, 208
"More Money for You and Me," 79, 80
"Mother-in-Law," 3, 55, 56–57

Motown, 54, 59–60, 62, 142, 185, 190
Moulton, Victor "Moulty," 189
"Moulty," 189
"The Mouse," 140, 141
"Mr. Bass Man," 192
"Mr. Custer," 98, 99, 109
Mrs. Miller, 116
"M.T.A. (Metropolitan Transit Authority of Boston)," 169
"Mule Skinner Blues," 100
"The Mummy," 91
Music, Lorenzo, 70
"My Bologna," 84
"My Boomerang Won't Come Back," 109
"My Ding-A-Ling," 229, 230
"My Girl Bill," 162
My Son, the Celebrity, 74
My Son, the Folk Singer, 13, 73–74, 168
My Son, the Nut, 74–75
"My Tambourine," 230

"Nag," 55, 192
"The Name Game," 59, 62, 63
Napoleon XIV, 6, 87, 93–95
The National Lampoon, 83
The Natural Seven, 212–213
The NBC Orchestra, 69
Nee, Bobby, 88
Nelson, Christine, 74
Nelson, Harry Edward, III. See Nilsson
Nelson, Sandy, 103
Nelson, Willie, 131
Newhart, Bob, 134
Newman, Randy, 212, 224
The New Vaudeville Band, 113
Nilsson, 223–224
"The Nitty Gritty," 62
The Nitwits, 221, 222
"No Chemise, Please," 24
"No, I Don't Wanna Do Dat," 177
Nolan, Bob, 97
Norvus, Nervous, 28, 29
The Novas, 97
NRC (National Recording Corporation), 120
Nunn, Robin Bobby, 46, 47, 48, 49, 51
"Nuttin' for Christmas," 9, 197, 198, 199, 200–201
The Nutty Squirrels, 19

Ode, 146
"Ode to the Little Brown Shack Out Back," 158

Oink, 207
O'Keefe, Johnny, 221
Okeh, 40–41, 42
Old Friends, 131
"The Old Home Filler-Up and Keep On-A-Truckin' Cafe," 166
"The Old Payola Roll Blues (Sides 1 & 2)," 194
"The Old Philosopher," 135
"Old Rivers," 143
The Olympics, 52–54, 55, 104
"One Dyin' and a Buryin'," 129, 130
"One Kiss," 48
"One Kiss Led to Another," 47
"On Top of Spaghetti," 169
"Open Up Your Heart (And Let The Sunshine In)," 15
Ostin, Mo, 115

Palmer, Earl, 103
"Papa-Oom-Mow-Mow," 55, 96
"Paperback Writer," 194
Pardo, Don, 85
Parker, John, 21
Parkway Records, 215
Parsons, Bill, 180
Paxton, Gary, 91–92, 93, 101–103, 104, 105, 120, 205
"Peanut Butter," 54, 100
Pearl, Minnie, 152–153
Pedrick, Bobby, Jr., 25
"Peek-A-Boo," 51
"Pepino's Friend Pasqual (The Italian Pussy-Cat)," 22–23
"Pepino the Italian Mouse," 21–22
Perkins, Carl, 25
Perkins, Joe, 158
Perry, Richard, 115
Peter and Gordon, 112
Peter, Paul & Mary, 170
Petersen, Paul, 218
Phillips, Bobby, 51
Phillips, John, 188–189
Phillips, Michelle, 188–189
Phillips, Sam, 61
Pickett, Bobby "Boris," 91–93, 118, 149, 204
Pike, Jim, 81
The Piltdown Men, 78
"Pink Shoelaces," 25
The Pipkins, 118
Pitney, Gene, 55
The Playmates, 157, 221, 222
"Please Christmas Don't Be Late," 17
"Please Mr. Johnson," 51
"The Pledge of Allegiance" (Skelton), 143
Pockriss, Lee, 82, 213

Pomus, Doc, 48
Ponchielli, 74
"The Popcorn Song," 156
Porter, Cole, 68
Prep Records, 120
The Preps, 81
Preston, Billy, 146
"The Pretty Little Dolly," 210
Price, Ray, 131
Professor Longhair, 55
"Psycho," 59
"Puddin' 'N' Tain," 64
Pugh, Mike, 171
Pullins, Leroy, 160
"The Puppet Song," 222–223
"The Purple People Eater," 7, 19,
    30, 31–32, 76, 204, 205, 224
"The Purple People Eater Meets the
    Witch Doctor," 35, 215

"Queen of the House," 130

Ragsdale, Harold Ray.
    See Stevens, Ray
"Rainbow Connection," 106
"Rama Lama Ding Dong," 190
Ramone, Phil, 50
Randazzo, Teddy, 40
The Ran-Dells, 88
Rappaport, Steve, 88
Ray, Ada, 62
RCA(-Victor), 19, 127, 128, 154,
    180, 202, 203
"The Real Thing," 230
"Real Wild Child," 221
Reed, Jerry, 18, 163–164, 165
Rendezvous Records, 103
Reprise Records, 115
The Return of Roger Miller, 127, 130
"The Return of the Red
    Baron," 105
The Revels, 97
Reynolds, Malvina, 168–169
Rhino, 43, 70, 95
Richardson, J. P. See The Big Bopper
"Ricky," 85
"Ringo, I Love You," 183
"Riot in Cell Block No. 9," 45–46
Ritter, Tex, 188
The Rivingtons, 47, 54–55, 96, 97
Robertson, Don, 31
The Robins, 4, 24, 39, 45–47, 55
Robinson, Floyd, 19–20
Rock, George, 198
"Rock-A-Bye Your Baby to a Dixie
    Melody" (Jerry Lewis), 139–140
"Rockin' Around the Christmas
    Tree," 200, 201

"Rockin' Pneumonia and Boogie
    Woogie Flu," 57
"Rock Island Line," 107, 218
Rodgers, Jimmy, 100
Rodgers, Richard, 71, 189
Rogers, Roy, 101
Rogers, Timmie ("Oh Yeah"), 141
Ross, Adam, 54
Ross, Jack, 138–139
Roubian, Bob, 156
Roulette Records, 11, 221
The Rovers, 173
The Royal Guardsmen, 105–106
The Royal Teens, 24
"Rubber Biscuit," 37, 43, 149
"Rubber Duckie," 106
Rubin, Don, 104
"Rudolph the Red-Nosed
    Reindeer," 17, 93, 197, 201–202
"Running Bear," 36
"Run Red Run," 49–50
Rusk, Jim, 210
Russell, Bobby, 168
Russell, Leon, 92
"Rusty Chevrolet," 208–209
Ryan, Charlie, 32, 157

"St. George and the Dragonet,"
    69, 201
St. Nick, 137
Sales, Soupy," 140, 141
"Sally, Go 'Round the Roses," 62
Samberg, Ben. See Bell, Benny
Samuels, Jerry. See Napoleon XIV
Santa and the Four Reindeer, 201
"Santa and the Purple People Eater,"
    204, 205
"Santa and the Satellite," 12, 204
"Santa Claus Is Watching You," 197
Saroyan, William, 14
Satellite Records, 61
"Saturday Morning Confusion," 168
"Saturday Night Fish Fry," 4
Sawyer, Roy, 195, 196
"Say Man," 219, 220
The Searchers, 50, 52
"Searchin'," 48, 181
Sears, Don, 166
Seeger, Pete, 168–169, 173
Senator Bobby, 82
The Sentimental Four, 135
The Serendipity Singers, 170
"Sergeant Preston of the Yukon,"
    120, 121
"Seven Little Girls Sitting in the
    Back Seat," 218
Seville, David, 11, 14–18, 21, 31,
    94, 202, 215

Shafer, Pat, 150
The Sharps, 54
Shauer, Mel, 78
"Shaving Cream," 117
Shawn, Dick, 141
Shayne, Gloria, 223
"She Can't Find Her Keys," 218
Sheen, Bobby, 64
Sherman, Allan, 13, 65, 70–76, 77,
    83, 100, 137, 168, 184, 208, 231
Sherman, Paul, 12
"Shimmy Shimmy, Ko-Ko-Bop," 40
"Shoppin' for Clothes," 50
"Short Fat Fannie," 185, 186
"Short People," 212, 224
"Short Shorts," 24, 32
Shropshire, Elmo, 207
The Silhouettes, 178, 189
Sill, Lester, 45
Silverstein, Shel, 162, 173, 195–196,
    227, 228–229
Simon, Paul, 7, 217, 218
Simone, Nina, 42
The Singing Dogs, 9, 202, 203
SKB Records, 104
Skelton, Red, 143
"Slippin' and Slidin'," 221
"Small Sad Sam," 81
Smash, 127, 128, 131
"Smells Like Nirvana," 85, 86
Smith, Fred, 52
Smith, Howard, 203
Smith, Huey "Piano," 55, 57, 58
Smothers, Dickie, 172, 173
Smothers, Tommy, 172, 173
The Smothers Brothers, 172, 173
Smothers Brothers Comedy Hour,
    172, 173
"Snoopy vs. the Red Baron," 105
Snow, Hank, 156
Snyder, Cliffie. See Stone, Cliffie
Soma, 96
"Somebody Stole My Santa
    Suit," 210
Sommerville, David, 81
Soul, 60
"Soul Heaven," 188
South, Joe, 35, 215
"So You Want to Be a Rock 'N'
    Roll Star," 194
The Space Girl, 19
Spark, 45
The Sparkletones, 24
Spector, Phil, 55, 64, 183
"Speedy Gonzales," 225, 226
Spellman, Benny, 56
"Spiders and Snakes," 162
The Squirrel Nut Zippers, 231

Stafford, Jim, 152, 160–163, 164
Stafford, Jo, 212, 213
Stan Freberg Presents the United States of America, 69–70
Starday Records, 35
"Star Drek," 93
Stax, 61, 62
Stephens, Geoff, 113
Stevens, Connie, 27
Stevens, Dodie, 25, 27
Stevens, Ray, 6, 7, 119–126, 164, 197, 204
Stewart, Harry, 208
Stiers, David Ogden, 70
"Still No. 2," 77
Stoller, Alvin, 68
Stoller, Mike, 4, 7, 23–24, 39, 42, 43–51, 52, 53, 59
Stone, Cliffie, 66, 155–156
Stookey, Paul, 170
"Stranded in the Jungle," 38, 39
"The Streak," 125, 126
The String Dusters, 153
Strunk, Jud, 176
Stump, Cinderella G., 212
Sue Records, 59
Sundquist, Jim, 100
Sun Records, 61, 69
"Surfin' Bird," 87, 95, 96, 97
"Swamp Witch," 161
Szarthmony, William. *See* Dana, Bill

"Take Off," 151
Taylor, Chip, 82
Taylor, Sam "The Man," 41
"Teenage Heaven," 187
The Teen-Aires, 187
"Temptation (Tim-Tayhsun)," 212
"There Is Nothing Like a Lox," 71
"There's Something on Your Mind," 57–58
"They're Coming to Take Me Away, Ha, Haaa," 87, 93–95
They're Coming to Take Me Away, Ha, Haaa, 94, 95
"The Thing," 87–88
Thomas, Dave, 151, 208
Thomas, Rufus, 61–62
"Three Cool Cats," 49, 181
The Three Friends, 185
"Three Little Pigs," 193
"Three Stars," 187
The Three Stooges, 145
Thunder, Johnny, 62
The Thunderbirds, 206
"Tie Me Kangaroo Down, Sport," 110–111
"Time Machine," 103–104

Tiny Tim, 29, 113–116
"Tip-Toe Thru' the Tulips With Me," 115
The Tokens, 25
Tom and Jerry, 217
"Tom Dooley," 169
Tonight: In Person, 170
The Toot Uncommons, 143
"Top Forty, News, Weather and Sports," 187
Torrence, Dean, 216–217
Toussaint, Allen, 3, 55–56, 57, 61
"Toy Bell," 229, 230
"Transfusion," 27–28, 29
The Trashmen, 55, 87, 95–97
Trigg, Patsy, 207
Tristram, Seventh Earl of Cricklewood, 113
The Troggs, 82
"The Trouble with Harry," 14
Turner, Jesse Lee, 19, 20
"Turtle Dovin'," 47
"Tutti Frutti," 189
Twin, 190
The Tympany Five, 4

Udell, Peter, 214
"Uh! Oh! Parts 1 and 2," 19
"Uneasy Rider," 163
United Artists, 52
Universe, 11
Urban Chipmunk, 18

Valens, Ritchie, 32, 36
Vallee, Rudy, 113
Vance, Paul, 82, 213
Van Dyke, Leroy, 156
Vanguard, 117
Van Winkle, Joseph, 99
Verne, Larry, 98, 99, 100, 109
The Vibrations, 39, 54
Vista, 176

Wahrer, Steve, 97
Wainwright, Loudon, III, 152, 173–175
The Waitresses, 210
Walker, David, 61
"Walking the Dog," 62
Ward, Joe, 198, 200
Ward, Robin, 225
Ward, Walter, 52, 54
Warner Bros. Records, 73, 74, 94–95, 143, 176
Weaver, Doodles, 5
Webb, Jack, 69
Weill, Cynthia, 190, 191, 223
Weismann, Carl, 202, 203

"Welfare Cadillac," 164
"We'll All Go Together When We Go," 231
"We Love You Beatles," 181, 182
"Western Movies," 52, 53
"Whadaya Want?," 46
"What About Us?," 49
"What It Was, Was Football," 136
"What's the Secret of Your Success?," 48
What That Is, 42
Wheeler, Billy Edd, 153, 158, 160
"When You're Hot, You're Hot," 163–164
White, Carl, 55
White, Jesse, 194
"White Lightning," 36
"Who Put the Bomp," 190–191, 192
"Who Says There Ain't No Santa Claus," 206
"Wild One," 221
"Wild Thing," 82
"Wildwood Weed," 162
Williams, Andy, 123
Williams, Larry, 185, 186
Wilson, Meri, 176
Wilson, Rocky, Jr., 55, 57
"Winchester Cathedral," 113
Winslow, Dal, 97
"Winter Dance Party," 35–36
"The Witch Doctor," 15, 19, 31, 215
"Wolf Creek Pass," 166
The Womenfolk, 169
Wood, Randy, 225
Wooley, Sheb, 9, 19, 29–32, 65, 76, 126, 204, 205
"Wun'erful, Wun'erful," 68
Wynn, Paul, 117

"Yakety Yak," 48–49
Yankovic, "Weird Al," 2, 5, 6–7, 8, 65, 83–86, 211, 229, 231
Yarborough, Glenn, 169
Yarrow, Peter, 115
"Ya Ya," 56, 60–61
"Yogi," 104
Yorgesson, Yogi, 208
"You Look Marvelous," 145
"Young Blood," 48
The Young Rascals, 54, 184

Zacherle, John, 89–91
Zadora, Pia, 64
Zahnd, Ricky, 198, 200
Zappa, Frank, 192–193
"Zing! Went the Strings of My Heart" (The Coasters), 49